The copilot wound his finger in wide circles, indicating that we needed to make a broad turn. As we leveled out, he shouted again into the headset, and the two gunners yelled "roger" in unison. They grabbed their ammunition belts, locked and loaded their weapons, then spun into position, watching out their side doors. The second officer left his seat to lean back into the cabin and shout, "You guys set?"

"Roger!" Smitty returned two thumbs-up. I sat mute. I couldn't even nod. My stomach still vaulting into my throat, I didn't think I could do this again.

The gunner next to Smitty tapped him on the shoulder and offered him his headset. Smitty took off his helmet and listened to the second officer yelling above the roar. Smitty relayed the orders to me. "We're comin' in hot. Two ambulatory, maybe more." He pointed at me. "Yer side down, Bubba. Be ready. We got no time." He returned the earphones and relayed a thumbs-up to the gunner.

Smitty unhooked his belt and approached my side, motioning me to unhook, too. He pushed me into the door beside the gunner and yelled in my ear, "Stand on the rail, Bubba! We're goin' fast!" He crouched behind me with his hand on my back. "Wait 'til I say go!"

MEDIC!

The Story of a Conscientious
Objector in the Vietnam War

BEN SHERMAN

BALLANTINE BOOKS • NEW YORK

A Presidio Press Book
Published by The Random House Publishing Group

Published in the United States by Presidio Press, an imprint of The Random House Publishing Group, a division of Random House, Inc., New York, and simultaneously in Canada by Random House of Canada Limited, Toronto.

Presidio Press and colophon are trademarks of Random House, Inc.

www.presidiopress.com

Originally published in slightly different form in hardcover by Writers Club Press, an imprint of iUniverse, Inc., in 2002.

ISBN 0-89141-848-2

Manufactured in the United States of America

First Mass Market Edition: June 2004

OPM   9 8 7 6 5 4 3

To the names on the wall

We were young
We have died
Remember us

Contents

APPRECIATION

My best friend and wife, Gwen Griffin Sherman.
My ear and editor, Joey Moschetti.

North and South Vietnam, circa 1968

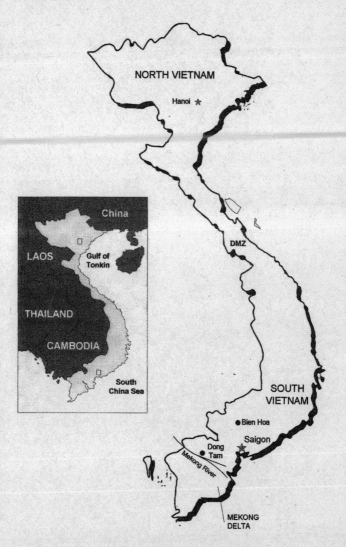

1

Bags

The bags are exactly where I should begin. They are where the war ended for fifty-eight thousand, and where it started for me. Black rubberized bags with reinforced plastic handles on each end, they were strong and durable, with heavy zippers you could pull with your whole fist.

Entering the morgue tent, one hesitated to take a full breath. My first duty in Vietnam was spent zipping up smells. The only solace was that the remains had quit screaming. Some bodies had the distinct odor of burnt cloth or flesh. Others simply gave off old sweat, bad socks, tobacco, or belly gas. Even a tent vaporized with Lysol couldn't cut the continuous olfactory blight of human waste staining the underwear of the shell left behind.

Our caring was meticulous, even while we tried, in our own way, to put our minds elsewhere. Each personal item was tagged, each button refastened. Neglected pockets and stripes were neatly resewn. Homely, wondering faces were shaved and cleaned. Without a sound, we each functioned with one mind, one obligation. Someone inventoried each coin, chain, watch, wallet, ring, and all were placed in small brown paper sacks. No one wanted their loved one coming home with someone else's personal stuff in his pocket or with field

1

dirt ringing his neck. And the army didn't want a home-town mortician opening the box to find a mess instead of a hero.

For every face locked into every rubber womb, I made a quiet promise to do this or that with my life for his sake. With some pride, I thought that as a medic I stood for part of the solution. I had come to this place to save a life, not take one. This plugging of rectums with cotton balls was a temporary setback. In one year minus one day, I could scrutinize my life for whatever meaning this horror held. A year from now I might even laugh out loud again.

"Graves Registration?" I asked the clerk. "But I'm a medic."

"New medics get the morgue tent first. Anything's better than the bush. Nobody *asks* for the morgue. But it'll pop your cherry. You'll be ready for anything after a few days of body-packing."

"Uh, I don't . . ."

"I know. The guys over there'll show you what to do. They're not grave diggers, either. Plain old medics like you."

"We dig graves here?"

"Nope. 'Grave diggers' are what we call the regular morgue specialists, lifers in Saigon at the big hospitals."

"Uh-huh." I scrambled to keep up. His words and feet were way ahead of me, heading down the dirt road.

"We don't get that many DOA anyway. It'll be pretty boring here. Just passing a few days, y'know? Only bodies we get are those who died in flight or across the street at 3d Surg. Most field KIAs go straight to Saigon. Then home."

KIA. Killed in action.

Upon entering the tent, the clerk handed me a blue tunic to exchange for my fatigue shirt, then disappeared without another word. Two lanky black medics worked over a corpse on a stainless steel table. They nodded politely but didn't speak. Their mouths puffed forward in a pout, like you had to hold your lips a certain way to concentrate. Their eyes were swollen, and I rubbed my own as the stench of disinfectant mixed with the humidity in the tent. I hung my fatigue shirt on a hook by the door next to their two. The stenciled names weren't showing. I didn't introduce myself, and they didn't offer.

The two of them taught me by show rather than tell. When they were done preparing the corpse, I helped roll him onto an open rubber bag. One of them placed the brown paper sack full of personal belongings carefully between the knees as the other zipped the bag from the feet up over the head. A chill rocketed from my toes to my neck at the sound. The two of them picked up the full heavy bag by the two side handles and slid it into a silver aluminum box, then closed the cover and snapped it shut.

The gurney bumped over the back threshold of the tent as they rolled the box out to be stored in a refrigerated steel building behind the morgue. Somebody else would ship him home.

Stacked at the end of the morgue tent were more six-foot-long aluminum boxes. Ten or twelve of them. Each one eventually took somebody home. Near the stack of caskets, an open shelf stored extra sets of large fatigue pants and shirts and piles of olive drab T-shirts and socks. An open bandage box held dozens of packs of varying brands and quantities of cigarettes.

I helped with the next KIA, who was about five years younger than I. This one's fatigues were wet and bloody, so we cut the clothes off. We carefully washed his arms, face, feet, even behind his ears and between his fingers.

Then we dressed him carefully in new starched fatigues from the shelves in the corner. We all scrubbed our hands thoroughly afterward.

On the second day we packed three more bodies, all dank with the musk of too many days in rice paddies. You couldn't inhale in our tent without the sharp medical scent of liquid soap and alcohol cutting through the stench of death. One of the medics showed me how he stuffed unused cigarette filters into his nostrils. It didn't work. The disgusting odor cut through everything.

The morgue tent could have been called Purgatory. The casualties weren't part of the fighting force anymore, but they hadn't yet touched down in their hometowns, where friends, family, and high school teachers would be there to greet them for the final time. Where they'd soon be war heroes.

Until then, inside this tent, the three of us took our time and paid attention to detail. These bodies were important. They were different from us only in that they were going home early.

In bags. Once closed, you couldn't see the bewildered faces anymore. You couldn't smell the blood, excrement, dried mud, or urine. Each one we zipped meant everyone had quit messing with him. No snipers or booby traps or command-detonated mines to slow his walk. No weight of cumbersome gear, weapons, and ammunition. No whistling rockets or mortars in his ears just before they hit. No sudden flinching or jerking. No fear. What a way to leave.

Repeatedly before me, on a cold stainless steel table, lay the one common denominator of escalated conflict: dead bodies. No matter what provokes nations to war upon each other—land, oil, trade, religion—this bagging of boys is as fundamental to war as haiku is to poetry.

High speeding metal
Slamming through muscle and bone
How war begins, ends

I scribbled the words on the back of a red toe tag. I didn't know it yet, but the tranquility of *this* Purgatory was far better than the screaming that preceded it, the hysteria I would catch up with soon enough in the field. For now, our shop remained eternally mute.

As soldiers, we were all isolated from the World. None of us saw the nightly news or read the newspapers. We didn't know enough to care one way or the other. GIs are not allowed opinions. Basic training whips the smartass out of every individual, one at a time, and creates a government-issue fighting soldier who doesn't have too many original thoughts. Real warriors are either alive and afraid, or dead and quiet. In the field there were no lines, no battles, no war strategies. Guerrilla warfare is nowhere and everywhere at the same time. My recollection of Vietnam has nothing to do with politics or Americans shouting in the streets back home. It's about serving in a humid foreign jungle, flicking horsefly mosquitoes, eating crappy food, trying to find a bit of shade or a beer or a soft breeze to slice into the humidity that hung on our necks. And about trying to stay alive.

My official papers said I was a noncombatant, which meant that I didn't carry a weapon. It didn't mean I wasn't going to get shot at, it just meant I didn't carry a weapon. But being a medic meant much more than carrying a weapon. It meant ten weeks of bloody movies, hypodermic needle drills, greased catheters slipped into wilting penises, splints made of tree limbs, fireman body-carries through mud, machine gun tracers colliding over crawling bodies, a morphine Syrette administered to a bare thigh in front of the whole gawking platoon.

Medics carried responsibility for more than dry feet, salt tablets, syphilis, and puncture wounds. A platoon leader relied on his medic to report on the morale and mobility of the troops. A medevac pilot relied on the medics to get out into the battlefield and back quickly. Operating room surgeons who had years of study and more years of practice relied on "ten-week wonders" like me to scrub, monitor vitals, sponge, pass instruments, administer anesthetics, even carve out and sew up wounds.

The grunts called me Doc, and it sounded like both Mom and Priest.

Medics were trusted to perform when needed. We treated abrasions, gave haircuts, soothed anger, and inspected rashes of unknown origin in all the typical places. We also confiscated marijuana; treated cuts, bug bites, and abrasions; and continually nagged people to keep their feet clean and their dicks to themselves. Yet no matter how much a medic bitched, he held your ticket home alive—if he knew his stuff. For that reason, I belonged to a proud fraternity.

I wondered if all new medics caught morgue duty as a way to desensitize us. You couldn't have one of us puking into an open wound. The clerk had said "temporary" duty. To some extent the whole war seemed like a fleeting mishap in my otherwise normal life. "Temporary" would have to be my mantra.

Working in the morgue tent may have been gruesome and smelly, but it kept us feeling reasonably safe. The hundred-degree heat started early, stayed through the afternoon, and hung on late into the evening. Inside the tent seemed even hotter than outside. If a monsoon dumped rain on us for fifteen minutes, the temperature might drop five degrees. Minutes later it climbed back up to over a hundred, with ninety-nine percent humidity. It seemed that even if the bullets and rockets missed, the weather would probably kill me.

I slept intermittently the first night after morgue duty. I awoke twice to sirens warning of incoming rockets. Half awake, I'd scramble into the bunkers. It felt much more like a nuisance than real safety. After a day of dead bodies, one can only experience a heightened level of fear for so long, then the nerves just go numb. The second night I remained in the morgue, passing time straightening clothes and supplies. When the sirens blasted again, at least I didn't have to wake up. And I was certainly in the right place if I bought the farm. Weary and bored, I wrote a note and took it out to the refrigerated building. I opened the last casket we'd prepared and dropped it in with the bagged body.

The third day I wrote something special and added it to three of the bags. The first two notes were simply "Smooth sailing" and "Good luck on the other side." But in the late morning I got inspired and wrote a full letter. I imagined the Stateside mortician opening the bag, reading it, and passing it on to the family. I asked if they had thought about this guy much before he died, and if they had thought about anything else since. I wrote about who and where I was, and that I wanted to know about the fellow whose body I had tended. I asked them to write and tell me about him.

I didn't get any replies. Didn't really expect any. I had dared to cross the line into somebody's grief without invitation. What could they write back anyway? But I had to do something to make the bodies real for me. Otherwise, we were stuffing limp meat into containers.

• • •

The bodies came sporadically. As we zipped away somebody's son, I thought that this one couldn't have been more than seventeen, at least five years younger than the guy wrapping him in a bag. He had perfect teeth. Must have had braces. I wondered what that had cost his folks. Looking down, I saw that what had been his last meal now stained my forearms.

I scoured my hands and arms clear up to the shoulders, standing at the sink long enough to hide my tears from the others. One of the two medics approached and put his hand on my back. I turned to look at him, trying to bite back my feelings.

"I'm Vincent," he said. "That there is Satterfield."

2

Papers

Selective Service System
CLASSIFICATION
Local Board No. 23

September 24, 1964

TO: Benjamin Ray Sherman,
    Selective Service No. 4 23 46 321

1. By authority of the Selective Service Regulations 100.4, you are hereby classified 2-S [student deferment].

2. This classification will terminate if at any time the reasons thereof cease to exist. It is your duty to report that fact immediately to this local board.

3. It is your continuous duty to report for induction at such time and place as may hereafter be fixed by this local board.

October 10, 1964

Dear Ben,

I truly look forward to our meeting. I haven't seen you since you were but a lad of four or five, quite active I recall. Your dear mother seemed to be the only authority you heeded. This is a good choice, by the way.

In preparation for our visit next week, I have jotted some notes for your consideration.

1. First, your question about not complying: Conviction for a draft law violation typically means up to five years' imprisonment at a federal penitentiary and a fine of up to $10,000.

2. You may apply for Conscientious Objector [CO] status by filling out a Form 150 (enclosed) and sending it to your Selective Service Board.

3. By reading, you can see that you are required to write an essay about your reasons, the religious nature of your beliefs, the development of those beliefs since early childhood, and any public or private expressions of your pacifism. You may also be required to appear in person before your board to answer their questions about what you have submitted.

4. 1-O status means alternative service. You state that you are not willing to serve the military in any fashion. That matches my status in WWII. I served five years in a

CO internment camp, not much unlike a prison. Nowadays, this classification is almost impossible to receive unless you are a member of the Quaker church, or one similar, or you are the son of a minister.

5. 1-AO status, noncombatant duty for conscientious objectors in the armed forces, was defined by the President in Executive Order No. 10028 on January 13, 1949, as follows: service in any unit of the armed forces which is unarmed; service in the medical department of any of the armed forces, wherever performed; or any other assignment the primary function of which does not require the use of arms in combat; provided that such other assignment is acceptable to the individual concerned and does not require him to bear arms or be trained in their use.

If you are drafted as a 1-AO, you would go to basic training just like a combatant soldier. The difference is that you would not be required to train with, carry, or use weapons. Most 1-AO's go directly to Medical Corpsman basic training followed by advanced training. But, this doesn't always happen. Your assignment is at the Army's discretion.

There is <u>absolutely nothing in the regulations</u> to prevent a CO who is classified 1-AO from being sent to a war zone. In fact, there is a high possibility. Of course, we do not know about this Vietnam action. It could heat up. We could see escalation there. Or it could all be over in a short time with the peacekeeping forces that have been sent there. Whatever the outcome, this will not be the last time America sends boys to war. You can be sure of that, and therefore must prepare yourself now.

The <u>most important thing</u> is that you make your intentions known as early as possible.

This may be a lot to digest right now, but all of it will become very important during your application process.

As are your parents, I am delighted you are seriously praying and contemplating about this service in the armed forces. I wish more boys would do this. I look forward to discussing the alternatives at length.

In peace,

Dr. Paul Delp

May 15, 1965

Local Board No. 23
Federal 1 Bldg., Room 423
9th & I Streets
Sacramento, California 95814

TO WHOM IT MAY CONCERN:

Enclosed are my application for Conscientious Objection to service in the Armed Forces, Form 150, answers to all the questions, and three letters of reference. Please know that I do wish to serve my country, but in an alternative capacity as a civilian. I am hereby requesting reclassification as 1-O and assignment to alternative duty upon my graduation from college, estimated to be in June of 1968.

Thank you,

Benjamin Sherman
Selective Service No. 4 23 46 321

Enclosures

[No reply]

May 1, 1966

Local Board No. 23
Federal 1 Bldg., Room 423
9th & I Streets
Sacramento, California 95814

TO WHOM IT MAY CONCERN:

1. I have not heard back from you regarding my status as a conscientious objector. I sent my application in May of last year.

2. I have a question about summer break from college. I need to work to pay for next year's tuition, room and board, but I do not want to jeopardize my 2-S classification. Should I continue taking full-time classes during summer?

Thank you for your prompt reply.

Sincerely,

Benjamin Sherman
Selective Service No. 4 23 46 321

[No reply]

June 1, 1966

Local Board No. 23
Federal 1 Bldg., Room 423
9th & I Streets
Sacramento, California 95814

TO WHOM IT MAY CONCERN:

This is my second letter following the submission of my application for alternative service (1-O).

I have not heard back from you regarding my status as a conscientious objector. I sent my application in May of last year.

Summer break from college begins next week.

I do not want to jeopardize my 2-S classification. Should I continue taking full-time classes during summer?

Thank you for your reply.

Sincerely,

Benjamin Sherman
Selective Service No. 4 23 46 321

[No reply]

September 3, 1966

Local Board No. 23
Federal 1 Bldg., Room 423
9th & I Streets
Sacramento, California 95814

TO WHOM IT MAY CONCERN:

I am currently classified 2-S, as I am a college student.

I have also applied for status change to Conscientious
Objection (1-O). My papers were filed in May of 1965.
So far I have had no reply to that application or to my
questions about whether I need to continue college during summer.

Could someone please write me?

Sincerely,

Benjamin Sherman
Selective Service No. 4 23 46 321

[No reply]

August 10, 1967

Dear Ben,

This is one of those times I really wish you had a phone but I know it's much more economical to live in the dorms during the summer. We heard terrible news last night that your long-time friend, Terry Nelson, has been killed in action on his second tour in Vietnam. I know this is a shock to you and it might be best to just drop this awful letter on the floor and get to a pay phone and call me collect. We're around this weekend. I'll be here when you call.

I'm not sure you knew that Terry got shot down flying his helicopter a few months ago. He received a medical discharge from the Service. I talked to his Dad last month and he said Terry tried to "pull it together." According to their neighbors across the street, Jim pulled some strings with his contacts in the War Department, and Terry re-enlisted. He joined his old unit flying medical airlifts about two weeks ago. They said that he safely landed a helicopter shot up beyond repair. All in it were saved but the pilot, who they found mortally wounded. That is pure Terry.

I remember your first YMCA football game when Terry threw you the winning touchdown using your "hidden pass" trick. And all those winning and losing football games that came after. I know you will remember years of YMCA then junior high and high school basketball. Also, the time when you and I went down to give blood when he had his operation. What a long night that was. Memories that will always be part of us.

I also remember talking to you about war and about your feelings on it. Soon after that talk, your church buddy Ricky Bright died as a Marine in Vietnam, a boy I didn't know very well, but this is one time I can truly empathize with how you feel. It turns my gut. As you know, I lost my twin brother in the Second World War. He was a flyer too, my brother Ben. That's all he ever wanted to be. All of that just came back on me today, the formal military funeral, my mother's face, the days of crying in the house.

Then I got that terrible phone call from Jack. He just said "Terry's been killed," then June had to get on the phone and tell me the rest. The neighborhood is planning a memorial service after the military funeral, but we don't know when yet.

Please call home soon, son. You know how very sorry I am to tell you this awful news. Please call home soon.

Your Dad

Selective Service System
CLASSIFICATION
Local Board No. 23

September 14, 1967

TO: Benjamin Ray Sherman,
    Selective Service No. 4 23 46 321

1. By authority of the Selective Service
Regulations 100.4, you are hereby classified 1-A.

2. You will be advised by this local board
as to the date you will present yourself
to the physical examination station for
pre-induction physical and screening.

SIGNED

Betty Doolin
Member, Local Board #23

October 11, 1967

Mrs. Betty Doolin
Member of Local Board No. 23
Federal 1 Bldg., Room 423
9th & I Streets
Sacramento, California 95814

Dear Mrs. Doolin:

I have not heard from the Board concerning my request
for reclassification as 1-O, alternative service as conscientious objector, which I submitted in May of 1965.

I have written three letters to the Selective Service Board,
with no word back from them.

I hereby request a personal appearance with the Board.
Enclosed are photocopies of my original application,
SSS Form 150, five more reference letters, and copies of
my last three letters to the Board.

Thank you for your attention to this matter. I look forward to meeting with the Board.

Sincerely,

Benjamin Sherman
Selective Service No. 4 23 46 321

Enclosures

Selective Service System
BOARD APPEARANCE
Local Board No. 23

November 28, 1967

TO: Benjamin Ray Sherman,
  Selective Service No. 4 23 46 321

1. You are hereby ordered to report to the Selective Service Local Board 23, in Room 420 of the Federal 1 Building at 9th & I Streets, Sacramento, California on the 5th day of December 1967, at 9 a.m.

2. Travel expenses ☐ are ☒ are not to be reimbursed by the Board.

SIGNED:

Betty Doolin
Member, Local Board #23

3

Finals

For a year before I got drafted, stacks of papers submitted in triplicate had assured the Selective Service Appeals Board that I would not under any circumstances "train myself to kill anybody, pretend to kill anybody, or walk around with a weapon intending to kill anybody." I thought I had made myself clear. The board, comprised of WWII veterans, disagreed. "After all," they insisted, "if we let everybody out because they didn't like it, we'd have nobody left."

They scheduled my meeting with the draft board during December final exams. While everyone else in the dorms crammed for finals, my spare hours were spent preparing answers for my meeting with the Selective Service Board. Many trips to the campus chaplain helped, but the frightening prospect of facing my board made no amount of information seem adequate. What would they ask? Could I defend my views with Bible passages, or would they want a long history of my nonviolence in school and church and sports? Would they ask deep philosophical questions I couldn't answer? I ran to the chaplain every time I woke with cold shivers. He seemed calm and positive about my chances.

"No one can force you to shoot anybody," he said. "They may threaten other not-so-lovely consequences. . . ."

"Like?"

". . . like prison. No worry, though. They don't want to fill jails with America's youth. They'll let you out. You'll be fine."

Although I worked almost full-time at Disneyland while attending college, all my money went to tuition. Broke, with only a Honda 50 motorcycle for transportation, I borrowed money for the cheapest Greyhound bus trip, a local, that went four hundred miles in twenty hours. I hauled along my school books, hoping to study for finals, but I spent the entire trip to Sacramento looking over the answers I had submitted months before on the conscientious objector application. I memorized every line so that if they tried to catch me at something, I could repeat my original words verbatim.

The draft board met at the central post office, an old government building with cold tall pillars holding up a pediment of sculpted gargoyles. Lions on pedestals glared at me. Inside, walls and woodwork shared a shade of brownish green and gray that fit with the smell of carpet pads mildewed from years of too much shampoo. Tobacco haze stained the windows and hung trapped in the tall hallways.

When I checked in at the Selective Service Office, the clerk didn't look up. She told me to put any papers in the wire basket and go wait in the hall. I sat on a bench, my only pair of dress slacks constantly slipping on the lacquered wooden seat. I straightened up a dozen times, not wanting anyone to see me slouch. I was supposed to be making a mature decision here. A sloucher couldn't be trusted to think for himself.

The sound of high heels clacking in the wide hallway stiffened my muscles.

"Benjamin Ray Sherman?" I sat very still. Using my

full three names always spelled trouble. "Benjamin Ray *Sherman?*" she asked louder. I was gawking. She had the thickest bifocals I'd ever seen. The sides bent into S's, with shiny pink jewels accenting the curves. She was wearing glass bookends on her face.

"Yes ma'am?" I wanted to disappear.

"The board is waiting." She pointed to an open door.

With no introduction, I went in and sat. A shiny wooden table and padded high-back chairs filled the bottom half of the room. Tobacco smoke filled the top. Three balding men sat smoking two pipes and a cigar. They were each reading identical papers. My papers. They had all my words in front of them. Words I had so carefully crafted, and words of wisdom from the seventeen books my college chaplain had given me to read. Biblical passages, quotes from Martin Luther King and Mahatma Gandhi and Jesus himself, and my own words.

> . . . *I am seeking this status of conscientious objection because I believe our conscience is often the truest guide in achieving some sort of understanding, love and compassion for our fellow human beings. And our conscience must be our guide if we are ever to achieve world peace, and peace of mind. . . .*

It all came down to this moment. Would these men believe the words they were reading? Would they even understand them? Could I remember everything? They had my papers in front of them. This was possibly the most serious final exam I would ever face.

Going into that room, I had never considered alternatives. It was me against the system from the beginning. They would ask me questions and I would answer them, and they would decide whether or not to believe me. Never had I considered bartering or compromise or any other possibility. It was, quite simply, the draft versus the conscientious objector. They wanted me to train myself to kill people. I would not do that.

But in the first thirty seconds with my draft board, they made it completely clear that there was no possibility of avoiding the draft, at least not without committing a crime or leaving the country. When they asked specifically about Vietnam, I said I didn't understand that particular war. They said the statutes had no provision for objection to a particular war.

I finally just blurted out that I would go.

"I'll serve," I said. I told them I'd be a soldier and wear a uniform and do push-ups. Be a cook, medic, clerk, or ambulance driver. Carry a radio, polish belt buckles, police the area, march in step, call everybody "sir," and stand at attention. I'd salute people I don't even know. I'd wash airplanes or change tires, mop, paint, dig ditches, scrub shower walls. Learn to shine boots, smoke, cuss, gamble, and drink coffee.

I'd go, I told them. I'd go. Only not with a gun.

They asked me hypothetical questions. What would I do if I were driving down a steep road with a bus load of crippled children and the brakes went out, with nowhere to swerve? Grandmother's house is on the right, a steep cliff is on the left. Did we mention the kids were crippled? There's a baby in the road straight ahead. Grandmother. Cliff. Brakes. Crippled kids. Baby.

"Now, Sherman. What would you *do*?"

"I wouldn't *shoot* any of them."

"No, Sherman. As a pacifist, how would you decide who would die?"

"What does deciding who will die have to do with pacifism?"

"Answer the question."

"Who left the baby in the road?"

"Never mind. What would you *do?*"

"I would have checked the brakes before driving the bus."

"Son, just answer the question."

"I'm not a philosopher. I don't know how to answer questions that have no answers. I told you I would serve. I'm just not going to kill anybody. I won't train myself to kill. I won't pretend that I'm a killer. I can't. It's against everything I know."

"Answer the question."

I tried a different approach. "Why is it that you have a nonviolent type driving the bus? Why not John Wayne or Audie Murphy behind the wheel?" I thought a little humor might help; they thought there were only two types of people in the world—heroes, and people like me.

"Would you stand by and let Hitler take over the world?" one of them asked.

"If you were a German during World War II," I countered, "would you have served on the draft board?" Pretty good reversal, I thought. It got their attention.

"Are you a communist?" one asked in earnest. The other two looked up and nodded.

"Can we go back to the bus? I'm better off driving the bus." I forced a smile.

They said no. In fact, they said *hell* no. The change in my status from 2-S (student deferment) to 1-A (eligible for military service) would stand. No chance for alternative service as a citizen, and no chance for noncombatant duty as a medic or clerk. They saw me as a soldier. My efforts to convince them otherwise had only sealed my fate.

Selective Service System
BOARD APPEARANCE
Local Board No. 23

January 1, 1968

TO: Benjamin Ray Sherman,
    Selective Service No. 4 23 46 321

Your request for reclassification has been
denied by a vote of 5-0.

SIGNED:

Betty Doolin
Member, Local Board #23

January 12, 1968

Mrs. Betty Doolin
Member of Local Board No. 23
Federal 1 Bldg., Room 423
9th & I Streets
Sacramento, California 95814

Dear Mrs. Doolin:

To whom can I appeal the decision of the Board concerning my appearance on December 5th of last year?

After traveling 400 miles from Southern California, during the week before final exams, I met with the Board for only ten minutes. Most of that time went to them explaining to me why everybody must serve in the Armed Forces. They did not ask me one question about my application.

Only three members were present, yet the vote was 5-0 against my request for reclassification.

Can you please help?

Sincerely,

Benjamin Sherman
Selective Service No. 4 23 46 321

February 22, 1968

Dear Mr. Sherman:

This is a note to tell you that officially you cannot have an appeal when there was no dissenting vote of the board. The three members who met with you informed the other two members of your appointment before they cast their votes. You could have offered any information you wished in the hearing room, with no time limit on your meeting with the board in any way, shape or form.

I am sending you this answer personally because there is absolutely nothing which can be done about it, but I want you to know that all members of the board are volunteers who spend many hours making very hard decisions about who should go to the armed forces and who should not go. They are all very upstanding citizens who shoulder a heavy burden which they would not have to shoulder if more young men such as yourself would volunteer for the Army the way your fathers did.

Now you think about it!

Sincerely,

Helen Hartig
Chief Clerk

Selective Service System
ORDER TO REPORT FOR INDUCTION
Local Board No. 23

The President of the United States

July 18, 1968

TO: Benjamin Ray Sherman,
    Selective Service No. 4 23 46 321

Greetings:

You are hereby ordered for induction into
the Armed Forces of the United States, and
to report at 9th and I Streets, Federal
Building (Branch Post Office Lobby),
Sacramento, Calif. on August 14, 1968 at
6:00 a.m. Sharp.

For forwarding to an Armed Forces Induction Station.

Helen Hartig, Chief Clerk
Member or clerk of Local Board

July 26, 1968

To my friends:

This is a form letter to let you know that your buddy Ben will be <u>Private</u> Sherman on August 14. Not too happy about it, but I couldn't appeal the board's decision to grant me status as CO, so it's "in the Army now."

I have quit my job at Disneyland but they say they will hire me back when I get out on August 13, 1970.

I'll send my address when I know what it is. In the meantime, try to picture me bald and unhappy. I don't think I've ever been either.

Peace,

Ben Sherman

August 1968

Dear Benj,

I gave a copy of the CO forms to the San Francisco Office of the American Civil Liberties Union and I guess they sent them on to the ACLU in New York City. They got some attention because a New York lawyer called me last night (can you believe it?) and said they would take your case!!

So, what do I do? I called my Mom and she said your parents were out of the country until after your draft date. I think you told me your draft board is still in Sacramento, so I'm sending this to your old neighborhood address just hoping. Please, you do not have to do this. There is legal help. And, if that fails, there is always Canada. Call me. I have the number in New York, and the people here have said they will provide you transportation. You only need to get to San Francisco.

Go next door and ask my Mom for money if you don't have bus funds. Whatever you do, please do not go!

Keep the faith,

Dave

4

Conscripted

In three days I went from playing Goofy at Disneyland to taking orders about how to brush my teeth from a redneck with an eighth-grade education. To receive this sentence, all I had to do was go down to the post office on my eighteenth birthday and do what the law requires of every young man—register with the Selective Service Board. Never mind if you're a young woman; Uncle Sam assumes you already know how to brush your teeth.

I felt that every young male *and female* in our country should serve in some capacity, choosing from a wide variety of options, including the military or the Peace Corps or countless other service-oriented endeavors. Our service could shave off a year from high school without much complaint from us *or* our parents. There would be no exceptions unless a person were mentally or physically unable to serve in some capacity.

But that wasn't how it was done, and even though I tried to create alternatives with a stack of papers and a dozen letters, it came down to somebody else making all the decisions. Once inducted, with uniformed henchmen looking to tear off your head and spit down your throat at the first flinch, there was an attempt to make it sound lawful and honorable by having everyone in line "take one step forward." But you cannot call that a choice.

Maybe it could be considered a decision to not lose a limb right at that moment. But it wasn't a choice.

On the appointed day, an out-of-service school bus took me and five others to a charter bus that took about fifty of us to a daylong induction in Oakland. From there, a military shuttle, a commercial airline, and another bus took us to what resembled a giant carport in the middle of a deserted field in Fort Lewis, Washington, just south of Tacoma. A screaming collection of angry gene pools welcomed us to ten weeks of misery called basic training, or boot camp. It turned out to be much more boot than camp.

In the wee hours following the long day that had begun the morning before, you couldn't call any of us very resistant. We shuffled into line and were ordered to stand still with our feet on each side of white numbers painted on bright red circles. Nobody said a word. The guys who had been yakking it up on the plane, bragging about sports and sexual conquests, were now mute and totally passive. We each stared down at our white number, trying to forget the humiliation of the induction physicals we had endured just a few hours earlier. I stood on number 14 on August 14.

Roll was hollered. We answered "Here!" and nothing else.

"You will not respond 'present' or 'that's me' or any derivation whatsoever, you fucking ignorant civilian piece-of-shit hippie assholes! Do you understand?"

"Yes, sir!"

"AHH CAIN'T HEAR YOUUUUUU. . . ."

After soggy toast and water-laced scrambled eggs, we were marched to a barn where we were ordered to strip naked and put everything we had worn or carried with us into a bag to be mailed home.

"If you're married, you may keep your wedding ring. Put everything else in the bag."

"Glasses?"

"Yes, Four Eyes, put those ugly Hollywood cheaters in the goddamn bag. Uncle Sam will issue you a proper pair tomorrow."

"Wallet?"

"That's right, ass wipe!"

"Social Security card?"

"Every goddamn thing in the goddamn bag, Gomer! Do NOT make me say it again!" The sergeant then took the question as an invitation to lecture the whole group. "Does anyone else have a stupid goddamn question? Wait! Stop right there. Don't fucking move a muscle. Before we do another goddamn thing, does ANY ONE of you stupid lowlife motherfucking civilians have another goddamn fucking question?"

Could've heard a tick toot.

"Good. Fine. Thank you very fucking much. Now maybe we can go on putting every goddamn civilian piece of shit you brought with you into the goddamn fucking bag." He turned away and threw his arms above his head in frustration, shouting to the wall, "Before I lose the rest of my fucking patience!"

They shaved our heads and issued olive green clothes and attitudes to turn us into a cohesive working unit. Our bodies were now government-issue, and our minds were supposed to follow close behind.

"If you somehow miraculously live through this training, you will be soldiers. If you do not, you will be dead. Far better in boot camp than in a real war zone where the lives of others could be put in jeopardy by your weakness." The beer-bellied drill sergeant leapt right out of central casting in Hollywood. Smokey-the-Bear hat. Spit-shined boots. Starched fatigues. Mr. Cliché marching around acting as if he were totally unique.

He bellowed and bawled. "Your ass is grass and I'm the lawn mower" and "We can play it my way, or play it the army way," which left us scratching our heads. He wore his IQ on his sleeve in the form of three stripes and a rocker, willingly and eagerly accepting his calling in life to whip us into shape physically, emotionally, and mentally. Our military lobotomies began as we placed all we had in one sack, mailed it home, then started our lives over from zero.

"Nothing you have brought with you is of any value here. That goes for attitudes, beliefs, prejudices, ideas, and desires. The quicker you learn that, the easier it's gonna be for all of us."

"If you are thinking about home, forget it! Jody already has your girlfriend's legs spread like a wishbone and she can't even remember your face."

"If you start thinking about sex in the next ten weeks, look around you. These are the only human beings you are going to see. If you wake up with a hard-on, slap it once firmly and go back to sleep."

"If you do not like the food, you will starve."

"If you do not shit when it is your turn, you will explode."

"If you do not like me, that is expected and part of the program. I do not want you to like me, because I do not like you. I do not like any fucking civilians. If you do everything you are told without question, I might shake your hand and wish you luck in ten weeks. And I might not."

I had gambled and lost. I thought I could convince the

draft board, but I didn't stand a chance with them. Then I bet my maturity against military insanity, thinking that because I had a little college knowledge and had been totally self-sufficient in the real world, that would sustain me. If all else failed, I thought my irrepressible charm, optimism, and keen wit would carry me through the brainless hell of basic training. I was wrong. Any humor and intelligence should have been dropped into the bag with the rest of my belongings.

It took me half of the first day to realize that personal sparks of life would be immediately stomped out by the drill sergeant. The only way to be, the only way to appear, physically and personably, was olive drab green. Shut up and stare straight ahead. Sink back into the landscape. If isolated and abused, suffer quietly without protest. Everybody would get his turn. And when the bloated oaf reveals his bottomless ignorance with yet another inane utterance, for god's sake, don't giggle.

"Tonight, ladies, we're gonna learn to pee, shit, shave, brush, and shower in five minutes, by the numbers, the ARMY way!"

"Yes, sir!"

"AHH CAIN'T HEAR YOUUUUUU. . . ."

Don't laugh. Don't think. What good will thinking do when given thirty seconds to effect a bowel movement with twelve platoon mates waiting in a straight line facing you? There's no time to do anything but count and shit.

Boot camp leadership strategy consisted of limited information, a full measure of fear, and immediate nondiscriminatory punishment. After seventy days of ridicule and torment, we were to miraculously emerge as fighting machines. In reality, on the last day of basic training we were a scattered, whimpering mob of scared boys who would pee in their pants if anybody yelled at us, most praying out loud for duty as clerks or cooks.

A couple of days in Vietnam would change all that. It surely did for me. Some of us would become more scared, some of us less. But none of us would remain little boys.

DEPARTMENT OF THE ARMY
Company D, 5th Battalion
First Basic Combat Training Brigade
U.S. Army Training Center, Infantry and Fort Lewis
Fort Lewis, Washington 98433

October 8, 1968

SUBJECT: Accelerated Advancement to Private E-2

TO: SHERMAN, BENJAMIN R.
    PVTE1 US 56 841 311
    Co E, 4th Bn, 3rd AIT Bde
    USATC Inf, Ft Lewis Wash

1. Having successfully completed Basic Combat Training and having demonstrated outstanding soldierly qualities, the former member of Company D, 5th Battalion, First Basic Combat Brigade listed above is hereby advanced from Private E-1 to Private E-2 on the date of this letter.

2. This accelerated promotion is made under the provisions of paragraph 7-19b, AR 200-600, and is the result of your dedicated efforts, your exemplary conduct and attitude, and your demonstrated qualities of leadership. The officers and men of this organization join me in congratulating

you as you receive this recognition of your accomplishment during your period of Basic Combat Training.

3. Copies of this letter are being placed in your official U.S. Army records.

JOHN R. GOODLETT
1LT, INF
Commanding

5

Refusal

"Lies," Lieutenant Hutch said.

"Sir?" I was staring down at his desktop and the poster-sized photograph that covered it. A glassy-eyed face looked back at me, a white guy with Afro hair so big it didn't fit within the edges of the paper. Why would the lieutenant have a poster of Abbie Hoffman under the glass on his desk?

"We're swimming in a pack of lies. Hell, I believe you, Sherman, but why should anybody else? This whole platoon is swimming in lies."

"I can't go any further with this, sir. I've never killed anything, much less a human. It's against everything I ever . . ."

"Draft board thought you were cooking it up to get out of the war," he interrupted. "I appreciate your coming in here and telling me straight, but there's nothing I can do. You can't just say you don't want to play the game. You know it doesn't work that way."

"I know, sir."

He nodded and waved his hand for me to sit while he thought.

Lt. Don Hutch commanded my advanced individual training (AIT) unit. After basic training, everybody went through another nine weeks to get their military occupation specialty (MOS), like clerk, radio operator, cook, mechanic, or in my case, infantryman.

"You'll need to flat refuse an order," Hutch finally decided. "Refuse to fire a weapon, something like that. We don't want a radical demonstration or anything, just a simple refusal. No big fuss. It's against military law to refuse an order. In a war zone you could be shot for it." He laughed and caught me staring again at the large face on his desk.

"That's me about ten months ago," he smiled. "I was in dental school when they drafted me. Can you believe that hair? You'll be put in the secured holdover barracks across the way."

"Secured, sir?"

"Okay. It's a jail barracks, guarded twenty-four hours a day. Bars on the windows. Everybody locked in by seven. Bed checks. All that."

"What do I do there, sir?"

"Oh, you'll have plenty of company. Homos. Bed-wetters. All kinds of freaks. You'll just *love* those guys. But during the day you can work in the orderly room. You type?"

"A little, sir."

"Well, you'll type a lot."

On the firing range during the third week, I put down the handgun I had been assigned and stood back from the shooting podium.

The sergeant barked something barely intelligible about six years in Leavenworth federal prison for refusing a direct order. I repeated that I wasn't going to train myself to kill anybody. Like falling dominoes, every soldier on the range stopped to turn and look at me. The sergeant called me a coward. I said again that I wasn't going to shoot the pistol. He raised his hand to slap me, then thought better of it and went to his jeep to radio our commanding officer. Training stopped on the gun range. Groups began to form.

It took Lieutenant Hutch little time to arrive. He directly approached me without even looking at the sergeant and ordered me to pick up the automatic pistol. I refused. He spoke the same words three times, each time adding a witness. Each time I refused. The guys I'd been living with in the training barracks gawked with their mouths wide open. I'd suddenly become one of the hated hippies beyond the base perimeter. Or worse, I was about to become a "holdover." I stood out, exposed, embarrassed, wishing it would all require less attention.

It seemed to take forever for the MP jeep to arrive. When it did, it came screeching to a sliding sideways stop, raising a dust bowl. Two eager-eyed barrel-chested linebackers leapt out and approached me as if the safety of the free world depended on their next few moves. Four rifle-range instructors stood at parade rest. Only the top sergeant moved, speaking out of the side of his mouth, not wanting to take his eyes from me.

"Fucking commie," he said, then turned to address the stunned gallery. "What are YOU looking at?" he bawled. "Your chicken-shit friend here is about to become somebody's girlfriend in the federal prison at Leavenworth fucking Kansas. Anybody wanna hold his hand for the trip?"

The rest of the platoon turned and dispersed, finding safe places to share a smoke and talk in hushed tones until the show was over.

DEPARTMENT OF THE ARMY
HEADQUARTERS
U.S. ARMY INFANTRY TRAINING CENTER
FORT LEWIS, WASHINGTON 98433

October 20, 1968

SUBJECT: Disciplinary Action

TO: SHERMAN, BENJAMIN R. US 56 841 311
    Company E, Fourth Battalion, 3rd AIT
    Brigade

On the 18th of October, 1968, you refused
a legal order to fire a pistol at the rifle
range. Affidavits confirming this insub-
ordination are on file at 5th Battalion
Headquarters pending conclusion of this
action.

1. As of this date, you are immediately
remanded to the custody of your company
commander to be placed under barracks arrest pending court-martial proceedings.

2. You are not to take leave until further
notice. You are restricted to the immediate company area during daylight hours
and the Military Police holdover barracks
at night.

3. Court-martial proceedings will be
postponed until a decision is made re-

garding your application for reclassification as a conscientious objector and reassignment to a noncombatant training
center.

Thomas R. Huntley
Colonel, Fifth Infantry Training Battalion
Commanding

The holdover barracks was on the outskirts of the company yard. It indeed had bars on the windows and doors, and its charm was enhanced by cold water only and no toilet seats. For the next four months I shared this hell with a group of recalcitrant head cases, dropouts rotated in and out of the twenty-two bunks. All of us were being held under lock and guard until orders came for us to return to camp, fly home, or go to jail. We were given no days off and could choose either to sit waiting in the barracks or perform some task for the training camp across the street.

My temporary assignment as an office clerk was a blessing that got me away from the idiots and kept my mind occupied. I learned to type by trial and error while the first sergeant stood behind my right shoulder and leaned over me to rip the seven copies and carbons out of the typewriter as soon as my fingers missed twice. We were bonded this way every morning until I could get through the entire morning report without restarting at least once.

Working as a clerk helped the hours pass quickly. My typing and filing skills improved, earning me some autonomy. I arrived early, made the coffee, stayed late, cleaned the pot, and didn't complain much. I managed to keep my spirits up. But hope waned that I'd get a reassignment away from the training company. Lieutenant Hutch made small talk and treated me like "one of the boys" around the office. I spent the evenings typing my request for reassignment as a noncombatant, and spent the nights sleeping four inches from barred windows, surrounded by jailhouse gutter talk and sporadic flashes of threatening teeth and knives.

We were more inmates than roommates. Roy Martin feigned asthma. Bob Robinson walked stooped over. Shepherd and Jimmy were boys from the Midwest who cried that they had to get home to save their family farms. They were applying for compassionate reassignments. Four of the guys said they were conscientious objectors. Getting to know them, I suspected they were more opposed to being killed than they were to killing. Smith and Friedman were said to be homosexuals, although nothing they did or said made me believe that claim. The sergeants gave them the worst time though, and they were discharged in two weeks.

Martin, the asthma faker, wheezed his way past a team of doctors, then even fooled a board of civilian specialists. When he got his discharge papers, he used the phone in my orderly room to call a cab, then went in to wait for the first sergeant in his office.

"Sherman!" the sergeant bellowed, and I shot out of my chair. He had returned from morning inspection to find his back door wide open, letting in the freezing winter air. The first sergeant had expected to give Hooper one final lecture on responsibility and duty. Instead, all that remained of Roy Martin steamed off the defecation in the half-opened middle drawer of the sergeant's desk. The rest of him had gone.

"Sherman!" The sergeant screamed as if he'd been mortally wounded. "Get in here!" Cleaning the mess with my boss glaring at me, I bit my cheek hard as I pictured the look on Martin's face as he squatted on the desk, his orders in hand, with a taxi fifty feet away.

Barely seventeen years old, Bob Robinson lied to get into the army and tried a more difficult lie to get out. He walked bent at the waist everywhere he went. MALINGERER glowed at the end of his bunk, stenciled in four-inch-high red letters on an official army-issue sign. Malingerer. I had to look it up. He barely managed to limp to the mess hall three times a day and couldn't do anything else. Stooped over, there was no way he could train. And no training . . . no war. His waking hours were devoted to whimpering in the fetal position on his green army blanket. Sometimes his soft wailing would put us to sleep at night, as well as wake us in the morning.

"He wasn't crazy when he got here," the first sergeant assured me. "But he's gettin' there now."

When they came to get him for Leavenworth, Robinson miraculously sprang to life, jumped out of his curled position, and ran screaming, chin up and shoulders back, across the shiny waxed floor, crashing through a thick, closed second-floor door. He flew off the landing and dropped in a lump in the company yard. We flattened our faces against the bars on our windows to get a clear look at the tangled mess strewn out below us. We overheard the MPs radio for an ambulance, trying to describe Robinson's condition. Splinters of wood and glass from the door were embedded in his arms, chest, neck, and face. His lower spine was twisted and appeared broken. He was frozen on the ground in the position he had fallen. Hearing his shrieks of pain and seeing his contorted face as they strapped him to a board and lifted him into the ambulance, someone commented that now he'd probably *really* walk stooped over. For the rest of his life.

After four months of clerk duty by day and holdover barracks madness by night, I got my reprieve. Somebody at the Pentagon finally decided to deem me noncombatant, and I flew away from Fort Lewis without so much as a "See ya!" from anybody. I landed in San Antonio, Texas, about fifty degrees warmer, for training at Fort Sam Houston as a field medic. My new battalion commander took one look at me in my wool uniform and shook his head.

"You bear a resemblance to hammered dog shit, soldier," he said.

"Thank you, sir." He leaned closer to search my meaning. "It's good to be here, sir." He grumbled some unintelligible Southern grammar, dividing each syllable with a cussword, then assigned me to a training company that would begin a week later. This meant I could rest in a barracks by myself for a few days. It was my first break in six months.

In the ensuing ten weeks I trained and earned an MOS as a field medic. They promoted me to private first class (PFC) and issued the papers ordering me to report to Alameda, California, for deployment to the Republic of South Vietnam. The war and I were about to meet.

January 22, 1969

Dear Mom and Dad:

Big day! Classification as I-AO came from the Pentagon. It is not exactly what I hoped for (1-O alternate service) but I am officially a noncombatant soldier for the rest of my two years. And, since I worked every day in the Orderly Room for Lt. Hutch, the time I spent under house arrest is not going to be bad time after all. It all counts as part of two years. The ~~saer~~sergeants here are sure angry. They took their turns to break my spirit. They think I am a chicken but I am not. My orders came just in time.

I report to Ft. Sam Houston in San Antonio, Texas, on the 2nd of February to go to medic school (~~nine~~ ten weeks) and then I will for sure go to Vietnam. I'm only trying to prepare you. As for now, I can actually take my first leave since I got drafted last August. I will be home probably before this letter. If not, it is because I am still waiting stand-by for a military flight. I of course have zero money since they postponed my pay while I was waiting.

I'm going to be a medic! Yay! No <u>weapon</u>!

See ya soon.

Ben

P.S. Pardon the mistakes. This Army typewriter is the oldest Royal in the free world. Can you believe I did all my reclassification paperwork on this thing?

**DEPARTMENT OF THE ARMY
HEADQUARTERS
U.S. ARMY MEDICAL TRAINING CENTER
FORT SAM HOUSTON, TEXAS 78234**

April 8, 1969

SUBJECT: Letter of Commendation

TO: Pvt. Benjamin R. Sherman US 56 841 311
    Company B, 1st Battalion
    U.S. Army Medical Training Center
    Fort Sam Houston, Texas

1. I take this opportunity to commend you for having been selected as a Graduate with Honor of Company B, 1st Battalion, USAMEDTC.

2. In a company of 214 trainees, you earned an achievement score of 945 points out of a possible 1,000 points, not only placing you at the head of your graduating class, but also breaking a record which has stood at USAMEDTC since 1954. Your success with the variety of tests administered and the high composite score attained by you indicates you are extremely well qualified as a medical corpsman.

3. Your military bearing, superior performance and academic achievements were prime factors in making this selection.

4. The successful accomplishment of our mission is assured when we have personnel with your ability and interest as members of the U.S. Army Medical Service.

CHARLES C. PIXLEY
Colonel, Medical Corps
Commanding

To Ben

As I sit at my desk and view your picture,
Now you are grown, but my mind is filled with
    memories
Of you in your youth, far from the mature,
Loving your boyhood, not aware of today's agonies.
So you registered for the draft as all good fellows do.
So your buddies started leaving, not to return.
Yet you were spared for but a brief year or two,
Our hopes soared only to crumble and burn.
Your notice, so final, arrived in due time,
In spite of objections filed so long ago.
My son, my boy, my pride and joy—
I face your leaving with mixed emotions.
I'm proud that you shoulder your responsibilities,
But my mind strays to the tenor of the past.
Long before you were conceived
There lived another,
A Ben Sherman who was my Brother.
I loved him too, as I do you;
Take care, my boy, take care of yourself.
I cannot take it again and again.
Our prayers are with you, all the way—
From August 14th to Armistice Day.

Your Dad

6

Incoming

At thirty-thousand feet, faces paraded in the dark beyond the airplane's wingtips. I pictured those malingering guys in the holdover barracks at Fort Lewis, and faces from boot camp and medical training. I wondered if any of them were going to be there when I landed. Were they still alive? Were they in Germany or Korea or Africa, or Stateside at some desk job? What were their names again? Were any of them out there?

What about school chums? Were any of them drafted and sent to Vietnam? Was anybody looking out his window into the black night wondering about me? What about Terry? Ricky? Had they looked out their plane windows and wondered? Had either one had a premonition that he wouldn't be flying home sitting up?

I did. The idea gagged me like a terrible smell.

When the sun reappeared, it lit nothing but an expanse of blue water as far as I could see. I endured the twenty-two-hour ride as the captive audience of a noisy veteran sergeant returning for his third tour. Lifers love to scare the giggle out of first-timers, especially draftees.

"Bamboo poles stickin' up at an angle. Right under the surface. You fall in that hole 'n you're a skewered shish kebab. Gooks smear their shit all over them punji sticks. If it don't kill you straightaway, it'll make you swell up 'til you're bloated like a toad."

I'd turn my head back to the window, ignoring his prattle, but he'd elbow me in the arm or jab his finger into my thigh to get my attention.

"They can figure out more ways for a body to suffer. Dinks'll come up with somethin' new every time. POWs be better off dead."

The chatter ebbed and flowed until finally, toward the end of the flight, he slept peacefully, his nodding head barely missing my shoulder.

As the big jet finally leaned right and lost altitude to land, daylight had come and gone. I wondered if my 365 days in Vietnam began when we left the United States or when we arrived here. I peered out again at darkness occasionally lit with dozens of orange and pink fireballs falling slowly out of the sky. The sergeant said the glowing flares were announcing our arrival. Two helicopters were keeping pace below and ahead of us, waving searchlights across a mass of textured green. Squinting through the smoky haze, I saw a carpet of green treetops. Then abruptly the jungle stopped. Some naked trunks caught the landing lights and disappeared, but the ground looked flat, barren, ugly, and lifeless. Red dirt passed by my eyes too fast for me to focus on. I glimpsed a span of brown water as the two choppers flew into sight again, noiseless trails of fiery red tracer bullets spitting from their noses. Then two more bursts caught the tree line and exploded on contact. The light show danced outside my tiny window as I pressed my cheek against the panes of insulation. I tried to look as far as I could, straining to know into what kind of lunacy we were landing.

"Must be the place," I muttered.

"You're right! Vietnaaaam! Drop your cock 'n grab your socks, kid," the sergeant rasped. "We're under fire."

He stuffed his order packet into his open shirt and quickly refastened the buttons. I tried to get my heart back down into my chest by swallowing air.

Our fat jet airliner bounced hard twice, then immediately screeched to a sideways skidding halt. Before anyone could do more than gasp in disbelief, the door swung open and fifteen screaming sirens answered our anticipation. A young officer shouted over the noise, "Get out! Everybody out NOW! *IN . . . COMING!!*"

"Here we go again," my seatmate droned. "We got hit at this same goddamn pad last time. Nothing fucking changes."

A whole planeload of virgins sat frozen in their seats, not even reaching to unfasten their seat belts. The comfortable, sturdy airplane seemed a lot safer than the clamor outside.

"Come on!" the sergeant shouted, pulling my arm as he negotiated the temporary stairs. "Get off the goddamn plane!" I took several stairs at a time. "Hit the deck!" he yelled when we got to the bottom. Something whistled far above us and went by. I winced, waiting. Nothing exploded.

"That's ours," he said at my grimace. He meant outgoing artillery. It felt like it was going out right through my chest. Then his eyes moved to a few soldiers huddled on the steps of the plane. "Assholes!" he yelled in my ear, grabbing my armpit to haul me up to a dead run.

"Hit the deck!" he yelled ten strides later. Down we went again, this time on the open tarmac. A blast deafened my ears. I couldn't hear him, but I wasn't lingering behind as he regained his feet and shot out toward a row of bunkers. I did not run crouched over. I did not serpentine or change directions even slightly. I ran like an Olympian, standing tall, head forward, arms pumping, knees high, full speed straight ahead.

As I gasped for each new breath, I sucked in damp air. Thick. Smelly. I couldn't seem to inhale enough oxygen to satisfy my fear. Bellowing with each puff seemed to help. I ran and wailed, ran and panted, ran and snorted, all with the veteran sergeant biting on my ear the whole sprint.

"There's no sumbitch place to hide out here!" he hollered, passing me at the same time. My hearing had returned. "Some dumbass telling those recruits to get down by the plane. Shit!" He veered left into a row of square huts with sandbag-reinforced walls. "If something hits," he panted, "it'll blow sideways 'n get 'em all. Plane too, for chrissake."

As we hustled into the safety of one of the bunkers, I looked over my shoulder to see a crowd of my traveling companions huddled right under the plane. Others cowered on the stairs. "Fucking replacements!" the sergeant spat. Then he disappeared into the dark of the bunker.

Moving through the bunker door into cavelike blackness, I heard a voice calling, "Who's a doc in here?" I squinted to hear better. He called again, but my eyes still hadn't adjusted. A doc?

"Didn't they send one goddamn medic?" the voice asked.

Medic. *Me!* something inside me hollered. *Shut up. You don't know what to do.* A light hit me in the face, then lowered to shine on the bleeding lacerated forehead of a soldier sitting on his butt in front of me. Before I had time to think, I dropped to my knees and applied pressure with the ball of my right hand. I asked the guy holding the flashlight to take off his shirt so I could use it as a bandage.

"Take off your own stupid shirt," he grumbled.

"Here, try this," a voice came from behind me. He handed me a pressure bandage, like the ones I had used in training. I followed a long brown arm to a pair of tired black eyes.

"Th-th-thanks," I stuttered.

"You gonna *move?*" he demanded.

My eyes adjusted to the dark. The patient had bars on his collar. God, not just wounded, but an *officer.* I looked closer at the open cut, which bled freely as I lifted the pressure. Training exercises began to repeat in sequence. My attention turned to applying gauze and grabbing a piece of neatly torn tape extended from the finger of the guy who handed me the bandages. I noted his tattered medic bag and muddy fatigue pants. He nodded approval, tearing more tape with a practiced snip between his forefinger and thumb.

"Good," he assured me quietly. "Good job." Packing his gear in his bag, he smiled. "You'll do fine here." He was clearly a medic, and had been for a while, but he hadn't stepped forward when they were calling for one.

As the all-clear horn sounded, I didn't see him leave. As the scare left me, I noticed that I was dripping with sweat. The air felt hotter and more humid than I had ever experienced. Cigarette smoke thickened it even more in the closeness of the bunker.

"How'd you do this?" I asked the dizzy captain.

"Cracked my noggin on the bunker door comin' in," he said, tapping its steel frame as we passed outside into the predawn gray. He straightened to about six and a half feet tall. The smell of diesel fuel burning human waste hung in the clamminess. "Happens to me all the time," he smiled.

"Give him a Purple Heart," someone joked.

"Purple Heart? Can I have your name?" asked a second lieutenant with a spiral notepad. "Injured in time of attack." He looked around for approval.

"Go screw yourself," the injured captain said as he walked away.

For the first time in the fifteen minutes since I'd arrived in Vietnam, no one was running or screaming or being shot at. I found a place to sit, leaning against a pile of duffel bags, and amused myself watching replacement troops wander around looking for their stuff. I wondered why the worn medic had ignored the calls for help in the bunker. A smack on the head from a low entryway was worth a Purple Heart to one guy and not worth the trouble to even look at to another.

I thought about home, my house on Murieta Way in Sacramento. I could see the small tin box my dad kept hidden under his socks. When he wasn't around, I loved to remove that special box to sort through the memorabilia. College basketball awards. An honor key from some club. Chains, bracelets, his senior class ring. He had world's fair souvenirs and tie clasps with interesting symbols, tarnished from age and neglect. The box also contained his brother's Air Force ID bracelet and flight wings. But my very favorite piece had a purple ribbon with a brass heart hanging from it. It had been handed to my dad at the funeral of his twenty-four-year-old twin brother, Ben. The discreet jewelry meant a lot to my dad, too much to talk about. He explained its significance once, briefly, barely able to speak.

My thoughts were interrupted by the old sergeant from the plane. "Got hit right after the all-clear," he said. He had found his favorite easy-to-scare audience again. "Twenty, thirty rockets," he pointed past my nose. "Wasted me right over there by that truck. Wanna see the scar?"

To avoid his eyes, I searched where he pointed. The flares were gone. The helicopters were gone. The men from the airplane were forming a long line near an official-looking building, and the big jet had already taxied to the end of the runway.

"Can't see 'em comin'," he observed. "Hear 'em whistlin' right before they blow you away." He jabbed at my shoulder to get my attention. When I turned to him, he clapped his hands right in front of my face. "Wham! Blam! Lights out, baby!" He laughed as I grabbed the manila folder of orders I had set down beside the bunker. I started toward the others and looked around for a place to pee. My second fifteen minutes in this country would have to get better.

"Keep your ass low 'n tight!" he yelled at my heels.

Nice talkin' with ya, I thought. Can I find permanent work in a bunker?

"Bunkers don't do nothin' if it's rockets," he answered my unspoken question. "Only save you from light ordnance. Mortars, maybe."

When I joined the line, a forklift carrying the rest of our duffel bags dropped its load in front of us. Several newbies had to jump to avoid the rolling baggage. I figured I'd better find my stuff first and pee later, although it better not be too much later.

"You b-b-been here before?" a fellow first-timer stammered.

"All my life," I said.

"Bullshit."

"Swear to God. I'm two-thirds Vietnamese."

"Bullshit."

Wonderful. Another conversationalist. I spotted the first familiar thing since landing—my last name stenciled on the side of an olive green duffel bag. I dragged it off to the side, stuffed my orders into the top, closed it, and threw it over my shoulder.

"Who's that sergeant?" he asked at my heels.

"My Aunt Estelle." My voice rose to soprano, a sure sign of stress.

"Bullshit."

I stopped and took a deep breath, letting the guy catch up.

"I don't know," I said, looking right at him. "Some lifer who gets his rocks off trying to scare us with war stories."

"Heavy, man," he said after too long a time to ponder. "Got any dope?"

A helicopter ride from the Bien Hoa receiving station landed me in a sprawling base camp called Dong Tam, the Mekong Delta's home to the 9th Infantry Division. My group shuffled into a tent open on all sides, where we were given an hour of "in-country orientation."

"Winning is staying alive!" the sergeant barked. "Staying alive is firepower. It is simply and totally about *fire*power, gentlemen. When the shit hits the fan, you're going to have a lot more of *our* shit in the fucking air than *their* shit in the fucking air." Then he detonated a helpless oil drum.

That was supposed to give us a lesson about igniting det-cord, but actually it served only to see how high we would jump. Next, we were warned about eating the fruit and drinking the water and wandering outside the perimeter. After the fireworks and the warnings, we stood in a straight line at a supply tent where we were each issued in-country fatigues, camouflage boots, a steel helmet, a canteen, and a tall stack of field supplies.

"Fold up them khakis real nice, boys. If any of you are still alive in six months, you *might* get to use 'em for R&R." The supply corporal cackled at his own humor. Everyone else was silent. He was my first example of what grunts in the field refer to as REMFs, rear-echelon motherfuckers.

At the end of the supply tent, each man was being issued an M-16 rifle and four grenades. Slipping to the back of the line, when it came my turn I explained discreetly to the supply sergeant that I didn't carry a weapon. He chuckled and referred me to the platoon leader, a captain, who was far less amused.

"You fucking WHAT?!"

I reached into my back pocket and removed the wallet that held the carefully folded letter from Congressman Moss. I handed the letter to the captain and immediately thought I'd made a huge mistake giving him my only copy. Sucking up his chest and blowing out a gust of wind, he tossed the letter back at me and pointed to the small building across the street, ordering me to get out of his sight before he "made an example" of me. I hurried over to an orderly room, where I showed the clerk my letter and asked where I should go. He assigned me to the morgue.

Congress of the United States
House of Representatives
Washington, D.C. 20515

29 April 1969

AIR MAIL

Pvt. Benjamin Sherman USA
2964 Murieta Way
Sacramento, California 95822

Dear Pvt. Sherman:

Enclosed for your information is the report from the Department of the Army which confirms that your application for discharge as a conscientious objector (1-0) has been disapproved.

I note that you have completed Medical Corpsman training and are scheduled for assignment in Vietnam. In response to the inquiry which you directed to Mr. Jerry Wymore, my District Representative, the Department of the Army assures me that Hospital Corpsman are assigned to hospitals which are not in the combat area and are not subject to ground attack. However, if you find after you have reported to your assignment in Vietnam that the circumstances are not as depicted, please do not hesitate to contact me at once.

Sincerely,

John E. Moss
Member of Congress

JEM:h
Encl.

7

Connie

An uninvited guest broke the morgue tent's reverence on my third day. MPs brought him to the door of our tent but didn't accompany him inside. Most people didn't come all the way into the morgue tent unless they were assigned.

"This here's Cornelius Jones," the MP announced from the door. "He's gonna be-*have* his own self or be right back in the brig." A powerful frame ducked under the tent door, rubbing his wrists. Vincent, Satterfield, and I were frozen by the sheer massiveness that immediately displaced an unfair share of the large tent's breathing space. It was hard not to stare.

The guy was dark as night and as tall and wide as an outhouse. He had power-lifting forearms and biceps, a boxed jaw, and hands like New York steaks. Cornelius Jones towered at least a foot above the three of us. We were awestruck as he moved about the tent, up and down, back and forth, taking inventory of everything in the tent except us.

Cornelius wasn't a medic. He wore the crossed rifles of an infantry grunt on his lapel. Dark green material on his sleeves outlined where his rank of corporal had once been sewn. The sun had faded the rest of his fatigues, but his two stripes had been removed, a sign of being busted to private. He returned to the tent opening and watched as the jeep spun on the gravel outside then roared off. Finally he turned to us and tilted his gigantic head left and right, creaking and cracking his stumpy neck like a dozen fingers breaking. It took him all of thirty seconds to firmly establish himself as a classic four-star bully.

He moved directly across the room to the only white guy.

"You eat pussy?" he asked, barely inches from my face.

"Howdy," I said, smiling slightly.

"You eat pussy!" he answered his own question, nodding before I had a chance to respond. I returned to cutting away a wet uniform from a dead soldier. The giant circled, shining with sweat and esteem. "All whiteys . . ." He trailed off into some sort of gibberish. I ignored him. He shoved my arm to get my attention. "I axed you a question!" I still managed to ignore him. "No *brothuh* would get his face *near* that thang." He added a limp as he walked away. I caught a "No sweat" wink from one of the other medics. Even with that, I was still feeling very much the minority. As my eyes followed Cornelius Jones, he spun around to shout, "Any man who'd eat pussy'd suck a dick, 'n there it is!"

We were more amused by the intrusion into our hypnotic routine than we were offended by his subject matter, but I still had a sinking feeling. Out of respect for his bearing and biceps, disapproval from any of us was not going to surface. Some grunts did tend to dwell on their favorite subject. He was allowed to jab at each of us all afternoon and then again the next morning. The theme remained constant.

I dubbed him Connie, which he took as a mispronunciation of his nickname Cornie. He seemed to put it aside, not wanting to be distracted from his continuous lecture on preferred sexual activities. He punctuated each revelation with the now familiar phrase, "Any man who'd eat pussy'd suck a dick, 'n there it is."

During a break from the smell and the big man's pounding, I explained privately to the others that I actually intended the nickname Connie as a shot at his masculinity which, I allowed, had to be suspect with all the concentration on dick-sucking. The two of them just rolled their eyes at each other and shook their heads. Not even a smirk. This was a tough room.

"Better jus' leave offa Jones," one of them warned. It was his first full sentence in three days.

As our shift wore on, the lewdness droned, but Cornelius wasn't getting to us. There was a noticeable transfer of power occurring in the room. He knew it but couldn't figure out what it was. Following one of his tirades, all eyes shot toward me, looking for my response. Like it or not—no words spoken, no attitudes positioned, no threats fashioned—I was becoming Connie's opposition. I kind of liked it. The power was shifting and it was clear. I figured he was just too stupid to know what was happening.

He ignored the others, circling to get my attention. He had done no work since he arrived. His time in the morgue had been spent either smoking just outside the tent flap or chattering to us about the follies of fellatio.

"You a faggot, whitey?"

I was scrubbing blood and mud off the table. I offered him the dripping sponge. He literally leapt back four feet. "Get that shit away from me!" The smaller of the two medics let out a giggle, and Jones shot him a quick right slap to the temple.

"Get off me, suckuh!" pled Satterfield. Jones jabbed the air at him, bobbing and weaving from left to right.

"You the suckuh," Connie spat back. "You the big

dick suckuh. Jus' like whitey over there." He stabbed
the air in front of my face. "Any man who'd eat pussy'd
suck a dick, 'n there it is!"

"Suck this," I said, grabbing a handful of my crotch.
It was automatic. Reflex. I'd done it a hundred times
on the basketball court. He froze and stared in disbelief. "You sure got a thing for sucking dicks, Connie.
What're you trying to tell us?"

Cornelius stood dumbfounded. The others were
snickering, but that was muzzled when he turned his
glare on them. His face looked like he had way too
much to think about all at one time, and this was causing him trouble. He peered at me, twisting his long black
neck without moving his wide shoulders, reminding me
of a turtle's head stretching out of its shell. He clearly
didn't like white people in general, and he didn't like me
in particular. And he *especially* didn't like being called
Connie. Not at all. The room stood still.

"I'm watching my family jewels with you around,
Connie."

Now he knew where his power had gone. Now he
knew what had been wrong all day. He glanced at the
others, then slid sideways toward the door, his lips wrin-
kled in disgust. "You sick," he snarled, turning to the
tent opening for a breath of air. "Y'all fuckin' *sick!*" He
turned back to look more at the tent than at us and repeated, "Y'all sick touchin' dead peoples all day." Then
he left.

For a few moments we all just stared at each other. No
bodies were coming in. A lone empty rubber bag rested
on one of the two prep tables. Was there any difference
between this and prison? As if being drafted, sent to
Vietnam, and assigned to a morgue weren't enough,
now this psychotic sociopath convict had been thrown
in to rub our noses in it deeper.

My mind was wandering all over the past four months. I was supposed to be in college, drinking beer. These tall skinny guys were supposed to be shooting college hoops. Instead we got drafted and, overnight, found ourselves in a barracks trying to pee with twelve naked men in line behind us. And that was only the first night. Now the MPs had escorted one Cornelius Jones in to make us happy. Who decides these things?

"You fuck!" was the last thing I heard before seeing stars. Jones had ducked back in the door and attacked from behind before anyone saw him. He smashed the back of my neck with both hands clasped. When my eyes cleared, I was on the floor looking up.

"White bastard!" he screamed. Then, with each syllable, he landed a kick to my midsection. "Muh-thuh-fuh-king-white-cock-suh-kuh." Rolling into the fetal position, I felt something pop. He kicked again. Another pop. I scrambled under one of the tables. He knocked the table over, crashing it in front of me.

"Jesus!" I cried.

"Jesus?!! *Jesus?!!*" he bellowed back, leaning down into my face. "What you want with *my* Jesus, you white-faced devil? Don'chu know Jesus is a *black* man?" He slapped the side of my head. "You hear me, whitey?" He slapped me again. "Ain't no Jesus in Vietnam!"

"Cut it out!" one of the others hollered. Jones grabbed something off the floor and spun around to face the other two medics.

"Shut up, niggah, or you be next," he threatened through clenched teeth. He was growing hysterical, shaking all over, slurring his words. He turned back to me. "Jesus a black man. Desert niggah. Come outta the Holy Land. Moses too. Desert niggahs, all of 'em." He slapped at me with his open hand to punctuate his point about the skin color of Jesus, Moses, Abraham, and as many saints as he could remember.

For the first time in my life, I felt a color difference. I couldn't remember ever feeling so totally white. The other two guys were clearly on my side, but they were caught between fear for my safety and fear for their own. Yet they stood their ground, yelling for him to quit. Most sane people would have run like hell.

"My mama called on Jesus to keep her from killin' me," he laughed. "Now I'm askin' my brown-skinned Jesus to give me permission to *cut* this muhthahfucker!" In the hand that wasn't slapping me, he clutched the long silver scissors he'd grabbed off the floor.

My exit was blocked. Cornelius Jones clenched his fist, and the slaps became slugs. Kneeling on the floor at my side, flailing away and cussing all the while, his howling was a vile sound that came from somewhere deep, like he was taking out on me a thousand beatings he had suffered. His voice cut through my protective curl deeper than the beating. It was shrill and piercing, the most demented noise I had ever heard.

The first few blows hurt badly and I tried to resist. But helplessness clicked in, and something inside me just let go. I felt washed with a surreal feeling of being outside the whole confrontation. It was as if I were looking down from some perch onto a ridiculous scene. I was trying to figure out what was happening rather than suffering the reality. Logic became a force. Something unknown and never before experienced was lifting me out of my own body. It was euphoric. Internal sensations swelled while external ones subsided. I was afloat . . . aloft . . . adrift . . .

For some reason, Connie didn't use the scissors. Instead, he scrambled to his feet and began kicking again. He missed a couple of times, kicking the overturned table instead of me, letting out demonic screams as he did. And though I was becoming oblivious to the pain and powerlessness of the situation, something began to slice through my passivity. It wasn't the physical threat as much as his *insanity* that was overwhelming. If I struck back, it would only grow worse. Most of his blows were soon missing anything vital, the damage having already been done with the first few kicks. His rage was overrunning itself. His voice was hoarse and cracking and his energy was beginning to wane. As soon as his frenzy reached the summit and began to fall off the other side, my own ability to remain remote began to drop rapidly as well.

In a tumbling of reality, it occurred to me that the end was approaching. My illusion turned to being stuck in a well, or a shaft. A very tight and deep constricted place. Caught. No exit. Surrounded on all sides by hurt, and only more to follow. I wasn't going to be able to sustain another blow and hold consciousness. At the very instant I knew I had endured more than I could take, I saw the shadow of a huge object slamming into the back of Connie's neck and head. I had forgotten about the other two medics.

In their panic, my morgue mates had effectively introduced Cornelius Jones to a flying silver-gray aluminum box. He went down fast, landing hard in a heap on top of me. Everything went absolutely still. Connie and me, the casket that flew, the overturned table I was cowering next to, and all its former contents lay in a twisted jumble of arms, legs, cotton balls, alcohol, swabs, and rubber gloves. Feebly rolling onto my feet with their help, I joined the two would-be assassins staring at Connie's inanimate body on the floor.

We were alone, the three of us, in a quieter morgue than even before. We were alone, with no one but us and

a lump of threatening flesh flopped at our feet, coma-
tose, bleeding slightly from the back of the skull. We
were detached, isolated in our thoughts. We were shuf-
fling through panic and guilt and our sudden uninvited
camaraderie.

No one spoke. I was still too afraid to even whimper
from pain. None of us wanted to give any kind of vocal
acknowledgment to what had just happened. For several
minutes that felt like hours we waited for the lump to
move, but it didn't. It didn't move at all.

Eventually finding myself at the scrub sink looking
down at my breakfast, I used my fingers to squash the
puke through the tiny drainholes. The worst pain I felt
was the piercing in my ribs while throwing up. I chucked
once and realized I had to arrest that urge immediately.
My gut could not withstand another retching. I stood
drooling and spitting into the sink, not looking back.
The scrub basin was a safer place to ponder what was
lying behind on the ground.

I'm sure Vincent and Satterfield were thinking exactly
what I was thinking: In a war zone there's no protection
from this sort of thing. If we called the MPs, they'd cart
Jones off for another couple of days in the brig. And
then what? What would happen to us when he was released? People came here and died. The point was not to
be the one in the bag.

The two gangly medics who had ended my ordeal
didn't have to think long. Without a word between
them, they lifted the table off the floor, cleaned up the
mess, and went back to work. They lifted Connie onto
the morgue prep table, sponged the blood from the back
of his head and neck, then packed him into one of the
bags. When I saw what they were doing, I walked to the
desk in the corner and grabbed a red toe tag. Without a
word, I copied the information from his dog tags onto

the card, twisted it around his shoelaces, and pulled the long zipper up over his face. I was slumping with pain, so the two of them lifted the heavy bag into the aluminum box and closed the lid.

The thick bags and the aluminum missile were designed to keep stench in during a long trip. This was also effective in keeping fresh air out. Cornelius Jones was headed home early.

8

Smitty

At first light, I limped to the morgue tent and waited for Vincent and Satterfield. I knew they wouldn't be early, but it beat tossing in my bunk. I peered out the tent flap a dozen times, watching soldiers walk to their assigned duties as if nothing had happened the night before. I waited an eternity, hoping we'd have the conversation I had rehearsed all night. Their actions were justified. He would have killed me. Nobody will know if we swear to trust each other, keep our word, and forget it ever happened. But they didn't come. I waited in the morgue tent alone with only my fearful heart and aching body.

As the sun peeked over the squat buildings of Dong Tam, light beams shot horizontally through the tent flap. A shadow ran across the tent, startling me. A man's frame filled the doorway. He didn't cross the threshold. He waved a bundle of papers in my direction, indicating that he'd prefer me to step out. There was no MP armband on his uniform.

"Private First Class Sherman?"

"Uh . . . yes, sir?" He looked menacing. Feet apart, jaw firm, drilled elocution. As he leaned into the room, I recognized the stripes of a ranking sergeant. Army sergeants hate being called "sir." "Uh . . . yes, *Sergeant.* Sorry. Sherman. Yes. That's me. I'm Sherman."

"Orders!" He waved the papers again, turning away from the odors of the tent. I tried to read the papers over his forearm, but he folded them, stuck them inside his shirt, and refastened one button. "Later," he said. "Sherman, I come to get yer happy ass outta this morgue." He grinned briefly, flashing gleaming teeth against tanned skin, then strutted toward the jeep he'd left with its motor running.

"Sergeant?"

"Sergeant First Class Robert E. Lee Smith, Jr.," he smiled again. "Yer personal goddamn guardian angel. Grab yer shirt 'n c'mon, soldier." Without thinking, I tore off the blue tunic and was buttoning my fatigue shirt as I jumped into the jeep.

"Robert E. Lee is a goddamn general's name," he bellowed. "But NCO I am, 'n NCO I'll stay. I *work* for a goddamn livin'! You can just call me Smitty. Everybody else does."

My duffel bag was perched in the backseat, clearly stenciled SHERMAN on the side. He'd been to my barracks, packed my stuff. He'd probably even grabbed my toothbrush and towel from the latrine.

"Where we going?"

"*Nuaces.* Navy troopship out on the river 'bout fifteen miles south of here." Dong Tam sat on the Mekong River. To get fifteen miles south, we'd have to drive through the jungle, outside the protected perimeter of the base. "*Nuaces* is a troop carrier. Can't dock at base camp. Too shallow here."

I noticed a marked drawl. "Where you from?" Always one of the first things one soldier asks another.

"Mis'ippi."

Mississippi fit. Ruddy red cheeks on a leather face, suntanned forearms, a blistered red neck, and rough worker's hands gave him the look of a country boy. He had a wiry frame that had been rode hard and put up wet a few times too many. He slipped his fingernail under the pop-tab of a Schlitz and pulled it without a hitch. Half the beer disappeared in a single lift. Smitty belched and finished it with another long gulp, crushing the can while still tilting it above his open throat, squeezing out the final drops.

"Beer?" he asked, smiling a wide menacing smirk.

"In the middle of the morning?"

"Get it while ya can," he said, offering me the lone soldier of a six-pack. "Who knows when we'll get another chance. Hell, it's happy hour someplace in the world!"

"We're going to a navy ship?" I asked.

"Gonna join our medical company. All us medics are stationed on the *Nuaces*. Commanding officer's a crack doc named Guenther. German guy. Helluva chess player. Plastic surgeon. Got drafted just like you. Not regular army, but a damn fine doctor."

"We'll be in a hospital?"

"A third of the time. Then a third in the field 'n the other third on medevacs. Ya like choppers?" He laughed in my face. I unconsciously patted the wallet in my back pocket where I carried the letter from Congressman Moss. I had it memorized. I would not be required to serve in combat.

Smitty jammed the jeep into second gear and lugged down the dirt street past rows of barracks. I tried to sip the Schlitz without spilling. He stopped at the gate and picked up two infantrymen carrying M-16s. I didn't know if they were hitching a ride to the ship or coming along to guard us. I hadn't been out of base camp, so I didn't know if we were venturing into unfriendly territory. They sat up on the backs of the seats behind us, automatic weapons at the ready, looking into the trees from side to side as we took a rutted road along the river. I'd been awake all night in physical pain, worried, wondering, guilty, afraid, and trying to breathe with a chest that felt like a bag of anvils. My tired eyes bounced in their sockets as we bumped through the jungle. Every rut in the road jostled a bruised or battered part of my body. Fifteen miles took us at least an hour.

A sudden burst from one of the backseat rifles whiplashed my neck. I ducked. My arms flew up involuntarily and I fell to my knees on the floorboard. Smitty swerved the jeep and braked, tipping us sideways into a rut. One of the grunts had shot at the treetops. Sergeant Smith charged over his seat, grabbed the kid's rifle, and smacked the butt on his steel helmet.

"Hey!" the kid protested. Smitty snapped out the ammunition clip, tossed it on the floor, checked the chamber to clear it, then threw the rifle with a thud into the boy's stomach. He wheezed, falling into the backseat. Smitty glared at him, then flipped back into the driver's bucket. He forced the floor shift into first, popped the clutch, and stepped on the accelerator all at once. Nobody spoke for the rest of the ride.

After a few more miles of pounding through the ruts, Smitty turned the jeep from the road, bounded even more violently through a dried rice paddy, then came to rest on a red clay riverbank. A flat barge was floating at the water's edge, tied with heavy chains to two concrete anchors on the shore. The humidity doubled where the jungle reached the water. I spanked a mosquito as big as a dragonfly that was trying to penetrate my pant leg. It left a spot of blood the size of a quarter.

The two riflemen tossed out my duffel bag, clambered into the front seats of the jeep, skidded a U-turn, and headed back to base camp. We could hear the M-16 firing off again thirty seconds down the road. Smitty and I walked out onto the barge.

"Yahoos," Smitty growled as he tapped a Camel against the watch he wore face-in to protect it. With one hand he flipped the cigarette to catch the wet sliver of his bottom lip while his other hand nimbly met it with a flick of his Zippo lighter. Leaning against my bag, pushing his hat over his eyes, he sucked on the cigarette until it glowed a long, steady red cinder. Smoke escaped briefly from his mouth and streamed neatly into his inhaling nostrils, then exploded in all directions through clenched teeth.

"Goddamn yahoos," he repeated, tilting his hat back to investigate me a little more closely. He placed the pack of Camels and his lighter between us. "California, huh?"

"Yeah. All my life."

"Nuts 'n queers."

"Yeah, queers and nuts keep moving to California from Mississippi." I smiled. I was always ready with a comeback when people bad-mouthed my home state.

He flinched a bit, then returned my smile. "What is it with California? Ya got somethin' in the water?"

"They *hang* queers and nuts in Mississippi. No wonder they all move to California. You can have them all back."

Smitty opened his eyes wide, raised his black bushy eyebrows, then squinted and laughed from his belly. "Prob'ly right, goddammit. Prob'ly right!" Then he added, in a sly warning, "Now don't get me to likin' ya, son. We ain't here to *like* nobody."

As I flamed my own filtered Kool with his lighter, I saw USMC engraved in bold letters on the side. "You get this off a Marine?" I asked.

"You get them smokes off a colored man?" he re-

Smitty

77

sponded. Kool cigarettes were a favorite of the black troops. I'd started smoking them in college while playing poker with the basketball team and had never tried any other brand.

"Last I looked, we were in the army."

"I was a Marine fourteen years."

I asked him how he came to be an army medical sergeant, but instead of answering, he smoked the Camel down, stripped apart the tobacco from the butt, and neatly toed the tiny wad of cigarette paper into the mud. I'd seen drill sergeants at Fort Lewis and Fort Sam Houston perform this same ritual. None of them smoked filters, and all of them habitually "field-stripped" their butts. When I tried to field-strip a filtered Kool, I wound up with a lapful of sticky, yellowish-brown stained gunk. From then on I stored used filters in my pocket until I could find a can.

Finally, Smitty deigned to answer me. "We got overrun at the DMZ, 'n I recouped Stateside in a Vet's for four months. We got hit by waves of screamin' Chucks," he grinned, appreciating his free flow of words.

"Chucks?"

"Charlie," he corrected. "The Viet Cong. Charlie. Chuck?" He eyed me for a moment. "Man, you *are* green. Where'd ya train?"

"Fort Sam Houston. Well, Fort Lewis first, then Fort Sam."

"They didn't call 'em Charlie?"

"Sure," I lied. He knew it.

"Radio talk. Viet Cong are VC. Victor Charlie."

"Uh huh."

"Chuck. Charles. Mr. Charles. *Hos*-tiles."

My head nodded at each name. But I didn't know. Our drill sergeants used generic terms—the enemy, aggressors, or something precise, like commies. They were training us for any war, any enemy.

"But I don't call nobody a gook. I hate them little bastards, don't get me wrong. But if ya reduce somebody, y'know, like prejudice—a slang name, like zipperheads, dinks, slopes, all that shit—it's just like nigger or chink or spick. Hell, I don't even like callin' a grunt a grunt."

I hadn't expected to hear a white redneck sergeant from Mississippi exempting himself from 150 years of bigotry. It seemed out of character, and it exposed my own prejudice against white Southerners.

"It ain't about racism goddammit, Bubba." He'd read my mind. "It's about reducin' the enemy. Never underestimate the bastards. They're very capable of blowin' yer happy ass to kingdom come."

That took him back to his war story.

"Scared shitless, all of us. Firefightin' like Fourth of July in Chinatown. Air full of lead. Un-be-*liev*-able. Melt the end of yer rifle. Tracers everywhere, bouncin' off shit, comin' from all sides. Bastards screamin' too. Whiny-ass screech. Worse than a landlord's cat."

He stuck his little finger in one ear and fiercely waggled it, grimacing as he spoke. "Rockets. Grenades. Mortars. Deafenin' shit. Goddamn headache for days."

He stopped to reflect, started to speak a few times, but winced and changed his mind. Finally he mumbled, "I got shot up 'n quit the Corps." He paused to light another smoke. "Guess they had a point. I looked like burnt toast for a while. Tripler Army Medical in Hawaii, then Fitzsimmons in Denver. Nothin' I could do. As soon as I could get up to walk down the corridor with a cane, they booted me out on my ass. Made me a civilian. And I hate civilians."

He knew what I was about to ask, so he cut me off.

"Couldn't hack it back in the World. Made the ol'

lady crazy. She was all over me like white on rice, but she knew I wasn't supposed to be home. I wasn't done yet."

I waited. It was clear he had more to say.

"Marines know fightin'. I'm a soldier." He stopped to clear his throat and spit. "We watched each other's butts. I was their platoon leader." He looked at the river as he talked, as if it were reflecting ghosts from the past. "Got our asses beat in. Too many of 'em, truth be told. Overran us. Happened everywhere, but we got some of the worst of it. Some Chinese New Year thing they celebrated by swarmin' over us like locusts."

The Tet Offensive of 1968 stands out as the worst American loss of the war. But none of us knew that in 1969. And nobody wanted to tell us how bad it could get again. The next Tet loomed around the corner, as anybody's New Year has a habit of repeating itself.

"Re-upped for six. Army took me, rank 'n all."

With each drag on his Camel, he swished air through his gums and teeth, making long, sucking saliva sounds. Smoke billowed from his nostrils and strained through his teeth as he spoke and spit. He'd stop to pick a piece of tobacco off the tip of his tongue, then take another long drag like a condemned man. When he smoked, Smitty looked like the Humphrey Bogart tough guy straight out of *Casablanca* or *The African Queen*.

"They were a top buncha guys."

"Were?" I asked before I could stop myself.

"Lost," he said. After peering straight at the sun as if to dry his eyes, he turned to me. "Y'all right, Bubba?"

"Fine. Did you say lost?"

Smitty ignored my question. "How're yer guts, Bubba?"

Moving my forearm from where it had been supporting my aching side, it hadn't occurred to me that the sergeant knew I'd been beaten up. I shook my head. Turning to squat and watch the river, Smitty lit a third smoke as the quiet heat of the afternoon caught up with me. Weariness from lack of sleep the night before had shoved aside my pain, but now a dozen shades of red and orange flooded the skin of my eyelids. My body abdicated, sinking as if cushioned by the metal grate of the floating pontoon barge. I couldn't feel its hardness. I felt almost safe as long as this ex-Marine from Mississippi watched the river.

I woke with a start as Smitty kicked my boot. "Up!"

A huge gray vessel was sitting directly in front of us, blocking my view of the river. It had slipped in while I slept a dozen feet away. Several crewmen peered over the rail and grinned as I came to my senses, clearly amused that I could nap while the huge, noisy ship pulled up to the barge. They knew a greenhorn when they saw one.

"Saddle up, Doc," Smitty ordered again.

Up the plank, to my first steps ever on a navy ship, I followed Smitty's lead and snapped a quick salute to a bored-looking navy officer. Smitty moved assuredly, obviously in familiar territory, as he led me across a deck then backward down several sets of vertical stairs. We twisted through oval steel doors. He had to come back for me twice as I gawked at everything left and right, up and down. We passed bay after bay of long rows of bunk beds. I wondered if I'd ever find my way out. The air cooled measurably as we progressed deeper inside, and the humidity seemed to disappear. My spirits lifted at the first livable temperature since I'd arrived in Vietnam.

"Cool," I sighed.

"Ain't exactly the army."

"No, sir."

"Don't call me sir, goddammit. I *work* for a livin'."

We stopped in front of a three-high set of bunks. "Eight hours in the rack is all ya get," Smitty explained, slapping his palm on the empty bed. "Ya'll be sharin' this with two other guys on different shifts. Put yer bag 'n gear under the bottom hammock 'n yer soap 'n shit in here." He kicked one of three wire baskets at the foot. "Got five hours left on yer clock. Get to it! I'll show ya the mess hall 'n latrine when yer up." He stepped out over the high threshold and left.

"I'm fine," I offered to his back.

Big lie. My kidneys were battered by the jeep's bony backrest, and lying on the pontoon hadn't helped. The night before I'd had trouble peeing as well as sleeping. No blood or anything, but my kidneys had taken some kicks and still ached. Needing badly to get rid of the Schlitz, I hustled through a couple of bays dimly lit by recessed amber lights in the bulkhead, only to come to a dead end marked MECHANICAL. As I turned to retrace my steps, the door opened abruptly and a burly man in a light blue work shirt stepped over the portal and nearly ran me over.

"I'm new," I said. "Gotta piss." A sop of wet stained my arm where his sweaty shirt bumped my fatigues as he pushed by.

"Follow me." In tight hallways filled with more three-high bunks and the trailing smell of my guide, I walked fast and breathed through my mouth to avoid the odor rising from hot breath, exposed armpits, and floating flatulence. Humanity sprawled left and right, up and down, hanging off the triple berths, a symphony of snoring, groaning, hacking, and wheezing. Three bays back, the latrine stood only ten feet in the opposite direction from where I had started. I thanked the sailor and he responded with a grunt.

My kidneys felt crushed, and pain prevented my natural process from beginning. My testicles felt as if only a couple hours had gone by since they'd been kicked. My bladder was poking out like half a volleyball. When I was able to place my mind somewhere else, on some object on the wall, my plumbing finally functioned and relief slowly spread all through me. First time I'd peed since the beating in the morgue. It's amazing how taken for granted a good piss can be.

Back in the sweatshop, I crammed into the berth under two others known to me only by the depth of the lumps in their thin bunks. I wondered if I could ever learn to sleep in such cramped quarters, but the soft rolling of the ship and warm, low vibration of its engines made even the tightness in my abdomen begin to loosen. We were under way. As the *Nuaces* headed up the Mekong, I practically fainted to sleep.

What seemed like only moments of rest ended abruptly with my feet being grabbed and twisted left and right. Smitty threw me a towel and rubber thongs and pointed toward the oval doorway. "Latrine's in there. Wear shower shoes. Place is crawlin' with infectious shit."

The towel was damp. "Somebody use this?" I asked.

"Nope. Everything stays wet out here on the water. Humidity's double."

I knew what he meant about the fungus. At the base camp shower back in Dong Tam, there were science projects thriving between the planks in the wood floors and up about twelve inches on the walls. By comparison the navy ship's shower looked squeaky clean and smelled like industrial-strength disinfectant. When it became obvious the water temperature didn't go higher than tepid, I ended my shower and tried to dry off with the damp towel that absorbed nothing. I pulled my clothes over my clammy body and was looping the last eyelet on my boots when a navy man threw his shirt off, kicked two deck shoes under our bunk, and, wearing his socks and jeans, fell asleep right next to me in less time than it takes to tell it. I got up quickly and glanced back at his hairy chest, neck, and shoulders. The faded tattoo of a blue and purple mermaid ran the length of his fore-arm. His sprawling stomach creased where the rolls gave in to gravity. A long lumpy wound between his nip-ples showed rough red stitches that looked new. I won-dered if he had come aboard on his own two feet or on a litter.

Coming up out of the cool lower decks into triage was like walking into a sauna. They saved the precious little air-conditioning for the operating room. I soon learned that for every procedure performed out in the open-bay triage, one operating assistant sponged the wounds of the patient while two others sponged the face and arms of the attending doctor. Large doors to the helicopter pad were permanently open to allow for emergency traf-fic. Two closed doors on one wall led to the surgery the-ater and an X-ray lab. Closed double doors on the other end opened onto a post-op ward with about fifteen beds for recovering patients. Keeping all these doors shut helped maintain a more comfortable temperature be-yond them, but triage itself remained hot and humid.

A dozen blue smocks were cleaning the four prep ta-bles and scrub sinks and picking up trash. No one wore rank, so I didn't know whom to approach. Smitty had told me where to go and said he'd meet me there. One lone patient sat on a table in front of an older man who seemed to be in charge.

"Sherman! Over here!" The older guy motioned for me to join them. "You just get here?" He prepared to uncover a bandaged thigh. The wounded soldier sat braced, watching intently, looking as if he might leap up at any second.

"Six days in country," I said. He took the bandage away and exposed torn flesh bleeding profusely from several shrapnel wounds.

"Scrub!" he ordered, nodding to the sinks against the wall. "Come back and sponge for me."

This I knew how to do. The morgue tent had not only prepared me for the worst, it also taught me about scouring. Yet something about seeing a real wound on a live human offered a new perspective. Pain was now part of the experience. The *living* proof of war sat right in front of me, gritting his teeth, clenching the sides of the table, looking down in disbelief at the messy jagged tissue lying open where his solid leg used to be.

The doctor doused the wounds liberally with a brown liquid, and the soldier's whole body went completely rigid as he shouted "Yeooooow!" Everyone in triage turned to look at us. They seemed to be questioning me. I looked back at the doctor and felt their eyes leave two by two.

"Get this guy gone, STAT!" the doctor barked to a young medic leaning on the head of the table. The wounded man now lay back stiff, straining against his outstretched leg. The doctor held his knee tightly to the gurney. "Let's go!" he ordered. I leaned in to help, replacing the doctor's grip with my own. He turned away and snapped off his surgical gloves, tossed them on the floor, then swiftly moved to the sink to begin washing again. "Get the clean room ready!"

"Yessir, Major." Three medics moved with determination through the door to surgery. One pushed the gurney toward the open door while I walked alongside, holding the wounded man's leg still.

Moments later, in the surgery theater, someone held a mask to the patient's face and asked him to count backward from one hundred. The third attendant unwrapped a cloth bundle of instruments. The patient dropped into a well of deep sleep before he could get to ninety, and I let go of his leg.

"I shouldn't have doused him like that," Major Guenther sighed. "Never can predict pain thresholds. Some wouldn't even flinch. Others flip right onto the floor." He handed me a safety razor and the same bottle of brown Betadine. "This works for shaving too." He indicated where to remove the leg hair from around each wound, then reminded me to scrub again first. After I had shaved the leg to Dr. Guenther's specifications, he released me to return to triage, where I remained, trying to look busy for the rest of my first shift.

Over the following three nights, you'd think I had become a barber. Every medic in triage seemed to have a specialty. I must have replaced the guy with the razor, because I shaved arms, legs, necks, scalps, and even the hairy butt of a talkative captain.

"Can you believe this shit? Hey! Major Goon-tah! Remember me?" The captain had been in triage before.

The medics referred to him as Captain Buttshot. He'd been wounded by his own troops. Not critically, but just enough to get him out of action, where his attitude and incompetence threatened the safety of his men. "Fragging" was never mentioned publicly or reported officially, but everyone knew it happened. Even though a captain would normally carry battlefield clout, he couldn't do much about getting fragged. It goes down among superior officers as a career-limiting occurrence. And it had happened to Captain Buttshot before.

I first heard about fragging in basic training, when the drill sergeant threatened us if we didn't show enough gung-ho spirit to suit him. The concept of fragging gave me shivers. It wouldn't be a big deal on the ship, but Smitty had said we'd also be supporting missions in the field. Would the fact that I wouldn't carry a weapon make me seem a liability out in the field? I remembered the orientation sergeant's speech about firepower being at the core of Vietnam soldiering. Would I even get a chance to prove myself?

Major Guenther suggested to Captain Buttshot that his men might be having a difficult time adjusting to his particular style of leadership. As a higher-ranking officer, Guenther could cynically assert such things. The captain ignored the suggestion and assured us all that he'd be back with his platoon as soon as we patched him up.

"Third time I been shot in the ass!" he boasted as I swabbed him for the razor. "Can you goddamn believe it?"

9

Scrub

The doctors were draftees too. Maj. Gerald Guenther had been plucked from his thriving private practice as a plastic surgeon. Capt. David Cohn had been drafted right out of his residency at a fancy Jewish teaching hospital in downtown New York City. The interruption to their careers wasn't exactly welcome, but at least they didn't have to endure the demeaning weeks of basic training that we had. They went through a few days of "learning military talk," then were commissioned as officers with rank based on their education and experience.

Major Guenther wore the highest rank and served as lead surgeon and quasi–commanding officer, but the only orders he issued were in the operating room. He read no army papers, gave no assignments, and didn't have an office except for the big oak desk in the middle of triage that we all used. If he sat at the desk at all, it was to write letters home or play chess. The hospital was run by people doing the jobs they were trained to do, mostly independent of military regulations, subject only to what the helicopters brought.

For a plastic surgeon who made his money on noses and eyelids, Dr. Guenther was very adept inside the body as well. His thick German accent was convincing as he described internal organs in Latin and often asked for instruments in German, always translating impatiently into English a bit louder than before. Dr. Cohn, the younger of the two surgeons, had great respect for the major's skills with a scalpel.

On my third early-morning shift, finally released from razor duty, I scrubbed for surgery prep and found myself in the operating room at Major Guenther's side, sponging his forehead to keep the sweat from falling into his work. Captain Cohn was observing as the major put a boy's ear back together by comparing it to the other ear in a mirror held by a medic. When they later removed the bandages to inspect the surgery, the soldier gasped at the improvement. "That ear never looked like the other one! Now I got a matched pair!"

I loved the surgery theater. It was crisply clean and clinical. It was cool and comfortable. It was professional. There were mentors here. Older, wiser, tidier, they were proficiency experts with clean language and scrubbed ideals who called each of us by our first name instead of our rank. In the operating room, I had a surreal sense that I was participating in priestly work.

The doctors constantly exchanged philosophies, occasionally interrupting their debates with orders for sponges or instruments. On the other side of the doors in triage one heard only idle chatter about who last got laid. In surgery I heard actual conversations, often of significance.

After Dr. Guenther finished the ear, two new patients were brought in. One was a scheduled forearm operation, the other an emergency chest wound that had just arrived by chopper. I scrubbed again and moved to help Dr. Cohn with the forearm. Dr. Guenther had been ready to leave, but he stayed for the chest wound. They picked up a conversation the two must have started earlier.

"I don't close my eyes for a minute," Cohn shook his head.

"The Vietnamese at the base are no different from the peasant farmers," Guenther countered. "Surely they prefer *us* to the guerrillas."

"If she's got a job on the base, what's she going to say? That doesn't mean she likes us much."

"She's cutting your hair. How long does that take? Twenty minutes? You're paying her five bucks. That's more than she can make in a whole day at the mess hall."

"I still keep my eyes open. I don't like her behind me with scissors."

Guenther's patient had a small black dot on his chest, and the surgeon prepared to open him. Compared to the messy forearm in front of Cohn, the major's job looked simpler, but it was serious trouble. Guenther's kid had a sucking chest wound and collapsed lung, and probably worse inside. The patient looked fragile as he lay on his back, already deeply asleep under the gas. His skin was pasty and jaundiced. He had no chest hair and appeared to be just a boy. A mask was held to his face by a medic who also looked pale. He'd probably had ninety whole days of training as a respiratory therapist. We had no anesthesiologist on the ship.

"The Viet Cong are rebels," Guenther insisted. "They're not really answering to anybody. They just come in and take what they want and snuff whoever doesn't agree with them." He had sponged the area for his incision and was about to cut. "Look at this kid. How old is he?"

"Isn't that exactly what *we're* doing, Doctor?" Captain Cohn asked. "Clamp here, Benjamin." He had both hands busy, with eight fingers all engaged on the patient's forearm. "Right here. Clamp this bleeder."

I followed his nod to a slowly oozing vessel and

caught it with the clamp, ratcheted down a few clicks, then let the grips slip lightly to lie alongside the open wound. Dr. Cohn's fingers were long and thin, articulate and balanced, most likely manicured under the gloves. My hands were fat baseball grips, fingernails chewed close to the nubs. I helped the best I could.

"Even though we're in a war," Cohn continued, "we're bringing a great deal of money into this country. We're giving away equipment, vehicles, farm machinery. Of *course* they act like they like us. These people aren't crazy. They know where their bread's buttered."

"But you think the regular citizens are *all* against us?" Guenther asked.

"Let me enlighten you with some history."

"Oh yes, Doctor. Please do."

"We Americans are the Great Liberators, fighting communism wherever it appears. Since it's always the poor and the ignorant, we don't pay much attention to what *they* want. We are the liber-a-*tors*. They're merely the liber-a-*tees*."

"Be fair now, David. Didn't they *ask* to be liberated?"

"Actually no, they didn't. The Vietnamese claimed their independence from the Japanese and French in '45. The French tried to recolonize, but we didn't think the Vietnamese were mature enough to govern themselves, so we supported the French."

"We were in Vietnam in 1945?" I interrupted.

"Not physically," Cohn explained. "A few advisers. But we pumped money into the military effort."

"Some say we funded as much as 80 percent of their war," Guenther added. "But I don't know if I buy that."

"It's a fact, Doctor. Toward the end in '54 we were paying for everything. That's why people say this all started with Eisenhower. It really began to cost us after the French lost the will to fight. By '54 we were covering *all* of the expenses."

"That's what you keep saying."

"Why did we send any money at all?" I asked.

"We hate the communists. Didn't you know?" Dr. Cohn let his sarcasm sink in. "We never did get along with the Russians, even as allies. And the population explosion in China has us scared to death."

"I've got a nasty bleeder in here," Guenther said. Cohn leaned over to see. "Here. Look right under here. Pulmonary artery got nicked. It should be all over for this kid. Ben, get Robert. Have him scrub." I stuck my head outside the door and motioned to Smitty, who had looked up as soon as he heard the door open. He went to scrub, and I returned to help Dr. Cohn.

"We started looking for commies under our beds during McCarthy," he was saying.

"His twin brother is head of the FBI," Guenther quipped.

"Careful, Doctor. You're our commanding officer," Cohn chuckled. "I don't get this 'Red Menace' business."

"Khrushchev screamed 'We will bury you!' right in the U.N. It was on television," the major explained.

"That's *not* what he said. That's what our *headlines* said. What he *literally* said was that Russian communists had no desire to *ever* return to war again after losing twenty million in World War II. He said, 'We don't *need* to fight you. We will bury you *economically* instead.' That's exactly what he said. 'We will bury you *economically*.' Our translators didn't get the whole quote, and the papers printed 'We will *bury* you.' Scared the West right into a Cold War. Colder than McCarthy on his best day."

"Well, if we keep spending millions on this war, Khrushchev may be right."

"That's a side issue. Communism can't have any real effect on wealthy, powerful countries. Not permanently. The best it can do is make comfortable, well-fed Americans look bad."

"Well, I have to give you that one."

"Communism, at least as *we* know it, succeeds only in poor countries where there's severe . . . forceps here, Benjamin." I popped his palm with the proper instrument. The more I watched, the more I learned to predict what he would need next.

". . . oppression?" Guenther finished his sentence.

"But what's worse?" Cohn asked. "Communists promising utopia, or Americans promising . . . let's see . . . what *do* we promise? Exploitation?"

Smitty was jamming his hands into rubber gloves as he backed through the swinging doors. "Communists? Y'all talkin' about commies? Them yella bastards are my favorite subject."

"I've got a bleeder here, Robert," Dr. Guenther said. "I need your help STAT."

Smitty wasted no time seeing what the doctor needed. He broke open a package of sponges and began rearranging surgical instruments, handing them to Guenther with two in his hand at a time, anticipating every move the doctor made. He looked at the patient briefly. "This little shit's got a hole in him, sir."

"Good diagnosis, Robert. Hold this pickup. It's got a suture half tied on the end. Grab it for me so I can . . . yes . . . there. Yes. Got it. Perfect."

"You two okay?" Cohn asked.

"We got it. Nice grab, Robert. Nice work. Hold here while I tie this thing off . . . yes. There. Fine." Smitty was as comfortable in the surgery theater as he was behind the wheel of a jeep or flipping a smoke up to catch his lip. "Dr. Cohn's lecture today is about the Russians, Robert."

"America's doing more to perpetuate the *need* for communism than all the propaganda of the Russians and the Chinese combined," Cohn continued.

"Well, at least the Vietnamese *business* community wants us here. We're saving their country for capitalism if not for democracy," Guenther interjected as a peace offering.

"Forty-two blizzard right, red bluff blackout, on two. Break!" The forearm patient was a little droopy but awake during the whole procedure, occasionally blurting out football plays or asking his Aunt Mae for warm chocolate chip cookies. Dr. Cohn worked carefully over him. The muscle tissue was cut in order to remove the shattered bone and steel fragments, then stitched together with dissolving thread. Bones were realigned, supported with steel rods, then screwed together by long, thin pins. The doctor whispered something about 70 percent use of his arm, but not loud enough for the dazed patient to hear.

The political discussion continued between Dr. Guenther and Dr. Cohn, spurred on by my questions. If you judged things by Smitty's reaction to some of the comments, we were bordering on treason. But even though I didn't understand all the politics, I felt a fraternal fellowship with the two doctors. We could speak our minds or ask dumb questions in the surgery theater. Shame didn't work here.

They talked about Ho Chi Minh, who they said was very popular with most of the people and led the freedom movement against the French and Japanese. And about how the treaty meant a unified Vietnam under him, but because he was a *communist* leader, the U.S. ignored the treaty and instead backed Premier Diem, who they said was hated by the people for being a ruthless dictator who hunted down and executed any opposition.

"How did Diem come to power?" I asked.

"Military coup," Cohn explained. "Fake elections we supported. He propped up landlords who were worse than before. Refused to unify with the North. Refused land reforms. Taxed the poor people like crazy."

"So Uncle Ho was Robin Hood?" Guenther suggested.

"And America backed the Sheriff of Nottingham," Cohn agreed. "We always seem to prefer fascists to communists."

"Come on, David. You're going too far," Guenther said.

"I don't know, sir," I said to the major. "What would you call the draft board?"

"Nice shot, Benjamin," Cohn chuckled. "Your move, Major."

"Touché," the major faked. "Et tu, Brute? Then die Caesar."

"How'd you get to be so un-American?" Smitty, the only nondrafted person in the operating room, was talking directly to me. I looked to Dr. Cohn for support and got it.

"By the time President Diem was overthrown by the military, the damage had been done," he said. "Typical of military juntas, a whole line of corrupt dictators took turns punishing the peons. The peasants saw America as their enemy and these temporary rulers as puppets. *We* don't see it that way, but here we are, destroying homes, burning land . . ."

"How can you participate in this war?" I finally had to ask Dr. Cohn.

"Sir, yer an officer," Smitty reminded him, his back to both of us as he helped Dr. Guenther.

"Yes, I *am* an officer. Commissioned by the United States to defend her against all enemies. I don't see anybody threatening New Jersey or Mississippi, Robert. Do you?"

"Sir, Ho Chi Minh is our enemy. I don't care how many people think he's Thomas Jefferson or George Washington. He's a commie. He's behind the Viet Cong, the most ruthless buncha gangsters . . . he's like Che what's-his-name in Cuba."

"Che Guevara," corrected Dr. Guenther.

"Right. I read that book *Che!* when I was recuperatin' in the World. It's about this commie who invented guerrilla warfare in Cuba. Castro's right-hand general. Planned the whole revolution. Organized the underground. Led the rebels. Armed 'n trained 'em. Kicked everybody's happy asses right outta Cuba, includin' ours. Got our butts kicked 'cause we didn't know what we was up against."

"You're right, Robert. That book should be required reading of every officer, top down," Guenther said.

"He had the support of the people," Cohn argued. "The people in rural Cuba who, by the way, didn't have a whole lot of love for the government. The poor people. He had their protection."

I interrupted. "What's the difference between the way Cuban and VC guerrillas fight and the way American rebels fought the British in the Revolutionary War?"

"Good point, Benjamin," Dr. Cohn nodded. "We hid in the bushes while the British fought in lines. We were in our own neighborhood, defending it as best we could."

"Difference is we were fightin' for democracy," Smitty said. "They're fightin' for communism."

Dr. Cohn hesitated, clearly not wanting to take Smitty to task. The respect between the two of them was long in the making. His voice became much quieter, even humble in a way. "I see poor people trying to defend their homes, families, temples, and farms against a huge world power."

"Ho Chi Minh is an old man by now," Guenther added.

"Not old enough for me, sir," Smitty insisted.

"There are rumors he's dead," Cohn offered.

"Not dead enough for me, sir."

"This is *his* country," Cohn raised his voice just a little. "*We* are the aggressors."

"With all respect, sir, if I catch that sumbitch in my sights, I'll aggress my M-16 right up his happy ass."

"Up his happy ass with a hot poker, yessir!" sang Cohn's delirious patient, right on cue. Smitty took a long breath and sighed. He knew these officers weren't spared the reality of torn-up wounded and dead and dying soldiers. But they'd had no experience in the field. They didn't know the enemy like Sergeant Smith did.

"Fact is, gentlemen," Dr. Guenther brought the conversation to a close, "the Viet Cong, whatever their politics, are killing their own people." He tied off the final stitches from the chest wound and pulled off his rubber gloves. "Robert, would you have the MPs outside the door move this boy to the security ward?"

"Yes, sir. This young'un ain't gonna *believe* where he is when he comes to."

The mask had been removed from the patient's face. I looked at my first enemy soldier. A guerrilla soldier. Charlie. The VC. He couldn't have been more than fifteen.

"Ya look a mite feeble, Bubba. What's the matter?" I could only shake my head and stare. "Man, ya don't look right. Better sit down someplace before ya *fall* down."

I didn't need to sit. I needed air. I needed space. I needed to think. This whole scene—the politics back and forth, the wounds, the blood and banter—all came crashing down when I saw the actual enemy right in front of me, unconscious, pale, dirty, nearly dead a moment before, now peacefully sleeping off the ether. Awake, he'd kill us if he could. It scared me that I hadn't known this intuitively. How could I be standing over this guy and not know?

I thought I'd educated myself on this war and this country during the years that I was preparing for conscientious objection. But the truth was, I didn't know anything about this place. I knew Cambodia bordered the west, but couldn't name any other neighboring country. Someone had called the ocean the South China Sea, but I'd never seen it. Did the Mekong River run east and west or north and south? What religion were these people? Buddhist I guessed, but I didn't know for sure. Were there schools here? What did they do besides rice farming? Could the mamma-san barber in Dong Tam be trusted with scissors?

Captain Cohn dropped his instruments on the side table and instructed me to close his patient's forearm. My mind was ten miles away and I didn't respond. He snapped off his rubber gloves and threw them in the sponge bucket on the floor between my legs. "You got a problem with that?" He scowled, then smiled broadly and turned on his heel.

"No, sir. What should I use?"

"Number ten fine," he said on his way out the door.

The nasty surface wound on Cohn's patient was now long and clean, sculpted perfectly by a skilled scalpel. All I had to do was throw some sutures in his arm and he'd be ready for a visit to the plaster-casting room, where they'd immobilize his arm for a few weeks. Smitty joined me at the table.

"Ya done this before?" the sergeant asked.

The half-alert patient suddenly looked very awake and tried to speak. I said nothing. I just nodded and gave them both my best "just relax" look. If I had spoken aloud, the crack in my voice would have given me away.

With a steady punch, I stuck the needle through his skin. It was soft. I thought it would be stiff and hard to penetrate, like the leather of a baseball glove. It was actually quite malleable, about the same as raw fish. I measured each stitch, concerned more with precision than the comfort of my patient, remembering the white lines along the scar of the man sleeping in my bunk. I poked a hole, then corrected by poking another a millimeter to the right or left, matching each stitch in symmetry. My figure eights were accurate and steady. Each tiny knot slipped perfectly into the small dot of blood marking the exit of the stitch.

I wondered how many times this guy would look at his arm and remember. Perhaps an appreciative lover would kiss his scar and praise his bravery. Someday his son would trace the scar with his finger and ask his daddy how it happened.

"Took ya thirty minutes to sew a five-minute job," Smitty teased, "but it's a damn fine seam." He showed his teeth and reached over to shake my hand. "Best I seen!"

10

Field

Medics took turns catching post-op ward duty on graveyard shift. On my third night of rounds I stopped beside a mummy. A clipboard hung from the end of his bed with a record of pulse, respiration, and blood pressure noted every hour since he had come wailing through the door, twisting and turning on a stretcher, his face smothered in field dressings globbed with fresh blood. Nowhere did his chart measure his acute pain, anger, disbelief, shame, and embarrassment. Nowhere did it graph the density, weight, volume, or depth of his fear. With his head shaved and his face covered with oozing gauze, he now mumbled for a cigarette.

"Naw. Sorry. Oxygen tank."

Two days before, he had made his entrance screaming for Mommy and the Blessed Virgin Mary, begging for one or the other to save him. Everyone in triage tried to help. The morphine had worn off quickly. A shudder crossed the room as his field dressings were removed and his face emerged, unrecognizable. Truly, you couldn't tell his nose from his chin. The major and two others worked for four hours merely to stop the tiny bleeding blood vessels and try to slide the bones into order. Reconstruction work might take years.

"I can smell it on ya, Doc," he begged. "God, I could use a smoke."

Escaping out the steel door from the ward onto the main deck of the *Nuaces*, in the wee hours of the morning I sat staring into the black night. I lit a cigarette and felt my heart sinking. What was waiting in the jungle? A few days in the morgue were supposed to desensitize me, but they had only scared me more. Tomorrow I would begin my first mission in the field. Infantry support. Smitty had given me the news that afternoon.

"We all take our turn," Smitty had explained.

"About being issued a weapon . . ." I stammered it more as a question than a statement.

"I know about that. Be too busy checkin' feet 'n dryin' socks to think about shootin' anybody."

I thought about the letter from Congressman Moss in my wallet. I almost took it out.

"Scared of gettin' shot at?" Smitty could read the look he'd seen before.

"No, sir."

"Goddammit. Don't call me 'sir.'"

"No, Sergeant."

"Whadya come to 'Nam for?"

"I was following orders." I actually meant that I didn't want to get in trouble again. The army had been kind enough to not convict me for treason, or worse, when I refused the order to pick up a gun in basic training. I endured house arrest and the abuse of the training sergeants. I'd proven, at least to myself, that I would not carry a weapon. But that would have to be where my disobedience ended.

"Well, keep followin' 'em."

"Yes, Sergeant."

"We're goin' to the bush together, you 'n me. I catch the duty just like everybody else, so don't start thinkin' yer special. I always take a rookie on his first hump."

• • •

The deck had cooled in the midnight air. I lit one cigarette off another. Would this be it? Would I panic in the
line of fire? Would I be a valuable asset to the platoon
because of my superior medical skills? Did it matter to
anyone that I got honors at graduation from medical
training? If shot at, would I grab the nearest gun and
blast away? Or would that bullet, that tiny piece of ac-
celerating metal with my name etched on its little frame,
find its mark tomorrow or the next day and put an end
to the whole question of killing or being killed?

Joey Sims, a medic working swing shift in triage,
found me against the wall just outside the door. He
knew I had my virgin voyage in the morning. He had
picked up on my lack of a weapon the minute he'd seen
me lying on my back, sleeping in the midday sun, as he
peered over the rail of the *Nuaces* the day I arrived. He
had a sixth sense for everything and everybody on the
hospital deck. After my first stint with Major Guenther,
Joey introduced me to the others and showed me the
routine of being one of the blue smocks.

"I heard of guys like you, but didn't think you ever
got out this far," he had said. "Why didn't you just take
a Saigon hospital trip?" I hadn't answered. I didn't want
to be different. I knew better than to stick out. He
dropped the question immediately, but I avoided conversations with him from then on. Now, out of nowhere, Joey squatted next to me and pulled from his
shirt a bullet he wore around his neck with his dog tags.

"I heard a clink, then a grunt behind me greased a
bush. Charlie flopped out, and when they checked him,
his rifle had misfired." He held the bullet closer to my
eyes. "This bullet got jammed in the chamber."

I examined it closer. It had JOEY etched on its nose.

"I'm short," Joey added. "Eighty-five days left!" He rolled the bullet between his thumb and forefinger and kept it in my face. "Ain't life a bitch?"

Our reality didn't have anything to do with geography or culture or anything even military. It had to do with surviving the days. Officers and enlisted men alike were not here to count the dead and wounded or the battles won and lost. In the war zone, nobody wore medals or marched anywhere the way they did in Stateside posts. Nobody even saluted anybody. I heard a guy get dressed down for saluting an officer in Dong Tam. The ass-chewing had mostly to do with snipers watching. Everybody walked around with the feeling we were being stalked. Meanwhile, we counted our days. Going back to the World with all of our body parts preempted everything.

The exceptions were soldiers like Smitty. Lifers seemed to be at home in the bush or on a chopper or even in the rear as support troops. They adjusted quickly and complained little. The army substituted for family and could do no wrong. Smitty summed it up by blaming the war on the politicians, not the army. "Never blame the war on the warrior," he said.

Night didn't last long enough. Before the sun had a chance to show itself, my new platoon stood shifting from foot to foot while a navy Tango boat prepared to carry us upriver. The infantry company commander, a young lieutenant, had not yet given the order to board. It was morning in Vietnam, barely daylight, and already ninety degrees and sticky.

Tango boats lined the barges tied to the side of the *Nuaces,* waiting for their passengers. These troop carriers were armored motorboats that could punch us into the thin, watery fingers of the Delta farther than any platoon could go by foot.

Tango boats had the ramp in front that I'd seen hitting the beaches in most WWII movies. They were water trucks that could be beached in a canal to drop the ramp and let troops out. Covered with armor, they had turrets for machine guns. A canvas roof covered the deck on some while others were left open. A couple were equipped with flight decks that could handle helicopters. I appreciated their defensive look.

My bag was resting between my feet. Smitty had carefully packed our two canvas medic bags side by side the evening before, putting exactly the same items in each, instructing me as he went. By sandwiching breakable bottles, Syrettes, and sharp instruments between the soft gauze bandages and adhesives, everything fit tightly. He shook my bag in my face when he had finished, not needing to speak his meaning. The bag didn't squeak. He threw it across the operating table to my chest and told me to tighten the straps. I slung it over my shoulder and snapped a bottom hook through a side belt loop, pounding it with my fist. Quiet and tight.

In the sterility of our hospital triage, behind the armored walls of a navy ship, Smitty and I were like boys playing war games. There were no real bad guys, just us, feigning fellowship while masking the expectations of the jungle tomorrow. We were smiling and telling jokes while we innocently packed our gear. He helped me act at being unafraid.

Now I stood with a whole platoon of armed soldiers, waiting on a platform, ready to step into my own bad dream. My predawn wondering gave in to reality. The soldiers carried stubby M-16s. There were two sniper rifles, long and lean with powerful scopes. Hand grenades tightly hugged the seams of every pack except mine. A

Yankee version of Pancho Villa, strands of feed-belts hanging from his chest, carried his fat-bellied M-60 machine gun like a baby in his arms, its tripod tucked underneath. Before anyone else boarded, he climbed up to sit under the navy machine gunner on the top turret of the boat.

They carried the firepower. I had a lot of gauze. One at a time, sets of eyes examined my gear, noticing something important missing. Without a word, the oddity of my presence crept along the barge. First my platoon, then others as well, they moved slightly forward or back, turned, tilted their heads, squinted against the morning sun's rays so they could see for themselves. I couldn't be the only medic in the world without a weapon. Could I?

The lieutenant whistled, and we slipped one at a time over the safety rails onto the boat. Men and their armor settled onto the surface areas of the open launch, leaning against packs filled with clothing, gear, a week's worth of food rations, and loaded clips of ammunition. When it looked like not one more soldier could fit and yet only half of the platoon had embarked, everyone moved their butts closer together until, one at a time, we each found a square foot of deck to call home.

Fortunately, no one spoke to me or to each other. Orders were already being waved rather than spoken. Nothing rattled. No one shifted. The tiniest clank of metal against metal made soldiers turn, frown, and cast a steely look in the direction of the offender. Someone rapidly tied something down tighter. No noise, dammit. No noise.

There were forty of us. Thirty-seven infantry, a first lieutenant, and two medics.

Our careful silence was broken when the idling motors gave a low rumble, then a louder growl. We were moving. Given the quietness of the troops, the roar of our engines was much too loud. Surely it echoed miles away. I closed my eyes tight and tried to block out the reverberating din. We cruised for an hour to where the water began to narrow and split into tributaries in several directions. Three turns completely disoriented me. The captain steered us into a left fork then a right and then another right without checking any charts or maps. He navigated solely by experience and the compass ball that floated in front of the helm. He leaned forward, scowling in an ugly pout. Only his eyes moved, darting, reading every ripple dimpling our path.

I sat with my medic bag on my lap, studying the men and machinery surrounding me. On my back was a pack with two dozen dry socks, a poncho, and backup medical supplies. I had a supply of C rations in small green cans, an extra canvas-covered canteen of fresh water, and a handful of red tags for the dead or wounded. A clerk on the *Nuaces* had given me last-minute instructions that I must complete a red tag for any casualties, including an inventory of the wounds and a list of any drugs administered.

I carried no clips of bullets, no handgun, no rifle, no grenade. I had no radio or compass, not even a pocketknife. My responsibilities had been drilled over and over: Keep people's feet dry. Never run out of water, salt tablets, or morphine. I packed even more bandages than Smitty said I needed. "Restore breathing. Stop bleeding. Make mobile." I had finger splints and aspirin, a snakebite ampoule, and Tums for the tummy. I hadn't moved an inch in an hour, and I was exhausted.

One at a time, I locked eyes with those carrying weapons in the boat. One at a time, they nodded back. Two things became agonizingly clear: Every single one of these guys carried more fear than firepower. And there's no chance I'm getting out of this in one piece.

My jaw ached from clenching my teeth. I rolled my neck around a few times to relax, then sat staring forward, trying to remember where I had come from and what might be there if I returned.

Another hour ticked by. Our course along the river was thick with trees. Someone whispered that we were very close to the Cambodian border. Before our earlier turn into the tributaries, intense defoliation had left bare dirt along the banks fifty yards back on both sides of the wide Mekong River. That ugly strip of red clay offered security. It kept us from always fearing what lurked behind the foliage. But no napalm or Agent Orange to clear the perimeter had ventured this far north. We were now creeping along where the jungle and small streams had become part of each other. Branches scraped the sides of our little boat. Our wake disturbed long, thin weeds bordering the banks and drooping into the water.

Midmorning sun beat on us as the motors slowed to a purr. We slipped into dense overgrowth, passing through spots where the jungle crossed overhead. The navy first mate perched on the bow and hacked away at low-hanging vines with a silver machete.

"Trees too close," Smitty whispered to me, his eyes darting across the bow, lifting his rifle from his lap. I clutched my medic bag as if it could save me. Several grunts removed their sunglasses. My ears started to ache from the strain of trying to hear something beyond the drone of motors. We seemed to be merely idling, floating as slowly as we could. The engines quieted to a dull hum.

Abruptly, a wide pool spanned out in front of us, exposing hundreds of yards of trees on all sides. "All reverse!" the captain hissed. "All stop!"

Six rifles snapped to infantry shoulders, pointing ahead. Each had already locked in clips of ammunition. Safeties popped off. The click and clack of steel ammunition carriers lodging into their rifle slots sounded like a hundred steel gates.

The tripod snapped firm under the M-60 machine gun. Two bolts clinked in syncopated locking-and-loading rhythm as our snipers were already eyeing their scopes. I stretched my neck to see and started to lift up, but Smitty's hand quickly returned me to my butt. As others began to rise from their seats, Smitty locked a clip into his M-16 and switched from his butt to his knees. I slowly looked over the brim of the sidewall.

A small, one-man sampan paddled into view. The papa-san smiled a toothless grin and motioned at the rifles to lower their aim. They complied as our boat captain called, *"Chieu hoi!"* The papa-san repeated, *"Chieu hoi!"* Balancing in his thin, skittish craft, he tried to appear unafraid of the threat in his face. He strained to keep his smile. The narrow sampan floated right to the bow and bumped into us. The papa-san reached out and moved his boat, hand over hand, to draw even with our lieutenant and first sergeant, who had moved forward to join the navy captain.

"VC?" our platoon leader asked, a .38-caliber pistol drawn but aimed away.

"Two klick," the papa-san said, raising his thumb and forefinger.

"How many?"

"Two klick," he repeated.

"How many VC?"

"Boo coo!"

"Moving?" asked the lieutenant, his free hand motioning slowly away from his body.

"Two klick!" the man repeated. The two officers conferred with the sergeant.

"What's 'Chew hoy'?" I whispered to Smitty.

"Means somethin' like 'I surrender.' A way of confirmin' this guy's on our side."

"Open arms," another soldier whispered. "It means open arms, like 'Man, I got no weapon.' We had a *Chieu hoi* in my last platoon. They're great at finding mines 'n shit. A Charlie deserter. Somebody said he probably set those mines the week before."

We let some laughter escape through our nostrils, and turning heads obliged us back to silence.

From the front of our boat one of the grunts leaned over and peered into the papa-san's sampan. He waved a signal to the lieutenant that meant "Nothing here," but no one liked having the small craft close to us.

"You go now," the lieutenant waved. "You *go*."

The old man pushed his skinny hull hand over hand to our bow, drew his long oar from the sampan's hull, then began to wave the water right and left behind him as he slid back to where he had come from.

I had no clue what any of this meant, and it showed. "A klick's a way of tellin' distance," Smitty whispered to me. "The click an artillery piece makes when ya move it up, down, side to side. A kilometer, 'bout a thousand meters. One klick on the map is right next door." I peered over the side of the boat into the jungle. Had I missed something in training? "It's okay, Bubba," Smitty grinned. "They don't teach this shit in boot camp. Gotta leave somethin' for me."

Smitty turned his comments to the lieutenant. "The papa-san's lying, sir. Either he's VC himself, sizin' up our strength, or he's bein' used by the VC."

"Yeah," Sergeant Bailey nodded. "They could be holding his family, or even his ox or some other shit."

"Whatever the deal is, two klick is bullshit," Smitty continued. "That close 'n they'd have lobbed one into the boat, greasin' most of us with one pop."

"Chances are he's just looking for a handout," Bailey added.

The lieutenant spoke low but loud enough so we all could hear. We were indeed near Cambodia. He said that fortunately, because Viet Cong guerrillas continually moved through the border area to protect the supply trail, the Cambodian Guard avoided confrontation and operated far more inland. The VC probably already had us spotted. Whenever we ran into them, they would be prepared. "We have our mission," he explained. "This is what we came for. We need to get out of this craft ASAP and spread out."

Within minutes, with all our gear on our backs, we were off the boat and cutting our way through thick leaves. The boat had drifted out a few feet, turned on its engines, and disappeared from sight. My heart sank when I saw it leave. Somehow it felt safer to be in the middle of the river.

The entire platoon was chopping through the thick jungle as if someone in front actually knew where we were going. I couldn't see twenty feet in any direction. Every two or three minutes somebody would raise his hand and we'd all crouch to listen. With a wave of a hand from the front, we'd begin walking again, beating back tree limbs, large ferns, and hanging vines, trying not to step directly into thick mud pools. Feet dry, I thought.

"Lock 'n load," the first sergeant had told us. "Full automatic, boys. We get lead in the air first, y'hear?" He had paced us twenty feet apart, but I pulled up closer to Smitty than that.

"Gimme some room," Smitty reminded. I waited for

him to move ahead and caused some bumping behind
me. I felt like such a rookie. Before we had traveled another hundred yards, I was following too close again.

"CDMs," Smitty said to me.

"CDMs?"

"Command-detonated mines." He wasn't put off by
my ignorance, at least not noticeably. It was obvious
that several others had gone before me in Smitty's jungle
college. "Charlie plants mines then waits. Rather get
two or three of us in range if he can."

"In range?"

"Twenty, thirty feet." He motioned his hands away
from his chest as if slicing a pie. "Depends on the type.
Most Russian-mades are about twenty feet."

Another lesson they didn't cover in training. Walk far
enough apart to keep Charlie from blowing us away in
groups. I would remember that.

With my face and hands stinging from the slicing foliage, we came to our first clearing. The sun seared my
raw cheeks. A pattern of rice fields stretched out before
us, perhaps ten or twelve in a row, each field about an
acre square, separated by long mounds of dirt levees. A
few farmers were bent over, working in each paddy.
They wore black long-sleeved shirts, black pants, and
round rattan hats that came to a point in the middle.
The little black figures against the lush green appeared
as if painted on canvas.

"All the farmers wear black pajamas," Smitty whispered over to me as we stopped at the edge of the clearing. "That's why it's hard to tell 'em apart from VC."

The point man of our platoon carried a two-barreled
shotgun. He also had an M-16 strapped across his back
as well as two sidearms, one on each hip, but no personal items, food, or provisions. Others carried his stuff.
His nickname Hoppy came from Hopalong Cassidy, the

two-gunned hero from the Saturday afternoon westerns. This Hoppy, however, resembled no movie star. The meanest-looking young man I've ever seen, his pock-marked face had deep scars from teenage acne and deeper creases from rough outdoor exposure. When I first saw him on the boat, I wondered which of his features made him look so scary. The coarse texture of his skin? His paper-thin lips? Eyes that seemed to sink way into his skull? No, it was his whole asymmetrical face. One eye opened twice the size of the other and his nose curved toward the smaller eye. His grinning mouth shot higher on one side than the other, and when he spoke, he laughed and spit juice from a wad of chewing tobacco. His mouth didn't ever fully close, exposing teeth whose colors were divided horizontally brown and yellow. Some were missing, and the rest pointed in several directions. I couldn't look at him for very long.

The platoon hunkered down at the edge of the jungle growth, tucked into the forest line. Our gunslinger Hoppy walked through shin-high paddy water across the field to an old man who looked, from a distance, exactly like the guy in the sampan except for the black pajamas. After some nodding and grunting, they moved together, talking and pointing, without much acknowledgment or reaction from the other workers. The old man didn't once turn to look in our direction. They stopped and squatted next to a smoldering fire near the tree line and talked for a long while, sharing a bowl of something steaming.

"Rice 'n vegetables," Smitty answered, again before I had a chance to ask. "Him bein' invited to eat is a good thing. To the Vietnamese, it's dishonorable to share food with an enemy."

"Hoppy's been a lerp for most of this hitch," Sergeant

Bailey explained to the lieutenant. "He's only been with us for a couple patrols."

A lerp? I didn't even have to ask. Smitty leaned forward to explain. "L-R-R-P. Long-range reconnaissance patrol. Guys who go out 'n live in the bush for weeks at a time. No food or supplies. Live off the land. Locals get used to havin' 'em around. Some even learn the language real good. When Charlie starts to move an operation, they're right where we need 'em. They go get a stashed radio 'n call it in."

"How long's the lieutenant been with this platoon?" I whispered. The young officer seemed reticent, looking to Sergeant Bailey before every move.

"Yeah, I been wonderin' that too," Smitty nodded, then let it drop. Sergeant Bailey seemed to be counseling the officer the way Smitty was teaching me.

After his honorable lunch and a brief chat, Hoppy walked carefully away, sloshing through the rice plants, looking over his shoulder at the farmer every few steps. He followed the exact route back that he'd taken out. Our eyes and weapons charted his course until he safely reached the tree line.

"About fifty Cong, sir," he told the lieutenant. "Here a day ago. Took rice, filled jugs with water, 'n humped due north."

"Fifty?" Sergeant Bailey asked. He seemed surprised.

"Fifty?" echoed the lieutenant. "Viet Cong or North Vietnamese regulars?"

"Yeah, I know," Hoppy said. "Don't sound right, sir. Charlie don't travel large. Sounds bogus to me."

North? That's in the opposite direction of the Delta and Saigon. I'm ready to return to the *Nuaces*. Anybody else?

"Lots of water, papa-san says. Speaks pretty good English. Grew up in the Philippines. He couldn't figure it out, either. He's pissed, though. Charlie took all the water pots from six hamlets."

"Water . . ." the lieutenant thought out loud, then turned to the sergeant.

"They have a million fucking tunnels in the hills on the other side, sir," the veteran soldier replied. "Not just tunnels for hiding. Whole gook cities over there." He lowered his voice as we all leaned in to hear. "Underground ammo factories. Tunnels like highways connected all over." The sergeant stared across the field at the papa-san, who had been watching us since Hoppy left him. "Maybe we caught an organized work party, sir. Maybe they're taking the pots to store all the water they can. Maybe something big-ass is up. Another Tet or fucking worse."

"Can he show us where they are?" asked the lieutenant.

"Can he, sir? Sure," Hoppy said. "But *will* he?"

"And how long will he be around if he does?" Bailey added.

Smitty nodded. "If he's talkin' to *us,* sure as shit he's talkin' to Charlie."

"Humpin' all that water, we shouldn't have any trouble catchin' 'em, sir," Hoppy said, then rose to his feet, abruptly ending the powwow. He moved directly to his position on point again. "Let's go chase some rats to their hole!"

Everyone grabbed weapons and packs. Hoppy grinned at one of the grunts carrying a machine gun. "It's a safari, man. Fuckin' A! Let's do *it,* before *it* do us!"

"Right behind ya, Hop," the grunt said, slapping the fat belly of his M-60.

"Lead in the air," added Sergeant Bailey.

We headed north, my first day in the field, about to cross over into Cambodia.

"Lighten up, Doc. It's less humid up there," Smitty grinned as he handed me a Camel. "They got a day on us. That means the smokin' lamp is lit." His Zippo flipped, flamed the ends of both our smokes, then snapped shut, barely missing the end of mine. His first inhale drew out long and deep, a signature of his temperament. He smoked as if each draw were his last. I started to ask a question, then saw that he was focused a thousand yards in front of us. Smoke streamed through his clenched teeth with a long audible sigh.

The smile left Smitty's face momentarily as he murmured, barely loud enough for me to hear, "Looks like we're gonna be swimmin' that goddamn river."

11

River

Sergeant Bailey jabbed his stubby finger at Smitty and me. "When we get to where we're gonna cross tonight, you two medics'll be first and last. Smitty, you got rank. You decide."

Smitty said he'd go over with the first wave. "Get it over with," he winked at me, never missing a chance to make me wonder. Could it be worse than going last?

The two sergeants talked about men and provisions, who goes with what, what would happen if we separated.

"Why is 'Who goes with what' such a big deal?" I asked, maneuvering for a chance to go earlier with Smitty.

"Two medics, two sides of the river," he explained. "One of us gotta be where somebody could get popped."

"Why all the fuss about equipment?"

"Everybody's gettin' wet. We're gonna cross that sumbitch without a boat, Bubba. Foot-long rats 'n snakes big enough to swallow 'em in one bite. Floatin' ox crap 'n mosquito larva 'n major-league shit like that. Could make everybody sick at once. Malaria. Dysentery. Yellow fever." He rummaged through his bag for something, didn't find it, dropped the bag, and went on preaching at me. "God knows what's floatin' out there. Could be mines 'n shit." He looked at me hard. "This

115

ain't no cakewalk, Bubba. No boat. No navy radar this trip. It'll be darker'n a miner's ass in January."

Everyone's mood changed to worrisome. The thick air was potent with apprehension and agitation. The dribble of chatter that usually shadowed army grunts stopped altogether. I wished someone would say *something*. I got nothing. My pulse beat within something that clogged the back of my throat.

My life had consisted of conversation and laughter, watching a little TV, listening to the radio, playing cards, chasing women. College dormitory life seemed not that long ago. Loud voices in the hallways. Grab-ass, water fights, late-night pranks, wet-towel flipping. Filthy jokes. Sexual conquests. Richardson's old Lincoln swaying into a turn with a carload of half-drunk liberated nineteen-year-olds howling at the moon and the coeds. We played at being all grown up and on our own. I didn't know what "on your own" really felt like until now.

Being young and in college favored the untamed. I liked acting a little stupid on a Friday night. But this was certifiably nuts. Every bush had a potential explosion in it. Every eye pierced the landscape in circling sweeps. Brows furled, necks stretched awkwardly forward out of wet collar rings of sweat. My nerves scratched against other nerves in places that had never itched before. And nobody wanted to hear about it. These guys were just as uncomfortable, but we were all scared silent. I had gradually regained my sense of humor after the initial shock of boot camp wore off, and up until now it had relieved many difficult moments. It kept me sane through basic training, the holdover barracks, and advanced medical training. Everything about the army could become an easy target for a joker. But now, I kept my mouth shut and tried not to step on anything dangerous.

The troops started moving again, spread out even farther from each other. Smitty advanced immediately as I scrambled to grab my gear. We were returning to the Mekong River, but not the same way we came from the boat. We now moved quickly, in the open, not through the trees. A small farm road lined the rice paddies. The spotty traffic of Vietnamese farmers, some children, and an ox now and then gave some assurance that we weren't in huge danger on the road, or at least alongside the road. We never actually walked *on* the road.

"Toe poppers," Smitty explained. I'd have to remember to ask him later, when I wasn't concentrating on every spot I stepped.

Our pace quickened. Hoppy kept moving farther and farther out on point until I couldn't see him at all. Nobody spoke. Every eye strained. I wondered what I was supposed to be looking for. Where was I? Who were these guys? Then came the fear. Deep fear. I just knew I would be blown into tiny little pieces. Each sound of a snapping twig caused my head to jerk from right to left or above and behind me. If I took a breath, a sniper would find me.

I imagined shiny trip wires like spiderwebs across the path. Hundreds of them everywhere. And how could I be the only one who noticed the two dozen pairs of eyes, like blinking neon lights, flashing out of various holes in the tree line. We were being watched. I was sure of it. And there was a pit with dozens of sharpened punji sticks waiting for me.

But it was just a fat mud hole on the side of a rice paddy playing tricks with the shadows of the branches above. My back muscles ached from constantly tensing. Something growing inside me was trying to poke its way out. My eyes were darting around, cold sweat clammy under my armpits and all down my back. Unresolved questions were tumbling over each other, pounding at my temples. What do I do if . . .

I'd ask Smitty, if I could just catch up to him.

After we'd been alone along the road for a while, a single line of silent walkers, two teenage girls passed from out of nowhere, holding hands and giggling right at me. I wondered what was so funny to them. Were they teasing the fear they saw in me? I had never been good at hiding my feelings. Were they my enemy, smiling and squinting at me with their deep, black expressionless eyes? Screw you, I thought. I don't want to be in your country any more than you want me here. I tried to lock my eyes in a solid stare. Menacing and foreboding. Bold and unflinching. They caught my change of expression and giggled even more. They probably thought I was trying to entertain them by making funny faces. Their giggles turned to laughter, and they scampered away. Could they see through the panic I felt? Did they know?

Smitty came back to check on me. "Drinkin' water? How're yer nerves? Ya look a little rough, Bubba. Whatcha thinkin' 'bout back here?" What *could* I be thinking? I didn't dare tell him. I asked what we were doing.

"Usually we avoid these hamlets. Skirt 'em. Maybe send a couple guys in to ask around, not look too intimidatin', y'know?" But we weren't avoiding anybody today. All adults we encountered were interrogated about the number and movements of the Viet Cong. We were in hunt mode. "Makin' our presence known," Smitty explained. "Usually we got Charlie outnumbered. We don't send everybody in. This is different. I don't like it. We're makin' too much noise today. We got a heat on."

"Why don't you *say* something?" I blurted out.

Smitty gave me an honest smile. He winked and

changed the subject, asking again about my water intake. How're my feet? Did I take salt tablets? Did I sweat a lot? This bein' my first tour, did it take stretchin' to keep up? He wanted me healthy, obviously. He cared about my being ready. And the way he avoided my question, it was also obvious he wasn't going to say anything to the lieutenant or Sergeant Bailey about how they were running the platoon. Not unless directly asked. By them.

A hamlet might have seven or eight thatched-roof huts, a central water well, a fire pit or two, eternally smoking, and a bamboo-fenced area for whatever farm livestock they owned communally. Each little hamlet connected to another, with rectangular patches of rice paddies surrounding all sides.

Bailey and the lieutenant had very different approaches to local interrogations. Sergeant Bailey lumbered in hollering, so everyone would stop what they were doing and recognize his larger-than-life presence. He demeaned the Vietnamese and demanded that they pay him respect. He pulled people physically and lined them against a hut to make his inquiries. He marched back and forth like a drill sergeant, rummaged through their sacks of belongings, and looked into their hooches. The Vietnamese greeted Bailey by bowing repeatedly with praying hands covering the fronts of their faces.

The lieutenant on the other hand talked with only a few and kept a distance from their hooches. He dropped to one knee to talk with a mamma-san squatting in front of her steaming vegetables and covered pit of rice, much like Hoppy had done. He smiled at her and broke off a few native expressions that made her giggle.

It was the good cop, bad cop routine. The mamma-san told our platoon leader that she knew nothing. "No bic! No bic!" she repeated. He smiled at her politely and bowed at the waist as he rose to leave. He looked over at Bailey and nodded at the mamma-san. She immediately jumped up and shrieked something in Vietnamese. Her body language indicated it would be better to talk with the good cop. She eagerly motioned the lieutenant to come back and kneel beside her. She jabbered in half-English until he waved her off.

"She don't know nothin'," Smitty said to me, adding that there were plenty of other Vietnamese watching our moves. "We don't belong here, 'n they know it." He eyed two young children at a well who watched us pass out salt tablets while men filled their canteens. "How would *you* feel if a bunch of eight-foot green men were walkin' through *yer* neighborhood?"

"We just honkies in the neighborhood," chirped a black foot soldier behind us.

"Honkies?" Smitty turned to face him.

"Where does 'honky' come from?" I interrupted, trying to deflect a confrontation.

"My ol' man says it's white folks come honkin' for their maids."

"Horn honkers?!" I was surprised. "Jeez, I always thought it meant something awful."

"It ain't endearment," Smitty observed.

"Naw, Doc. Nothin' wrong with 'honky,'" the grunt smiled. "We got worse names for y'all."

"Niggah, get out the way," said the next black man in line for water, shoving the grunt to one side.

"Uh huh, bro," he said. "See, Doc? There's plenty of that to go 'round."

"Try to get along, girls," Smitty said half seriously.

"Yessuh, Massuh. Yessuh, Mis'ippi," the second man joked back, the early history of the American South dripping from his words.

Smitty glared at him, then broke into a smile. "Don't call me 'sir,' goddammit. I *work* for a livin'."

The soldier glared back for a moment, then returned the smile. Smitty knew that everybody bled the same color out here, and so did the grunt staring him down. This momentary standoff, however tame, caused a chill that shook me back to the crushed skull and tagged toe of Cornelius Jones and the two black medics who had defended and then protected me. Wasn't I just as guilty for participating? Accident, unintended reaction, mistake, self-defense, and all other situational ethics notwithstanding, the guy was dead.

No one would bust me for being loyal to fellow medics who had surely saved my life. I kept quiet, protecting them as they had protected me. Even so, anxiety over what I'd done, or hadn't done, badgered me. My arms and legs began to shake, and I could feel my heart pounding everywhere in my body. The guy was dead. Somebody would want to know how it happened. The army had reports. Casualties were recorded. Files, orders, names, dates, places were sent to the Pentagon. What about the MPs who brought him over? Did I really think the army could be so disorganized? I had typed morning reports at Fort Lewis. We tracked every soldier, every day, sick call, on leave, over-the-wall, just like a prison. Would no one trace the cause of death of a guy as high-profile as Cornelius Jones? I must have been crazy not to go screaming to the authorities immediately.

But I hadn't said a word, not even to Vincent and Satterfield. Just thinking their names now had me shaking. Where were they? Why didn't they come back the next day? What would I say to the military court-martial judges when all this came out? I had just followed the next indicated step, exactly as I had done every day since I got my draft notice. One hour at a time. I can do anything if it's only one hour at a time. I should have said something then. I should have at least told Smitty. I could be in the deepest trouble of my life, and it had nothing to do with the Viet Cong we were hunting. Or who were hunting us.

Connecting the dots from hamlet to hamlet, the platoon continued to move north and west without hesitation. Those who stopped to make inquiries quickly hurried to catch up with the rest of us. I kept walking and watching. Some of the men ate fruit offered by villagers, and we always took on more water when available, filling canteens to the brim. We moved fast, covering a lot of ground. The boys in the platoon were beginning to smell blood.

The afternoon flashed by and dusk became dark. The lightless cavern of being many miles from electricity surrounded us like a canopy. Hoppy met us as we squatted along one bank of the Mekong, finally preparing to cross. Smitty and I wrapped our medic bags in a couple of light tarps he carried to use as litters or protection from sudden monsoon rains. The others bundled their packs and weapons in their shelter halves. Hoppy removed his fatigues and boots, and Sergeant Bailey took them to wrap and carry for him.

"Gotcha. You set?" Bailey asked.

"Frog's ass watertight?" Hoppy cracked.

Hoppy was standing naked except for his boxers and dog tags. Bailey walked him to the bank. Toting a large knife in one hand, our point man slipped into the river without a sound. From his mouth, he extended a wheel of fishing line attached to one end of a stick of bamboo he held between his teeth. It gave off a whir in spurts as he breaststroked out of sight into the black ink of night.

Once I thought I heard his leg kick surface water, but it could have been a wave slapping the bank. Or it could have been almost anything. Frozen with apprehension, I watched the black water long after he disappeared.

We waited until the slack in the fishing line popped horizontally out of the water. Sergeant Bailey plucked the end with his thumb and it resonated a thin vibration. He held his fingers gently next to the line and felt Hoppy's responding thumps. He untied the line from the tree, wound the end of it around the end of a rope, and knotted them together. He tied the other end of the rope securely to the tree, then gave the line a long slow tug.

"Where'd that rope come from?" I asked Smitty. I hadn't seen anybody carrying rope. I knew I didn't have room in my pack for anything besides my food, water, and dry socks.

"Scrounger got it from the friendlies," he said, referring to the guy in charge of "acquiring" needed items from friendly Vietnamese or other sources. Our army entrepreneur. I didn't know who this platoon's scrounger was, and didn't need to know, but my medic bag with its drugs and paraphernalia never left my shoulder.

We all watched as the rope slipped into the river, slowly passing through Bailey's hands. When it stopped moving, he tugged softly, and the rope tugged a predetermined signal in response.

"That's still Hoppy," Bailey smiled. I tried not to imagine who else it might be.

Sergeant Bailey quickly scooted down the bank on his butt. He pulled himself into the river, rope in one hand, rifle and pack high out of the water in the other. In an instant, he too vanished into the black.

"I'll be countin'," Smitty whispered to me. "Go next to last, hear me? Hop'll be back for ya. Go one before him." His voice was calm and serious as he positioned himself in line and whispered, "If ya don't hear my bird chirp, let go the rope."

"Let go?"

"Hear me, Bubba? If my bird ain't chirpin', let go. Float to the China Sea if ya have to." He slapped the side of my face hard with his open hand, then slipped into the river.

Each guy made it into the water without much of a splash. They knew what they were doing. Their packs were tight. Their lips were tighter. My eyes adjusted to the black night, but I could swear it was getting darker by the second. Each man seemed to be gone as soon as he slid into the river. I strained but could hear nothing.

We waited about three minutes for each man to arrive on the other side. With forty of us, this was going to take a couple hours.

"Lieutenant," the machine gunner whispered. "Needin' a smoke bad."

"Sure, go ahead," the young officer replied. "But let me get a little farther away before you light up and get your head blown off."

The gunner thought for a second, then got it. "Well, can I at least take a piss?"

"Piss when you're in the water," someone else said.

"I'm next then, goddammit!" he said and slid into position by the rope. Not only did he have to carry his pack and M-60, he also had an ammunition belt slung around his forearm, holding it high above the water.

"Jerk'll probably light up halfway across the river," someone huffed after he'd gone.

The radio operator slipped past me and sunk into the black with our only communication. Now we were isolated from the rest of the platoon. As the numbers steadily dwindled on our side of the river, the hairs on my neck stood taller. The ninety-degree heat and humidity actually felt chilly. I had goose bumps on my arms.

Two to go. Two of us left on the bank. The soldier in front of me impatiently waited for the signal tugs, but they didn't come at the usual interval. Something pulled on the rope but not as a signal.

Hoppy and his bowie knife slid up onto the bank. He startled me, but having him on my side made a difference. I immediately felt more secure. Hoppy looked ugly and mean enough to scare anything away with just a growl.

The soldier in front of me went into the water. Three minutes later my turn would come. I started toward the declining slope, holding the rope for balance. Several times I had wrapped and rewrapped my two bags tightly together with Smitty's tarp. I propped the bundle on one shoulder and tried my grip on the rope with the other hand. Satisfied, I waited. Either a very gentle rain or a heavy mist felt cool against my face and neck as I anticipated a tug on the rope.

Something hard jabbed the rear of my shoulder. Hoppy leaned forward and offered me a large flat piece of wood. "Put your shit on this. It'll float bitchin'."

"Bitchin'?" I couldn't help myself.

"Yeah, bitchin', man," he smiled, showing crooked teeth. "Heard you're from California."

"Uh huh."

"Me too. Laguna Beach."

"Oh my God. You a surfer?"

"Yeah, well, sorta. Not much. I mean, I could, y'know. Not like a hotdogger or nothin'. I sorta lived at the beach, that's all."

"No shit?"

"If I'm lyin', I'm dyin'. Catch ya on the flip side, Doc. There's the signal. Get outta here."

I pulled myself into the water and started off, my stuff floating beside me on Hoppy's little wood barge. The water felt thick and warm in spots. A cool drift would pass through my path, then turn tepid. It was comfortable. Pulling myself along the rope, I counted seconds. Three times to sixty and I'd be there. Hand over hand, slowly, steadily. My ears strained in the dark, but I heard nothing except water parting around me. No stars or moon lit the night.

I lost count as I felt the river's weight increase. The water turned cool. Gradually the current encouraged my legs out from under me and tugged them downstream. I flexed, twisted, and held still a moment to catch a breath. My exhaustion surprised me. The rope made crossing easy, and the current didn't pose much of a threat. But my heart was beating so hard that anybody could hear it a mile away. I crawled my legs over the rope behind me to feel more secure, then swallowed several huge breaths and adjusted my tight hold on the wood plank. My packs still sat high and dry.

It seemed that I'd gone far enough to reach the other side and should hit the bank any second. The pull of the current ceased, and the water warmed again. I wiped my eyes to try to focus and squinted hard, but saw nothing. I started muttering to myself. Mustn't panic. Take your time. Never been afraid of the dark. Hasn't been three minutes yet. Wish I'd kept counting. Floating easily again. Gotta be close.

A whistle. Smitty's birdcall. It sounded so close. Mustn't lose my stuff now. Easy for the most part. I can handle it. Only a little farther. Nothing bit me. No floating sludge. No ox crap. Can't be more than a few feet. Smitty's whistle sounded right on top of me.

I heard it again. What a sweet sound! That warble of his spelled welcome in my ears.

"Yo, Doc! Sherman!" Sergeant Bailey called in a loud hiss.

"Yep."

"Shush, okay?" He pulled my packs off the piece of wood. Someone else pulled me by the armpit onto a flat mud landing.

"We got company," he whispered.

"Huh?"

"The rest are upriver two klicks. Stay here with me 'til we get Hoppy."

"I heard Smitty."

"No you didn't. He's with the rest of 'em."

"I could've sworn . . ."

"Shut up, goddammit!"

I moved away from the river's edge to unwrap my packs and quickly find dry socks. Every move made noise. Bailey tugged the signal on the rope. It went slack and began to float away with the current. I crouched beside him, helping to haul the freed rope slowly toward us. My eyes had adjusted to the darkness enough to make out the river and the bank and the silhouette of the sergeant.

"That Hoppy's like a big fucking fish," he snickered. The rope slid sideways at an increasing angle, as if we'd lost him. Then we felt the weight on the end. He wasn't helping us at all by swimming. Crazy Hoppy was enjoying the ride while we pulled. Sergeant Bailey whispered that Hoppy would probably water-ski up. Just then our catch floated into the bank to our right. The sergeant gave a final tug as I reached forward to offer Hoppy my whole forearm. I stretched but saw him turn in the water away from me.

"Hoppy, here," I whispered. His body turned over, and I could barely see in the dark that his wrists were tied together to the end of the rope.

"Fucking shit!" Sergeant Bailey exploded in my ear. Pushing me aside, he lunged and grabbed the two tied arms and, with a painful groan, hauled the lifeless body onto the landing between us.

"Shit!" he sputtered. "This ain't Hop."

The lifeless body was half the size of our point man.

"This is a fucking *gook!*"

We could barely see in the dark, but nothing about him looked like Hoppy. I thrust three fingers to the jugular to find a pulse, and they slid into an open throat wound. My whole arm snapped back. "Shit!"

"What?"

"This guy is very dead, sir."

"I'm not a sir, you fucking idiot. And I can see he's dead, for chrissake."

Tipping him on his side, his mouth and nose oozed swamp water and blood. He was wearing only a pair of army-issue boxer trunks, way too big and held up by a hank of twine tied around his waist.

"Gotcha!" hissed behind us.

"Jesus fucking Christ!" yelled Bailey on his return from leaping out of his skin. "You cocksucker."

"Let's split, man!" Hoppy laughed, completely naked except for the knife in his hand. He leaned forward and deftly sliced the body from the rope, shoving it into the river with his foot.

"What . . ." I wondered out loud.

"Jesus!" Bailey sighed again, trying to catch his breath. He threw Hoppy's clothes at him. They were completely on his body before I could fetch my gear.

"Tell ya later," Hoppy answered. "Git up 'n git out." He picked me off the ground and shoved me forward. "We ain't alone out here."

Sergeant Bailey came to his senses and began chuckling and cussing at the same time. "God fucking dammit, Hoppy. You scared the living crap outta me. How many times you gonna pull this shit? I'll probably die in Vietnam of a fucking heart attack."

"Let's hump, doggies!" Hoppy laughed out loud, leading the way.

Grabbing my bags and throwing them over my shoulder, I followed close behind them. We skirted along the riverbank, stopping often while Hoppy searched the darkness of the river and the jungle and then changed our course slightly. I took the first couple of breaks as opportunities to retie my bootlaces. Keeping up with Hoppy did not come easily.

We walked together until dawn started to show on the horizon, then our spacing automatically began to lengthen. When enough light allowed us to see each other, the sergeant fell in behind me. Like Hoppy and unlike me, he carried a weapon at the ready. I walked as if between escorts, carrying only my precious medical gear. I wondered how they felt guarding a conscientious objector who added nothing to their firepower. What did they think about me being out here with them? I clutched my medic bag and worried about having to put its contents to use.

We kept up a quick pace, saying nothing, half running, often backtracking as Hoppy followed signs in the deep jungle. He examined everything from the ground to the tops of the trees. He froze, peered at the thick foliage as if he could see right through it, changed directions, backed off again, waited, reversed, then took off at a fast clip on another course. My sense of direction completely deserted me. An hour after first light but before the sun had shown, we finally stopped. My wind abandoned me. Afraid I'd never get up again, I stood like a zombie while the other two collapsed to rest.

"We stay right here." Hoppy pointed at the surroundings. "The platoon should be here any time now."

Even though I couldn't light up, I opened my pack to see if my smokes were dry. Carefully folded in a side flap, I found my calendar. It had a picture of an American flag with 365 squares forming the stripes and the stars. Called "short-timer calendars," they came in different forms, like a full-frontal naked beauty with the squares swirling around and around until the final days ended in pubic heaven, or a Chinese dragon with days 2 and 1 ending at its bulging flaming nostrils.

I turned away from Bailey and Hoppy so they couldn't see my pitifully few days scratched off. Black marks blotted out the numbers of days 365 to 355, barely beginning the first row. I took out my pen and happily marked out two more days. Only 353 to go. The sun rose on my twelfth day in country. Time passed a lot faster in the field than it had in those long first hours in the morgue.

As Hoppy had predicted, in a few minutes the rest of our platoon popped one at a time out of the jungle.

"How long you been here, Hop?" asked the lieutenant.

"Just got here."

"You were moving!"

"Yep! The skinny Doc here kept up some kinda cool."

"Way to leg it, Doc," Sergeant Bailey added. "Not bad for a rookie."

I nodded but was too tired to acknowledge the compliment. How had we passed the rest of the platoon? And what about the body floating in the river? My clothes and socks were soaked with sweat, and some kind of welting skin irritation had started to crawl up the inside of my thighs.

"We're gonna cool it here for the rest of the day and

try to make some major movement tonight," the lieutenant said. "Doc, you look like shit. Better sit before you fall on your face." I dropped my pack and my whole body fell in right behind it. Yes. I could rest. I could sleep a while. I could die.

As my body shut down, my eyes closed and immediately pictured a brown body twisting in the dark river. I couldn't keep them closed. My right eye socket felt as if something had jarred loose behind it. It twitched. I couldn't focus. Normal soldiers fret about losing limbs. I was worrying about a spastic eye.

I chased dry mouth with so much fresh water that another swallow would make me puke. Every exposed part of my flesh was ruby red from the stinging ferns we'd been flinging our bodies through since the morning before. From a lower corner of my bag, my hand found the salt tablet bottle, and I swallowed four tabs with another gulp of warm water. Reaching to loosen my boot-laces and rub my aching ankles, I found several leeches fighting through the folds in my socks. I gave each a good squeeze, flinging them back to their habitat. Rolling to my knees, I reached out to offer a handful of tablets to Bailey and Hoppy, who received the salt readily. Neither of them bothered with the water chaser.

Nobody spoke. We sat in exhaustion and numb observation. The jungle offered eerie solace. A morning mist held the ground tightly as shadows in the trees began to sharpen and run out long with the rising sun. It was beautiful. Long black shadows on low-hanging fog. I'd never seen anything more lush and peaceful, even in pictures.

I figured sleep would come when I was bunked safely on the *Nuaces*, after a large meal and a huge bowel movement. My eight-hour sleeping shift under two fat, farting seamen seemed like heaven to me right then.

Finally tilting back to give rest a try, I bumped hard on a rock and nearly knocked myself out.

"Nice head butt," a familiar voice chuckled behind me. "Why don'cha just dive into that rock?"

"Smitty," I managed to say. "Where you been?"

"Better bag some Z's here, Bubba. We're lookin' at another long hump tonight."

"Where are we?"

"North, 'n west. Made good time. Not easy keepin' up with Hoppy."

"I wasn't gonna let him outta my sight."

"Smart move. We ain't alone out here."

"I heard your bird chirping," I slurred, as my consciousness gave up to a spiral of shapes, my head swimming in the inky river of the night before.

Smitty winked and repeated the whistle, unmistakably the same signal. Confused and exhausted, I fell asleep.

12

Sniper

It felt like I'd slept a hundred hours when the rustling of gear woke me. The midday sun was blistering my cheeks. My arms itched and face had tightened with the beginning of a sunburn. Smitty dozed a few feet away, propped against the wide trunk of a once-magnificent tree now disappearing under a tangle of giant ferns and vines. Tanned arms folded neatly across the M-16 rifle on his chest.

Mississippi Smitty. Lifer. I studied his frame, the architecture of a man built for life outdoors, devoid of amenities. One could only wonder what he'd seen. Wounded, shipped home, discharged. Re-upped. He told me later that he always wanted to sit on his porch watching the Mississippi River roll by, but when he found himself there with his leg in a cast, he realized that the only people he gave a shit about were over here.

My life bore no resemblance to Smitty's. I had a fun job at Disneyland. I lived in a party house where dozens of friends came and went at all times of the day and night. We took nothing seriously except running out of beer. This war, millions of miles away, came to life only briefly for us on the evening news, and we had been getting pretty tired of the interruption it posed. Stupid people joined the army. Unlucky saps got drafted. Nobody I knew really understood the demonstrations against the war. They only hung out at them to pick up girls who might believe in world peace by way of free sex.

None of that meant beans in Smitty's world. Here in the jungle, he personified the army lifer. Strong, wise, stealthy, adept, shrewd, erudite. All qualities I lacked. The human equivalent of a Swiss army knife, effective as well as efficient, Smitty ruled as the king of competence and control. He looked like coiled steel wrapped with cowhide. I felt like an ex-Disneyland employee with chafed thighs, shredded arms, an itchy butt, and blistered cheeks. In the World, I could be Smitty's boss. I wondered if he ever had thoughts like that. I considered rousing *him* with a kick to the boot like he had awakened me, then thought better of it.

I remembered his bird whistle at the river. How did that happen? Sergeant Bailey insisted twice that Smitty had been moving upstream at that moment with the rest of the troops. It wouldn't be like Smitty to leave the platoon. I hadn't seen him, but I heard him whistle. I know I heard it. That little warble he did with his tongue flicking the inside of his teeth. Backwoods code. It had to be Smitty. And he'd be pissed if he knew that I'd totally forgotten his warning about letting go of the rope in the river unless I heard his whistle. Up to my armpits in fear, drifting alone in the black of night, I wouldn't have let go of that rope if Ho Chi Minh himself had been on the other side whistling the Hanoi Hymn.

Smitty smiled in his sleep, no doubt saving helpless rookies in his dreams. Like he had done when he pulled me out of the smelly morgue the morning after we stuffed Cornelius. A tremor shook through me as everything about the beating and the horrible results boiled up from where I kept trying to bury the whole thing. I wanted to talk about it. I wanted to tell Smitty. It would be bad if he found out some other way.

The noises around me indicated we would soon be on the move. I closed my eyes again, trying to stave off the inevitable for at least another minute or two. Why can't they all go away? Why can't this all just go away? If I close my eyes tight enough, can't I be on a beach with a cold beer? The beach, the beer, the morgue, the river, the mysterious whistle . . . all vanished as being a soldier again fell in on me.

I limped over to wake up Smitty, but before I had moved three steps, his eyes opened and sharply considered why I approached. Two blinks later, he had a cigarette stuck to his bottom lip and the Zippo flaming toward it.

"I thought we were waiting for dark," I whined.

"Let's git," Smitty said, reaching for his gear. "Shit changes, Bubba." I hadn't even tied my boots as he moved away. The whole platoon mobilized without another word. We spread out, moving back into the jungle with our backs to the burning sun and the Mekong River. I stopped to pee, and everyone walked out of my sight. It was only for the briefest moment, and I knew where they were, but it felt extremely perilous. One minute I'm watching a line of urine splash into the bank of the Mekong as I pushed with all my gut to reach the water. The next, I'm standing by myself. Grabbing my packs, I hustled to fall back into line, zipping my pants as I ran.

Smitty scolded me when I told him what I'd done. "That's the number one dumb thing out here, Bubba. Think of the coyote circlin' 'n watchin' the sheep. What's he waitin' for?"

"The stray."

"Out here, ya don't ever wanna be too close *or* too far from anybody else." He thought for a few seconds and added, "That goes for personal shit, too."

Never too far away. Never too close.

• • •

The platoon had traveled through the thick of the jungle for about an hour when we heard a sharp *pop!* and one of our riflemen fell from a single sniper shot.

Smitty reached him first. An entry wound passed under the neck and above the sternum, square in the middle of the wrong place, like somebody had been aiming. I approached with caution, not knowing if Smitty wanted me there. Others in the platoon were hastily moving out and away with no attempt to be quiet. Brush cracked and feet kicked at the dirt as they hollered at each other and at Charlie, making as much noise as possible. A few bursts of automatic rifle fire, and every hair on my body stood at attention. I lay on my face in an instant. The others sounded like a hundred and forty men on Clydesdales. I stayed prone a few yards from the victim, hoping Smitty wouldn't notice me.

"Bubba, come here." He waved me closer. "Look here." I crawled forward. "AK-47 round." He was pointing to the exit wound. "It rifles clean through." He demonstrated by twisting his finger in my face. I nodded again but wasn't paying any attention to what he was trying to teach me. I'd been around enough broken bodies to not be too unnerved by the wound, but the chaos flying around distracted me totally. Men were flailing through the brush, kicking their legs high, boots stomping on the hard ground or splashing through marshy ponds. Everybody jockeyed for position.

Pop! Pop! Pop! Oh man, theirs or ours? Is that coming in or going out? Am I supposed to keep ducking every time a blast goes off nearby? I hit the ground again.

"Get up, for chrissake, Bubba! They're a hundred yards from here." I began to push up. *Pap! Pap! Pap!* I fell flat again. It sounded like ours, but what did I know?

Pappity. Pappity. Pappity. Pappity. I hadn't heard that rapid fire before. The wounded man, Smitty, and I were right at the center of this circling storm. Take a deep breath. Blow it out. Think slowly. Concentrate.

I had one of those running-around-naked dreams, except this time it occurred in the middle of the day, in the jungle, in a war zone, totally awake. I got to my feet. Exposed, I curled my neck forward as close to the ground as I could get it. My ears full of frenzy, my brain racing, and Smitty chattering at me as if I could actually learn something in this state, I felt like screaming. Who gives a shit about AK-47 ammunition? I wanna know what we're gonna do with this guy. Is he dying? Why isn't he moving? Who shot him? Where's everybody going? For chrissake, are we still in the line of fire?

"Shit, Bubba, pay attention. I'll tell ya when it's incomin'." Smitty didn't flinch once when the guns went off. "American M-16s tumble the bullets all around inside." He rolled his forefingers one around the other. "An entry wound might be small, but an exit wound'll blow a manhole." He made a gesture like a fisherman bragging about a large catch.

He flopped the guy over. The body didn't respond. Smitty, gimme a break with the chatter and look at this guy's skin.

"Sometimes those tumblers just bounce around in there forever 'n never come out. Damn! I'd rather be shot by an AK, wouldn't you?"

"Sure," I said, rolling my eyes. "Are you nuts?"

"What?" He looked at me, then remembered I didn't know a thing. "Hey, this guy's KIA. Never even felt the ground hit him. Look . . ." Smitty grabbed the man's neck from behind and poked his finger into the tiny entry wound high in the chest.

This was cold. I didn't know this soldier. But he made

a difference to somebody. Fortunately, I didn't know *any* of these guys. I saw the body sinking into the dark river again. And then I saw the bloody skull in the morgue. My stomach exploded into my throat, and I swallowed as hard as I could to get it back down. I couldn't breathe.

"Toe-poppers'll blow yer foot right off 'cause Mr. Charles only uses our M-16 rounds in 'em. . . ."

"Chopper's dustin' off at the river," the radio operator interrupted, flopping his heavy radio between us. "Only safe zone to land. You 'n me'll have to hump this KIA back to the LZ." I had a blank look. "You 'cause that's what you do. Me 'cause we need to call the chopper in when we get there." He patted his radio. "Thomas. Wally Thomas." He introduced himself like we were standing around yakking at a fraternity party. He reached out, grabbed my hand, and shook it up and down. "After they grease this sniper, Bailey says they'll cop a position here 'n wait for us. Looks like one old papa-san dink. We still ain't caught up to the pack." Then he turned to a small group of grunts who had remained near us rather than hunting with the rest. "Who wants to ride shotgun?"

One of them stepped forward, pointed his M-16 toward the river, grabbed his gear, and started walking. Nodding as he passed us, he said nothing as he loaded a new ammunition clip into his M-16 and moved out of sight. Luckily, we hadn't plunged too far into the unknown. The river ran barely a mile away even though it had taken us an hour to get this far. The trip would be quicker now that we knew the VC were moving in the other direction. Thomas helped me heave the casualty onto my shoulder.

I lugged the body the whole hike without a breather. Thomas didn't offer, the rifleman watched the path and the trees, and I didn't complain. Their jobs. My job. I remembered how it looked and smelled and tasted in the morgue tent. How still the air, how dank and dark and heavily fecal. I saw this guy's face behind a zipper. Peaceful, content, just wondering what the hell, if you please, had happened. With my entire shirt matted in drying blood, I couldn't wait for a chance to wash all over.

High speeding metal
Slamming through muscle and bone
How war begins, ends

Wally Thomas knelt by the edge of a long clearing next to the Mekong, near where Bailey, Hoppy, and I had met the platoon. He fired up his radio and spoke into it. I dropped my cargo gently onto his back, holding his neck as if he were a newborn so his head wouldn't bounce on the ground. I removed my shirt and slipped down the bank to wash my chest and arms in the river.

"Breaker, this is One Man Down. Gotcher ears on?" Thomas looked at me and grinned. "CB talk. My dad's a trucker."

We could hear the chopper noise loudly in the radio as a matching cadence came from the south. It was close.

"This is five-ninety offa Echo Hotel. You gotta clean end zone?" a voice crackled from the radio.

"That's a big negatívo," Thomas said. "Poor little lambs. Gotcha long 'n lean, but can't say how clean."

"What's the ball game?"

"We were in the game. Golden Gate inland. Can't confirm. Lone Ranger 'n no Tonto. Half the swingin' dicks are lookin' to offer the big hurt."

"Pop smoke in ten," came back from the chopper.

"We'll look-see. You say your ride ain't changin' status? Over."

"That's ten-four, Eagle Hummer. Our ride ain't said a word." I stood nearby, impressed that somebody actually understood what Wally was saying.

Thomas lifted his radio into my face. "This is *my* machine gun, man. My fuckin' tomahawk! I can bring pee with this hunk of wires. Artillery, medevacs, replacements, gunships, napalm, the whole nine yards of military firepower. Easy as talkin' into this little box." He laughed, then added, "Even food if we need it. I love my fuckin' radio." He grinned at me. "I *love* it. Bet I could get us pussy with this thing!" He laughed again, then looked at the casualty at my feet. "You gonna red-tag this guy?"

I had forgotten. I pulled a tag from my pack. "What's his name?"

Thomas looked at me in disbelief. "Jesus, Doc . . ."

"Jesus what?" I asked.

"Here, I'll do it." Thomas traded me a smoke grenade for the red tag. "Go around over there 'n pop smoke when I wave atcha." He pointed to the opposite side of the clearing, at least a hundred yards away. I wasn't thrilled and it showed.

"Go! I'll stay with the radio 'n KIA."

As I started off on my own, unarmed in a battle zone, my thoughts turned to our escort, whom we hadn't seen in a while. I hoped he was nearby. I *really* hoped he knew it was me stomping around in the bushes. Shivers crinkled around my ears at being totally by myself again in this place where people routinely died violent deaths. Smitty's example of the stray sheep and the wolves haunted me. And the guy now at Thomas's feet hadn't been a stray. He was walking beside us one minute, then lay flat dead. "Never even felt the ground hit him." Not at all like the long-winded death scenes in old movies, where the hero's sidekick, cradled in his arms, leaves a list of regrets and apologies and remembrances. Hollywood showed some decorum in the way it knocked off cowboys and soldiers. This "dying before you knew what hit you" had no poetic appeal whatsoever. Whatever happened to that long last letter home? "Tell Mom not to cry for me, Billy."

When I reached the other side, Thomas waved. I removed the pin and threw the grenade well away from me into the clearing. Four, three, two, one, *pop!* Deep red vapor spewed out and caught a soft breeze, quickly filling most of the landing zone. On cue, the chopper emerged in front of me. Red swirled everywhere. The percussion of the long blades slicing the air right above me reverberated in my chest. The blades of a Huey cutting the wind sounded exactly like a machine gun. I threw myself facedown in the swirling dust.

When I finally got to my knees, I could barely make out two soldiers leaping from an open door before the skids had fully touched. The front windshield reflected the bright sky, and I couldn't see the pilots inside. The chopper glared right at me, like a huge menacing mosquito with the ends of a machine gun sticking out of its ribs. A sudden burst spit orange chaser bullets into the field away from my position and sent me sprawling again. Rise, drop, up, down, tall, flat. Now I knew why we did all those squat thrusts and push-ups in basic training.

The medics ran low to the ground toward Thomas. I started running back to him, too. They had the body on a stretcher and were flopping back onto their chopper just as I crossed the landing zone. These medics looked a hundred years old and scampered like they were ten. They didn't even glance back, just crawled into position and belted themselves in as the chopper lifted off. The big bug flew out over the Mekong River fifteen feet above the water.

Thomas and I waited as the smoke lifted, then saw our escort rise from the weeds and motion to us from across the clearing. In the heat of the afternoon, the three of us double-timed through the jungle, back to the platoon.

Smitty was sitting in the same place we'd left him. When I told him how quickly the chopper had come and gone, he explained that not only do chopper jocks hate flying into an unsecured LZ, but "Hell, we're in Cambodia, for chrissake!"

Being extremely tense, I was more inquisitive than usual, and Smitty was patient with my chatter. He took every question as an invitation to teach me his profession.

"Gormley was staked out near ya'll," he assured me. "Knows what he's doin'. Third tour for him too, y'know? Sittin' still 'n watchin' for anything movin' outside yer perimeter. When ya popped red, he prob'ly threw yella or purple someplace else."

"Why?"

"Pilot knows what color he's landin' on. Charlie don't. Charles sees smoke, he just knows something's happenin'. He'd sooner lob a rocket into a chopper than cut us one at a time. We blow smoke in two, three spots to mess with him. Thomas prob'ly gave him Bear Bryant or the Tide, whatever. Anyhow, an American'd be lookin' for red."

"Bear Bryant?"

"Alabama, Bubba. The *Crimson* Tide. Where ya been?"

"Why all the double-talk? Why not use the codes we learned in training?"

"Chuck took the same classes," Smitty grinned. "He's got his ears on too."

"Ears on?"

"He's listenin' to his own radio. Monitorin' ours all the time."

"Thomas said our ride wasn't changing status."

"Yer ride. Yer passenger. Perkins." He saw my forehead crinkle. "The dead guy, Bubba. Perkins."

This was the first time I'd heard his name.

"Ya *did* tag him, didn't ya?"

"Uh huh. What's Golden Gate?"

"Can't use klicks on the air unless callin' in artillery. Charlie knows klicks anyhow. That'd give away the rest of the troops. Golden Gate means a mile. Most of us come through Alameda Naval Station right by Oakland."

"So did I."

"Spend any time in the City?"

"Sure. I spent a lot of weekends in San Francisco. Grew up in Sacramento."

"Before ya shipped out, did ya go see the Golden Gate Bridge 'n wonder if ya'd ever see it again?" I nodded. "Everybody does," he continued. "How long did it look?"

"Not very."

"Yer gettin' it. Golden Gate means not very far. Like, next door, y'know? Less than a mile."

"Echo Hotel and five-ninety?"

"Echo Hotel's the *Nuaces*. Five-ninety's the chopper number."

"Eagle Hummer?"

"Same letters, Bubba. The *Nuaces*. Another way to say Echo Hotel." Smitty looked puzzled. "Don't know any of this military shit, do ya, Bubba?"

"They just taught us the regular . . ."

Smitty drew a long breath and began to lecture. "Look, Bubba, I said it before. Charlie ain't no dink. He's been kickin' people outta this country since, well . . . since before dirt." He placed an unlit cigarette between his lips and faked his customary long drag. "Makes ya think, don't it?"

Gunfire ended my lesson.

"Here comes the shit," Smitty hissed. "God-*damm*-it! See what I mean?"

It wasn't too close, but an exchange was cranking up somewhere. I was beginning to be able to distinguish the sound of various weapons. The bursts of M-16 rifles accompanied the much lower chortle of the M-60 machine gun.

"Let's go," Smitty grunted, running toward the noise. Every muscle in my body said stay put, but I fell in behind him anyway. We picked up a dozen more troops moving through the trees. When it abruptly became quiet again, we stopped short, skidded to our knees, and listened.

"Doc! Goddammit!" someone shouted from fifty yards ahead. Another soldier's pain joined the chorus off to our left. He was definitely one of ours, screaming a long list of curses. A Vietnamese couldn't know that many American cusswords.

"Hold tight!" Smitty responded, then ran crouching low, out of my sight. I couldn't catch him. He ran too wily and I too deliberately, watching every tree pass as if something lurked behind each one.

"Medic!" I heard again, this time closer, to my right.

"Who's there?" I called.

"Here, Doc! We're over here." That name again. Doc.

I half crawled to the hollering, wondering if he knew I wasn't really a doctor. My grandfather was a real doctor. Everybody knew him. Iowa GP. Delivered a thousand babies. Dad's dad. Doc Sherman. I was an impostor out here.

I found three of our guys leaning over a fourth. One was trying to stop the bleeding from the wounded man's shoulder by pressing on it.

"Let me," I said, opening my pack and pulling out several pressure bandages at once. Some flew in the air. "Shit!"

One of the soldiers gathered the bandages off the ground and handed them to me. The others backed off to resume ready positions, turning their backs to us, spreading out. More screams. Two in front where the first had come from.

"Mother of Christ, sonofabitch! Somebody get over here. I been hit, goddammit! Over here. Please, God!" Every word shot right through me. "Jesus Christ! Ow fuck! Medic! Can you for chrissake hear me?! Doc!"

I concentrated on the open shoulder wound in front of me. It was well enough away from the heart and lungs, yet dangerously losing blood all the same. Shirt ripped away, helmet and rifle nearby, the soldier's pack had been stuffed behind his head. He said nothing, didn't even grimace as I pulled the T-shirt scraps away and applied a sterile gauze bandage to the wound. His eyes weren't focusing as his face lost color.

"Whatcha got?" Sergeant Bailey asked, kneeling behind me.

"Shoulder. A mess." He glanced over my shoulder then returned his eyes to watch all around us. "Who's yelling over there?" I asked.

"This guy looks white," Bailey observed.

"Shock. Loss of blood. I got it stopped for now, but he's outta here. I can't do anything but stuff him."

"We got two others going out," Bailey said. "We'll come get him when the LZ's secured. Stay here. I think it's over for now. Somebody must've got the fucking snipe."

"Who's yelling?" I asked again.

"We got 'em covered, Doc. You pay attention here." I turned to look at the sergeant, who nodded back at the guy on the ground. "He really looks like shit."

The other guy was still screaming ahead of me off the path somewhere. Bailey disappeared in his direction. I tried to close my ears as I worked to rearrange the bandages. My guy wasn't saying a word.

"Jesus! Jesus! Mother Mary! Please God, help me!" His pleas sounded close enough, but I couldn't leave the shoulder wound. Oh man, please stop screaming. More gunfire exploded farther away. It sounded bigger. Maybe Hoppy's 12-gauge. Where's Smitty?

"Medic! Medic! Doc, over here!" Then all was quiet. The sudden silence, and all that it implied, was even worse than the screams.

My guy's color wasn't improving. I held pressure on the wound and the bleeding stopped, but my mind raced. Couldn't get to the chopper holding bandages to his chest. Had to make him mobile.

Something clicked in my head. Pictures started pouring in. I knew how to do this. Had done it a hundred times. Wound is in a bad place for wrapping. Pull some kind of truss around and under his arm, over his shoulder. Make a sling to keep his arm still. Even better, fold his arm in the shoulder wrap, flat to his chest, to hold the bandages in place. Wish I had help. Whoever had been screaming before started screaming again.

My guy wasn't coming around. Airway open, but breathing shallow. No pulse in the wrist. Weak and then none in the neck. Color fading fast. Loss of blood to the face. Got the leak stopped. So what else is it? I threw my ear onto his chest. Nothing.

I left the wound long enough to lodge his helmet under his feet. Get the blood out of his legs. Treat shock by lifting the legs. I quickly returned to holding pressure against the wound.

With my free hand, I pulled a roll of Ace bandage from my bag to start the truss. I reached under to raise him, still holding pressure on the shoulder. My right hand underneath him caught a quart of blood. Turning him slightly, I saw what I'd missed. He had an exit wound the size of my fist. He'd been lying in a pool of blood from his back while I pressed on his front.

"Shit!" I reached for more pressure bandages. His breathing slipped from quiet panting to shallow gasping. His neck let go and his head fell sideways into the blood-soaked mud beneath him. His chest stopped moving altogether. I felt no pulse at his neck. I pushed harder, and his neck collapsed into my fingers. His arm hung limp.

"Shit!" I rolled him over to inspect the larger, ragged wound. I stuffed square gauze pads against the hole. Each one instantly soaked red. Christ, help me here! This is a mistake. Why hadn't I looked under him? Somebody help me! Shit! Shit! Stop the bleeding!

"Drop it, Bubba, *drop* it," Smitty yelled from behind me. "That one's gone. Can't help him. Need ya over here." I tried to protest as he physically lifted me away from my first field patient. Blood fell freely from my right palm onto the ground between us as Smitty pushed me over to a leg wound that hadn't been touched. It was the soldier who'd been screaming earlier, and he again filled the air with a comical combination of profanity and prayers.

"Mother of fucking Christ Almighty scumbag pissin' gook shit shot my fucking leg off! Help me goddammit!"

"Shut up, Harper," Smitty ordered, to no avail. Harper escalated his cries of terror, and now added threats.

"Dammit to fucking hell, Doc, my leg! Fucking gooks shot off my leg!"

"Yer leg's fine, buttwipe. Give it up." Despite the words, Smitty's tone was reassuring.

"Don't touch me, goddammit! Fucking hurts like shit, you dick piece of crap. Don't fucking touch me. Fuck it to hell, I'm serious as shit! You bastards hear me?"

"Let us help ya, Private Dipshit. Quit movin' around!" Harper was trying to shield his wound from us, pushing our hands away while we were trying to dodge him and get to his wounds to control the damage. If one of us touched him, he'd lash out in reaction to the pain.

Femur break. Compound fracture. Open wound ten inches long. With my help, Smitty managed to tear part of Harper's pants away with his knife. "Get that fucking knife away from me!" he screamed. "You ain't takin' my leg off!"

"Hang on, Harper," Smitty spat. "Quit grabbin' at me or I'll cut yer stupid Yankee *head* off." This got Harper's attention. Even in his panic and pain, he stopped to consider Smitty's rank and meanness. The sergeant spread his wide grin and laughed in Harper's face. "Yer gonna make it, asshole," Smitty said as he stuck a morphine Syrette through Harper's pants into his good leg, emptying the contents into his thigh in about two seconds.

"Goddammit, Doc! What the fuck?" With a quick pull, Smitty extracted the Syrette and laced the needle through Harper's pants, bending the end over itself. This would indicate to the folks on the receiving end that this soldier had been drugged. He kept cussing while Smitty held his leg still and just waited, watching him and counting. "You stabbed me with that sucker, you son of a bitch. You touch me again and I'll . . ."

Harper stopped hollering and started smiling. Whoa. High as a water tower in West Texas. He was screaming like crazy one second, then turned all serene and mushy the next. His lips tangled around his tongue as he tried to speak, so he quit trying. Smitty laughed in his face again. "You were sayin'?" Harper managed a silly grin.

Able to work now, Smitty and I were a matched team. It reminded me of the operating room on the *Nuaces,* where Smitty anticipated Dr. Guenther's next request and was there with the instrument before the doctor knew what he needed. Smitty handed me the scissors. I handed him the tape. He tossed me several packages of gauze, which I opened with my teeth and repeatedly placed on the wound while he pulled tape and I tore. We had the bleeding stopped in a few minutes and wrapped Harper's leg to prepare it for a heavy splint for transport. The medevac medics would have the leg splint and stretcher.

My thoughts drifted back to Fort Sam Houston, Medical Corpsman Training. Our training sergeant, standing stiffly on the company street, gave us his final lecture before we departed for the War.

"You learned all we can teach you, men." The drill elocution still riveted our attention after ten long weeks. "You've done well. We've *all* done well. But listen to me one more time." He paused a long uncomfortable moment.

"What have I told you Gomers a hundred-and-a-half times?"

"Restore breathing! Stop bleeding! Make mobile!" we chorused as rehearsed.

"You *will* do that *well!* I be-*lieve* you. And you *will* do everything you learned here—every technique, every field drill, every maneuver—you will do *everything* ab-so-*lute*-ly perfect." He paused this time to make eye contact with each one of us. "And you will do *all* of these things with tears in your eyes . . . and your stomach in your throat."

God, he was right. I couldn't swallow. My eyes were full and stinging. That shoulder wound caught hard and sticky in my mouth and throat. I had blood all over me, and the handful I had rubbed on my fatigue pants stuck against my leg. That drill sergeant had definitely been here.

"LZ's clear!" Bailey hollered nearby. "You guys stay put. We got some beef here to carry Harper out." Four grunts jumped in to snatch him up, two cradling his leg while Smitty led them carefully across the bumpy terrain. I grabbed his gear and followed them to a small clearing. Two choppers swooped in nose first, then abruptly lifted their underbellies to perch on the ground, one in front of the other, like tandem ships coming into port. Their blades continued running, sucking spray from the swamp below. Five soldiers ran or limped bent over toward them while medic teams carrying stretchers darted away from the choppers. One of the litter teams came with the leg splint for Harper. I recognized a medic from the *Nuaces*.

"Joey!" I shouted over the noise of the engines.

"Tie this down!" Smitty yelled, pointing to the leg. "Compound femur."

"Roger that, Smitty," Joey replied. "We got the word comin' in."

"Affirmative," Smitty yelled. "Now move yer asses. We're not secure down here yet."

"Sherm!" Joey hollered at me. "This is a new guy." He nodded toward his partner, who was deftly applying the leg splint.

"Hi, New Guy!" I hollered back, putting Harper's gear between his legs on the stretcher. Harper grinned at everybody.

The new kid looked fifteen and scared shitless, but he knew his stuff with leg splints. In only a couple of minutes they had finished securing Harper and were off running, Harper propped on one elbow and waving to his buddies as he neared the chopper.

Another team carried a soldier holding his bandaged head. Another carried my slain patient, flat on his face, arms dangling limp in rhythm with the gait of the hustling carriers. They lifted him onto his back to the litter basket attached to the side of the helicopter. A green tarp stretched from his feet to over his head. Straps were tied across his neck, ankles, and waist. Smitty squatted down next to me.

"I thought Bailey said only two guys," I sighed.

"Two for stretchers. Plus the one we lost. Four others ambulatory. They're outta here."

The one *we* lost.

"Seven guys then?"

"Eight. One ya took to the river, remember?"

I had already forgotten.

"Maybe nine," Smitty said. "Nobody's seen Hoppy."

It took a couple of hours to regroup. Thirty-one men were spread out all over the jungle. A small squad had gone to track the sniper. Others had circled the landing zone to secure it from further fire. A few tended the wounded as the choppers were called in.

Smitty and I traveled from man to man. He looked directly in their eyes, felt their neck or brow with the back of his hand, grabbed an arm, or patted a leg. He had explained to me privately that sometimes a wound was embarrassing and the guy wouldn't tell anybody. Some didn't want to be a burden, and others felt like they'd done something wrong by getting hit or twisting an ankle. So now we checked each man, doctored a few minor abrasions, and handed out aspirin. Everybody complained of a headache. I was stingy with my aspirin because I had only a small tin.

"Give 'em all out," Smitty said. "We'll get more later. Hell, Bubba, it got pretty damn *loud* out here."

The lieutenant had a severe bruise high on his cheekbone that bled in the center and swelled to the size of a golf ball. He looked like a hapless boxer who had just lost a decision. A low-hanging branch had smacked him as he went leaping through the woods trying to keep pace with Hoppy.

"He flat flew," the officer said. "I couldn't stay with him. Then I caught that branch and found myself sitting on my butt alone. I'm no Hopalong Cassidy. I thought, screw this, I'm going back."

I tried to look at his cheek, but he turned away. "Just a bruise, Doc," he said. "Leave it. Is he back?"

"No, sir," I answered. "Hoppy's missing."

"He's not fucking missing," Sergeant Bailey spat. "He's out there ahead, looking for signs. Doing his fucking *job*." The sergeant looked squarely at me.

I looked away. His accusation stung. My first field patient was dead. I had missed the exit wound. I had propped up the legs of a guy who was bleeding to death from a wound to his upper body. I had pressed on the front of a man who had a giant hole in his back. And Sergeant Bailey seemed to know exactly all the ways I had screwed up. I lost a guy who maybe could have made it.

"What hit us?" I tried to change the subject.

"One little dink papa-san stuck in a tree," the sergeant said, looking across the landscape. "Had us pinned and we couldn't get to Harper. Dropped the kid right where you're sitting and stuck him like a piece of owl meat."

"Human bait," Smitty said.

"Fuckin' A," the sergeant agreed. "I think we got the little slope-ass prick. Didn't see him fall, though. Hoppy took off right over there." He pointed to a stand of trees not far from where we were kneeling.

"Ya think one sniper did all this damage?" Only Smitty had the rank *and* the guts to question Sergeant Bailey.

"Whaddaya mean?"

"Two guys we treated were sniper rifle wounds, like Perkins. Clean in, clean out. That coulda been yer snipe, Sarge. But Wilson's shoulder took an M-16. Exit hole you could drive through." Wilson. My first casualty had a name. "And two of the ambulatory looked nasty ragged. Again M-16s. Unless one sniper's shootin' three rifles in five directions all at once . . ."

"Or one of our guys . . ." the lieutenant suggested. Our guys had put a lot of lead in the air as soon as Harper got hit, so it's possible some errant bullets could have done the damage.

"Got at least three?" Smitty asked. "In the front?" He paused, searching each of us. No one answered. "Not likely, sir. The guys hit with the 16s were in front of the pack. Ya wanna bet they all shot each other at the same time?"

Now nobody knew how many had hit us. Smitty's combat lesson to me about our M-16s and the enemy's AK-47s covered more than just entry and exit wounds.

By understanding what weapons can do to a casualty's body, Smitty could estimate the number of enemy faced.

"Three, maybe four," he said. "And two of 'em had M-16s."

American weapons were made to be more permanently disabling. Somebody somewhere had invented a softer lead that tumbled or burst apart when it hit anything solid. An American manufacturer designed it specifically for Vietnam. Apparently, M-16s had been swiped by our enemy and were being used against us. M-16s were also often referred to as piece-of-shit weapons that jammed whenever they got hot. They were good for one or two clips in a firefight, then they needed to take an hour off. I preferred my medic bag. Morphine works every time.

I turned to look at the field and the jungle beyond. Out in front of us stretched a meadow of tall grass growing in a wet marsh. Rimming three sides was a thick overgrowth of trees, bushes, and vines entangled in a tapestry mesh. Gentle winds had blown away our signal smoke, the exhaust from the diesel engines, and the dust the chopper had raised. In the serenity, I saw only lush green and the flat water of the paddies, circled by trees, as pristine as if nothing had disturbed them for centuries. I was touched by the incredible beauty.

I had experienced total violence and, in the same moment, saw unconditional natural grace. How could God ignore human catastrophe while so easily returning nature to its original state? Were we *so* insignificant? I stood there barely able to swallow or breathe, mouth wide open, gathering in everything. Something bottomless started bubbling from inside me, something guarded, fierce, and hysterical. Whatever was surfacing, my whole body shook and retched. Unnoticed by all around me, I dissolved into heavy waves of uncontrollable weeping.

"Let's move," the lieutenant ordered.

As the soldiers passed, I hid my face by examining something in my pack, letting them line out in front of me. Walking in the rear, I shuddered and sobbed and tried to mute my choking, until darkness and a ten-degree drop in temperature eased my lament. Drying my eyes and biting the inside of my cheek, with each step I fought the urge to collapse in tears.

The look and feel of my hand full of sticky blood returned. It was like Lady Macbeth's "damned spot" and the bucketload of blood that haunted her into madness. I inhaled deeper to ease the shortness of breath and stop my stomach from churning, but it only made me dizzier. I felt the caked blood on my pants, against my thigh, sticking and releasing with every step.

I could barely make out the butt of the guy moving in front of me. Close enough, but not too close. Far enough, but not too far. I concentrated on stepping right and left exactly as he did, planting my feet in each of his steps, ducking the ferns as they flipped out of his grasp into my face.

All night it felt like we were getting nowhere. Each time we came out of the trees into a clearing and moved across, one at a time, it seemed like the same clearing as before. Then we'd duck right into the same jungle, onto the same trail, through the same trees. All the while I could feel eyes watching every move I made. My intuition screamed at me to stop, dig a deep hole, slide into it, pull the dirt in over me. As my imagination took off on its own, I realized that for all the new emotions I was feeling this day, I had temporarily forgotten the one that was at the foundation of them all—fear. I began counting how many steps I could walk without taking a breath. Twenty . . . thirty . . . forty . . .

If the sun rose for me in the morning, it was still only my thirteenth day in country. Three hundred and fifty-two to go. My body might make it through a year, but my heart had stopped sometime yesterday.

Gradually, morning shadows brushed us as we increased our pace. Forty soldiers had stepped into the Tango boat. Forty had crossed the river. Now we were thirty-one, heading east, deeper into Cambodia. We had two dead, six wounded, and one important point man out in front of us somewhere. Hopefully.

13

Charlie

The meaning of "humping the bush" became clear, and I was carrying only half the gear that the others were. As sunlight stripped across the treetops, the platoon stopped to eat a breakfast of C rations, our first legitimate meal in two days. We ate like it was Thanksgiving at Grandma's. Small, dark green cans of turkey loaf, meat stuck to the sides with congealed grease. A can of bread with rings in its crust where the lid had pressed for months, or years. Cold pork 'n beans in red sauce, complete with the obligatory quarter-inch slab of pork fat. Three sugar cookies in a stack, mysteriously uncracked.

"Y'know we're sittin' right on Ho Chi Minh's birthplace? Ain't lyin'. Born in Kim Lién less than a hundred miles from here." Smitty pointed over his shoulder, then swung his arm around in the opposite direction and added, "Went to school in Hue, up there somewheres."

I concentrated on eating as much as I could, not knowing when we'd do this again.

Several of the guys removed their boots to inspect for ticks and leeches. Smitty scooped up their wet socks, whipped them around in the air, then tucked them through the canvas strap that ringed the brim of each soldier's steel helmet. By the time we would start walking again, the wet ones would be dry enough to roll and return to the packs. I changed my own socks and helped

157

Smitty with the others. It was the medic's ritual. We did it at every break. The men didn't even pay much attention. They just automatically dug into their packs to retrieve a dry pair.

"We're in Uncle Ho's hometown, Bubba," Smitty continued when we sat back down. "We shoulda learned from the French." He pushed my shoulder. "Hear me?" I nodded, fell on my medic bag, and shut my eyes.

I had lettered two years in varsity soccer before the draft got me. Basic training, though emotionally dispiriting, had made me physically stronger. I was in as good a shape as I'd ever been. Could run, crawl, climb, jump, push-up, squat thrust, and duckwalk as fast and as far as just about anyone in my platoon. But in the heat and humidity of the Southeast Asian jungle, my body felt hammered. I was fatigued, soaked, battered.

Smitty kept on talking. "We could win this if they'd let us, if the politicians would just leave us alone 'n let us fight this thing. We keep chasin' Charlie all over his own damn neighborhood. Li'l gangsters. Intimidate their own people. Disrespect their own laws 'n their own religion."

I opened one eye. "Stick a fork in me, Smitty. I'm done."

"The farmers are more scared of Charlie than of us. We chase the li'l shits away 'n they move back in 'n torment their own as soon as we're gone."

"Shit, Smitty, enough already. I can't move my legs."

"Me either," he said, offering me a hand up. "Let's go."

We spread out once more in the light of day. I yanked my dry socks off my helmet and rolled .them as we walked. The platoon didn't seem as eager to move as before, now that we'd seen the shit hit the fan without warning. Repeatedly, someone in front would raise a hand, and a wave would sweep over us as we each tried to become invisible.

Smitty concluded his lesson. "You remember what yers truly Bobby Lee Junior tells ya, Bubba. Charlie ain't no dummy." He slugged me in the medic bag as he sped up to pass me and several others.

My first brush with the enemy had taught me all I needed to know. We were getting whipped. Charlie wasn't stupid at all, especially on his home field. He had the advantage. The only way I could personally wrestle any dignity out of this lopsided game would be to get myself out alive, and hopefully help the guy next to me get out alive too.

Were the others thinking the same things? About what had just happened? About the World? About not ending up like Perkins, who was walking alongside us one minute, looking left and right just like we were doing, then *pap!* and he was gone?

Nobody talked. Nobody smoked. We moved deliberately while our ears strained to hear anything other than the sound of soldiers swishing through the foliage.

When the sun reached the top of its arc, we regrouped for water and lunch under a thick, protective grove at the entrance to a long valley. We weren't hungry again this soon but ate anyway. A few grunts fanned out to protect our sides so the rest of us could sit close and talk quietly for the second time that day. Smitty and I again checked feet, hands, and faces for blisters, sores, abrasions, heat rash, and other minor ailments. We dispensed salt tablets to everyone. Smitty had told me to watch each man swallow at least two, because some didn't like to take pills even though these were very necessary in the heat.

Smitty recommended to the lieutenant that we wait

here through the heat of the day. "Everybody's spent, sir. We could use the rest. Who knows what Charlie might throw at us if we catch him."

"*When* we catch him," Sergeant Bailey corrected. "We're closing in on them dink bastards, Lieutenant. I say let's push." Signs of Charlie's movement had become more numerous. Bailey smelled blood and wanted to pick up the pace. But the lieutenant listened to his medic first, as well as to his own exhaustion, and decided to hold for a while.

"Set a perimeter, Sergeant," he instructed Bailey. "We're here until dark." Bailey didn't seem overly disappointed. He turned his attention to putting more men at various posts to protect us from ambush in any direction.

I had often thought about writing the recommended "last letter" home, but up until now hadn't seen the point. After we stopped and the events of the past twenty-four hours caught up with me, I found myself writing a note to my family to be delivered only in the event that I ended up dead. I couldn't believe how quickly it came. I thought it would take forever to put everything I felt and thought and believed and wanted them to know into one carefully written epistle, but it didn't. I sealed my "last words" in an envelope, carefully addressed to my mom and dad. I closed my eyes and tried to picture my folks reading it at the round Formica kitchen table where mail, newspapers, family plans, arguments, philosophies, most meals, and all news, good or bad, were shared.

Dear family:

If you're reading this, I'm pretty much totally dead. You know that already. You also know that war stinks. Nothing good comes when people shoot each other. It leaves a complete mess. War is just fear and ego and power. And it isn't going to go away by holding hands and singing peace songs. Somebody's going to have to invent a way for us to not be so afraid of each other. The older guys seem most scared of all.

Some over here think that everybody in this country is our enemy. If that's so, then I guess I've seen my share. Nobody has come at me with a gun or anything. They wait and watch, and then shoot us one at a time. That's probably how I got it, too. But that's exactly what the boys in our neighborhood would do if someone came over and tried to wipe us out. And you would help them. You'd feed them, arm them, hide them, and do what you could to confuse the invasion. You'd also be pretty mad at any of your neighbors who helped the invaders. I can understand that. I don't hate these people.

I love all of you, and I tried my very best to come home in one piece like you wanted me to. I just didn't. Please don't think I did anything foolish. I'm no hero. I am only your son and brother, who is now with some of his best friends.

Love, Ben

I gave the letter to Smitty.

"Nice timin'," he smiled, slipping it into the bottom of his medic bag.

"It's nothing. Tried to keep it short."

"Roger that."

"You write one?"

"Affirmative. First tour. Gave it to my brother to put in his safe-deposit box." He smiled wider. "Says 'To be opened only upon the untimely demise of Robert E. Lee Smith, Jr.' Untimely demise. Ya like that?"

"Yeah, mine says something like that."

"Everybody's got a bullet somewhere with their name on it," Sergeant Bailey joined our conversation. "When your number's called, you meet that bullet."

"Joey Sims wears a bullet around his neck," I said.

Smitty and Bailey winked at each other.

"What?" I asked.

"Nothing. Don't sweat it." Bailey gave Smitty another look.

"Bubba, yer still new out here. Gonna find that people who wear shit around their necks 'n take trophies like ears 'n shit, well . . . they ain't . . . well, let's say there's a code they ain't followin'."

"A code?" I asked.

Out of nowhere, Hoppy appeared.

"What's happenin'?" he asked in a hoarse voice.

"Christ! Hoppy!" someone gasped. Everyone snapped around and gaped. The lieutenant came out of his own hiding place to greet our point man.

"Boss Phantom returns," Hoppy laughed, waving his hands above his head and dragging one foot like Frankenstein's monster. "Hey Bailey, your perimeter sucks, man."

The sergeant immediately departed to kick some ass.

Our point man stood bare-chested. His fatigue pants were now shorts, cut off above the baggy pockets. An olive drab T-shirt served as a bandanna that covered his head and draped down his neck. His helmet, shotgun, and handgun were all missing. He carried only his long hunting knife on a piece of heavy twine around his neck. His chest looked rough and red.

"You tell *us* what's happening," the officer said.

"Nothin' at all, sir," Hoppy croaked. His voice

sounded terrible. "Just a whole downtown society of Chuck types. Seven, maybe eight klicks northwest. Probably a thousand or more, that's all."

"Jesus H. Christ," the officer sputtered.

"Gimme some water," Hoppy demanded before he continued. He drained half a canteen then threw it back. "Like papa-san said, sir. A whole bunch of them motherfuckers been stockin' up on shit for their underground city right in them hills. Right there." He pointed ahead of us with determination. "Looks like a million ants crawlin' around."

The hills were close enough to touch.

"All of 'em soldiers too. No mamma-sans or kids or any old farts. Ain't no village, sir. We got us a full-on military outpost up ahead."

Everybody stared at each other. Hoppy gulped down a can of C rations someone opened for him.

"I saw 'em," Hoppy continued, shaking himself. "Scary as shit." He looked around at each of us. "I'm tellin' ya, they're like a buncha goddamn insects up there. Comin' 'n goin' as they please. Like nobody's within a million miles of here."

"What's the call?" Bailey asked, rejoining the meeting.

"If we can, we slide outta here," Hoppy said with no optimism in his voice. "Outnumbered at least fifty to one. I think we can mess with 'em a little first, though."

Oh good. My heart started working its way up my esophagus again.

"We can?" someone asked.

"They know you're here," Hoppy answered. "I been watchin' 'em watch you since we got hit."

Hoppy grabbed for a cigarette out of Smitty's pocket, and Smitty flamed it for him. "Smoke 'em if ya got 'em," he called out for everyone. "Don't look like they're gonna do shit 'til they bring us in closer." He squatted to one knee. Cigarettes flared all around. It looked like a forest fire.

"How many we lose?" he asked Smitty.

"Two. Six wounded. We're thirty-two countin' you."

"How're we for runnin'?"

Smitty shook his head. "Spent, mostly. Ate twice today. Could go the other way most definitely. Ain't much fight in these guys right now."

Hoppy thought for a few seconds, then turned back to the lieutenant.

"Followed seven scouts all yesterday afternoon 'n night, sir. They kept circlin' to see where you was goin'. I kept watchin' 'n they kept movin'. Never copped a position. Just waitin' for you to advance, I guess. Y'all stayed put 'n they totally missed me!" He laughed at himself. "Cruised right through 'em." He stretched his arms and simulated a surfer. "In the tube. Bitchin', man."

"We pack it in?" asked the lieutenant. "Retreat?"

"Naw. Not right away, sir. Been thinkin' this out. That's why I come back."

"Okay, shoot."

"They know we can track 'em. They're leadin' us right to their front door. They don't want more gunships in here."

"But they get *off* blowing away choppers," Bailey said.

"Yeah, I know," Hoppy went on. "That's what I thought too. But goddamn, they've been awful careful not to get noticed, not to pick off any of you after that first Alpha Bravo near the river."

Smitty turned to me and whispered, "Ambush. A-B. Alpha Bravo."

"But you would've made some flap if they'd stopped, right?" Bailey asked, even though he knew the answer. He wanted to reassure the lieutenant's frantic look.

"Never had to. They kept movin' kinda like they meant to lay tracks on purpose. I think they want us all. I think they're leadin' us right into another ambush so they can get 'em a major grab."

"A grab?" I whispered to Smitty.

"POWs," four of them answered in unison.

Sergeant Bailey put it together. "They pop two guys and wound a few, just to get our attention. Then scamper away leavin' tracks my mother could follow. Over thirty POWs in one maneuver ain't bad, even for Charlie."

"Okay, lie low," the lieutenant said, his voice higher than before. "We'll get some help from command on this one."

"Sir! No way, sir," Hoppy blurted without blinking an eye. The lieutenant stared at him, more fascinated than annoyed.

"I mean, sir, we're in Cam-fucking-*bo*-dia."

"So? We need to know what kind of help we can get. We can raise gunships." He looked around for Thomas the radio operator, who was standing right behind him.

Hoppy continued. "Look, sir, you radio anybody now, Charlie's gonna know his safari's a wipeout. He'll go to plan B 'n call a few hundred of his buddies on the hill to cruise over here 'n wax our asses."

Bailey added, "We got no idea what kind of Cambodian border patrols are out here. Don't know if they're friendly to *us* or the gooks."

"Then let's get out of here," the lieutenant concluded.

"We can do that, sir, and take our chances that we can outrun these fucks," Hoppy said.

"In their jungle?" Smitty added.

"We're in a squeeze, sir," Bailey said. "At least that's what Charlie thinks."

The lieutenant stood abruptly and started pacing a

few yards away, thinking to himself. He looked nervous.
After a few moments he delivered a fine testimony.

"Fellas, I've been in country sixty days. All that time
has been with this platoon. Until yesterday, I hadn't lost
anybody. All day, after what happened, all I've been
thinking about is what I'm going to say when we get
back. I've been thinking all about me. My explanation.
My excuses. My career. Facing the commanding officer." He stopped to regain his composure and look into
the face of each man listening.

"In fact, all the way through OCS and the first fifty-
nine days, the center of my attention has been me. I felt
pretty up for this job." He swallowed hard a couple
times to let the frog out of his throat. This guy was really
young. At least two or three years younger than I. And
out here with all the responsibility.

"I flew over here knowing everything the army could
teach an officer about leadership. I'm a quick study." He
paused again. This wasn't easy for him. "But now I
know how stupid I am. I don't know *any*thing. There's
nothing I can do about the guys we lost yesterday. And
worse, there's nothing I can do to avoid it happening
again. All the books, leadership training, military protocol, politics, field maneuvers, marching, battle strategies . . ."

"None of us do, sir." Hoppy tried to be supportive.

"Yes you do, dammit!" He was dead serious. "I knew
everything two days ago. I know *nothing* today." He
paused. He certainly had our attention. "Except two
things. I've got to let you guys make the moves." He
paused again. "And I've got to get the rest of us out of
here alive. That's all I care about right now."

Bailey and Hoppy started to say something but he
raised his hand. "I don't mind being the link to HQ. I
don't mind taking whatever shit we get from above. I

can talk military. I can get with the hype, the gung-ho, the codebooks. But from now on, you guys are making the moves. You hear me?"

The sergeants nodded automatically. I nodded with them, then caught myself. Why the heck was *I* nodding?

"And that's pretty much an order." He turned to Hoppy and smiled.

A big, ugly grin spread over Hoppy's face, and he offered the lieutenant his open palm to receive the honorary low five. "What I really think we need, sir, is another radio."

"Huh?" Thomas asked. His antenna bobbed above his head as he adjusted the radio strap around his shoulder.

"We need to call in a total balls-out air strike, sir. And we need to do it a hundred miles away from here."

"A hundred miles?"

"You know what I mean. Five miles. Far enough away that Charlie can't zero in on our location."

Sergeant Bailey helped. "We keep one radio here to dial in the hits to the other radio that's calling in the strike."

"Keep changin' frequencies to keep Charlie runnin' all over the dial," Thomas added.

"So Chuck don't know who's talking to who," Bailey continued.

Hoppy summed it up. "Even without the mixed-up signals, it's gonna take two radios anyway. We're too far from the nearest artillery base." He quickly drew a wiggly line in the dirt with a section sticking out to the right. "I think we're right here, not too far from the border. This little piece of land is actually Cambodia, but it juts out right into 'Nam. Takes too long for the gooks to walk around, so they just cut across from here to here." He made another mark with his stick. "Tay Ninh is ri about here someplace. At least twenty-five miles inland. That's close enough for the really heavy guns. We gotta bunch of those in Tay Ninh. But it's too far for radio contact. We gotta split the distance."

"Without calling for help, where do we get the second radio?" the lieutenant asked.

"Leave that to me, sir. I saw Charlie with one of ours." Hoppy chased some cookies with the other half canteen of water and added, "You boys sit tight 'n I'll be back at O-dark-thirty. If you hear any poppin' at all, get outta here. I'm a wipeout. Southeast. Do *not* go near the river 'til you're at least ten miles southeast of here. They'll expect you to head to the river." Instructions complete, he disappeared.

Bailey changed his sentries. Smitty and I kept to ourselves rather than check for dry socks. It felt better to stay very still when we knew Charlie was watching every move. In the stone silence, our lieutenant sat down to write letters to two families in the World.

14

Strike

We rested uneasily, aware that our hosts knew exactly where we were. Everybody crawled under cover. Following the others, I stuck vines around my helmet and used a piece of burnt wood and some mud to rub black over my face. In the overgrowth of the jungle, you could totally disappear without much effort. Wally Thomas joined me in a bush built for two, and I could hear the faint sounds of radio babble leaking from his headset. He scanned frequencies and caught some foreign language.

"Man, I wish I understood Vietnamese," he said. "I'd like to know what these suckers are sayin'."

"That doesn't sound like Vietnamese to me," I said.

"Whaddaya mean?"

"Just been around it for a few days in Dong Tam. I heard the mamma-sans talking while they were cleaning the barracks and mess hall. I studied phonetics in school, and all their sounds have kinda whiny diphthongs."

"Dip-thongs?"

"Yeah, two vowels together. Like Smitty always double-dips each vowel. He makes a diphthong out of every syllable. Southern drawl."

He thought about it and smiled.

"This sounds more like French vowels," I suggested. "Isn't it called 'French Cambodia'?"

"Yeah, Doc, could be. Wonder how close they are." My exact thoughts.

Just before sundown, Hoppy returned with a second radio. No shots had been fired. I was surprised that the radio didn't have someone's arm still attached.

Gormley and Smitty volunteered to join Hoppy as the forward observers. The perfect trio. The best equipped and most seasoned. I'd seen Gormley and Hoppy totally disappear into the jungle, and Smitty seemed to be a bit of a magician himself. Even so, I didn't like seeing Smitty fall in behind those two, leaving me as the only medic.

When it grew dark enough to afford cover, the rest of us moved in pairs along a tree line, zigzagging south and east away from the valley and the hills. And away from the tributaries that led to the Mekong River. We crossed back into Vietnam, heading directly toward Tay Ninh. When we reached a small river, we crossed using the buddy system, keeping each other close. This time we used no rope, no meticulous safety. We all just hit the belt-high water at the same time and waded as hard as we could in all our clothes.

We walked faster and more deliberately again, putting distance between us and a city of communist guerrillas. The light waning, our lieutenant held his compass in front of his face until he couldn't see it anymore. Then every few minutes he'd stop and peek at it through his hands with his flashlight.

After four hours of nonstop moving, as it turned pitch black, we halted. Bailey and the lieutenant determined that we were well away from the enemy. We began to prepare our position. The riflemen secured our perimeter. The machine gunner propped his beast on its tripod, aimed it in the direction we had come from, and sank back into a comfortable leaning position. He knew we'd be there a while. I made the usual rounds without Smitty, checking for dry socks and bandaging blisters, handing out more salt tablets. Content that I'd done all I could do, I found a bush and backed into it. For the rest of the night we watched.

I had been impressed by the lieutenant's honest approach to our situation. And now, he sat close enough that I could start a whispered conversation.

"I guess some people think we're winning," I said. "Then there's the rest of us."

"How long you been in country?" he asked.

"Thirteen days, sir."

"Well, for a rookie, you certainly summed it up, Doc."

"I guess it's pretty hard walking the wire between us and the commanders."

"I'm not sure the brass knows any more than we do. All the talk is negotiations right now."

"How's that?"

"Paris. The peace talks."

"Sir?"

"You don't know about Paris?"

"Oh, sure. The stuff in Paris. Yes, sir."

"You don't know what I'm talking about, do you?"

"I guess not."

"North Vietnamese, South Vietnamese, Americans—I think the Russians are there, and Britain and Canada—all sitting around a big conference table. They talk a lot. Newspapers write stories. We offered to give over the DMZ if they'd return all the POWs. But they didn't want that useless plateau. They want the fertile land of the South. Rice farms. Cash crops. Trade centers. Shipping industries."

The radio operator slid up to the lieutenant and told him he'd received a short coded message from Smitty: Gormley and Hoppy had greased the seven scouts. All dead. "So the game is on," Thomas added. "When they don't report in, hell's gonna fly." Thomas crawled back to his spot.

We both sat thinking to ourselves for a while, then the officer asked, "How come you don't carry a weapon?"

"CO, sir."

"Quaker?"

"No, sir. And my dad's not a minister. That would've been too easy."

"Draft board say you could be a medic?"

"No, sir. Refused my application, then denied my appeal five-to-nothing."

"That's why I went to OCS. Figured I'd keep myself out of here if I went to officer's school. Bought it hook, line, and sinker. Pretty stupid, huh?"

"Begging your pardon, sir, but yes."

"And how'd you get to be a medic?"

For the next few minutes I told the second lieutenant about having to refuse an order to pick up a pistol in order to get the army to take my CO request seriously. And about that landing me in the holdover barracks with the other rejects. And how I'd bombarded the Pentagon with change-of-status paperwork while I was working as a clerk in the orderly room. "After the papers were filed, I had two appointments. One with a shrink, the other with a chaplain."

"No shit? To make sure you weren't nuts and ... what? Spiritual?"

"I guess. Army shrink asked me about my home life. About my mom and dad. We talked for several hours.

He asked if I wanted to go to Vietnam, and I said I didn't but that I knew that's where most medics went. He wrote on my form 'Knows the difference between right and wrong and adheres to the right.' That was it."

"What a relief, Doc. Glad you're not a psycho."

"Yeah. So much for therapy."

"And the chaplain?"

"Well, sir, that didn't go so well. The chaplain was a major. First one I'd met. And a major hawk. Told me the story of Sergeant York, the conscientious objector in World War I who threw down his morality, picked up a gun, and blew away dozens of the enemy to save his buddies."

"Gary Cooper and Walter Brennan," the lieutenant noted. "Saw that movie."

"He actually took an army hymnal off his shelf and read me all the words from 'Praise the Lord and Pass the Ammunition.'"

"No shit?"

"It all sounded pretty rehearsed. He said I should be honored to place my country over my own personal beliefs. I said I thought America was *founded* on religious principles. He started telling me what Jesus wanted me to do."

"Jesus?"

"Jesus would want me to defend my country. Jesus would want me to be brave and heroic. Jesus would want me to kill communists. I told him, 'Not my Jesus.' He *really* hated *that*. Then he went on to the hypothetical 'What would you do if . . .' stuff. So I asked him what he would've done if he were a German in 1937. And he said that was different, that Hitler killed millions of Jews and tried to take over the world."

"You didn't toss in the Nuremberg trials?"

"Oh, man, I forgot. Where were you when I needed

you? I tried quoting a bunch of people—political leaders, church leaders—and he kept interrupting. I finally told him he was the worst excuse for a Christian I'd ever met."

"A major? You said that to a *major* chaplain?"

"He threatened to take me out back and whip my ass right there in the company yard. Oh wait, excuse me—his exact words were, 'I'd like to take your little coward ass out back and give it a good whipping.'"

"Did he sign your form?"

"Nope. I wanted to cash it all in and take the first underground rail to Canada."

"The underground?"

"I have a buddy in San Francisco. My next-door neighbor growing up. He's with the ACLU or something and does some draft-dodger stuff. He's always wanted me to get out of the country." I could picture Dave Anderson's handwritten words imploring me not to go: *There's still time for you to jump. I'll be here when you do. Think about it. Don't go. It ain't worth your legs.*

"What's *his* draft status?"

"Never registered. Never went to Selective Service."

"And they haven't caught up with him?"

"Not yet. Not that I know of. He just turned twenty-six."

"Why didn't you call him?"

"Couldn't let one army asshole ruin me. I've been a Christian all my life. When I applied for CO status as a civilian, my college chaplain stood right beside me. Guided each step. Helped me think through my answers. An old professor friend of my dad's helped too. They both took me seriously. We talked for hours about pacifism and violence, about the differences between this war and World War II. He'd been interned in a CO camp all during that war. Those guys really suffered for their beliefs, for making a stand. I didn't want to disappoint all the people who'd helped me."

"Or yourself."

I thought about that for a while.

"Sherman?"

"Yes, sir?"

"Jim."

"Sir?"

"My name's Jim Cook."

"Ben."

"It's an honor to have you in my platoon, Ben."

"Yeah, I guess."

"You're like a hippie in the army."

"No, sir. Just a guy who doesn't shoot people."

"A lot of us are."

Wally Thomas was responding to his radio. "Sir? Yes, sir. He's right here, sir." He leaned over to us. "Lieutenant, I got HQ in Tay Ninh. I think he said Colonel somebody."

Lieutenant Cook slid away and began a disjointed series of conversations that lasted off and on all night. He and our commanders in Tay Ninh talked in American gibberish, each side creating new codes as they spoke. First they used football jargon, then geographical references to states in the Union, then television shows.

About half an hour before first light we got our second call from Smitty. In code, he indicated the channel he'd be switching to. Thomas followed him to that channel, then relayed Smitty's information to another command post miles away, the one that HQ at Tay Ninh had called to help with this operation. Given the distance and the need for more accuracy than long-range missiles could provide, army brass had decided that they would call in the air force.

Now a new voice was talking to Thomas. "It's the air force!" he grinned. "I got us another full-bird colonel!"

Out of the sky at dawn, like the Japanese flying into Pearl Harbor, air force bombers laced a nondescript hillside in the eastern region of Cambodia with enough explosive tonnage to kill all life for a hundred years. As they made several passes, I could hear Smitty's Mississippi twang calling changes in direction to Thomas, who relayed the information to the air force commander in charge of the strike. Squawking from the radio, the colonel sounded like he was enjoying the show.

"Un-fucking-believable!" he said, at least fifty times.

Then came the jets. For more than an hour we heard the distant, screaming whir of air-to-ground missiles followed by the resonance of their impact. Once or twice there were huge rocking secondary explosions, where they had hit ammunition or fuel. We were closer than we thought. I could swear I felt the ground trembling.

When the blasts began to subside, it reminded me of waiting for the last kernel of popcorn to pop. Lieutenant Cook motioned to Sergeant Bailey, who quickly squat-hopped from man to man, detailing instructions to get everything ready to move. Cook grabbed my arm and said, quiet enough for only me to hear, "Still didn't shoot anybody, did we?"

The last far-off rumble yielded to deep quiet. Nobody moved. We sat packed and ready to go, listening for any twig, any breath of a noise, from any direction. We heard nothing. No wind. No rain. No hollering. No rustling. No choppers. No distant *rat-tat-tats* from gunships or *blats* from rocket launchers. There weren't even any birds or mosquitoes.

Two long hours after the noise ceased, Hoppy and Smitty rejoined us, soaked from top to bottom, breathing hard from running. They were carrying Gormley in Smitty's makeshift litter blanket. He was dead.

"Get us outta here," Smitty rasped as their casualty fell to the ground between them.

"Go, Thomas," Lieutenant Cook ordered.

"Ready to beat feet, Papa One," Thomas barked into his radio.

"Backatcha," came from one of the chopper pilots. "Confirm your squat. Copy?"

"Roger, Papa One. Five TDs, an extra point, and one down."

"Run two klicks, from Chicago to Denver. Find us with a nice, clean Lima Zulu."

"Jesus, they're here already," Thomas said.

Two klicks, two thousand meters. Chicago to Denver would be due west. The chopper was already waiting in a clear landing zone. Five touchdowns and an extra point meant thirty-one of us for transport. The one down was Gormley.

I grabbed the foot end of Gormley's litter. Smitty and I were off running. His shirt and pants were soaked with sweat. He looked spent. Seeing his exhaustion, others offered to help take Smitty's end, but he waved them off. He knew his job, and he had never learned how to spell "quit."

15

Politics

Before I had time to reflect on how much ground we'd covered, a caravan of medevac choppers lifted us out of the jungle and headed to the *Nuaces*. In another hour I had eaten the largest breakfast of my life, taken the longest cool shower, shaved close, and changed into clean underwear and fatigues. Smitty and I shared an oasis of calm astride a prep table with a chessboard between us. We were the only two in triage. Still wired and far from sleep, I dropped my fatigue pants and rubbed a ton of Vaseline into my chafed thighs as Smitty contemplated his next move. I had him cornered and he knew it.

"Gormley?" I asked Smitty.

"Don't know," he said, "except he got his throat cut. Got too far from us. Almost tripped over him runnin' back." His mood was stern and grumpy.

"Smitty, I need to know some things."

"Yeah me too, Bubba."

"Are we winning or losing?"

He stiffened his back and stretched his neck, leaned over to grab my fresh, cold Coke, and finished it in one long series of gulps. Looking around as if he had spicy news to share, he leaned forward, looked me straight in the eye, and asked, "Whadda *you* care?"

"What?" He caught me off guard.

"You 'n yer no-weapon shit. What is that, anyhow?"

"I'm a medic . . ."

"No. *I'm* a medic, Private. Yer just weight."

"I can't believe . . ."

"Believe it, soldier. That's the way it is." He raised himself from the table, pushed his king off the side of the board, and let it drop to the floor. "Hippie bullshit." He walked out onto the deck.

I didn't think it was possible, but triage turned even quieter. I slowly, deliberately placed each of the chessmen in the padded cells of Dr. Guenther's ivory box. Lost in remorse, I didn't move from the table. No one came in, not even other corpsmen. Were they avoiding me? Had word spread that Smitty wasn't pleased with my performance in the field? Maybe Sergeant Bailey had reported that I hadn't checked the exit wound.

Two hours passed like two days. I trembled through a few shaking fits, then just sat and stared, replaying the scenes I had witnessed, trying to dissect my own actions. I moped, stung by Smitty's sudden explosion. How could I have been so wrong? I had really thought we were . . .

What was I thinking? I'm in the army. Never too far away. Never too close.

"Bubba," Smitty called to my back. "Come on out here 'n have a smoke." He motioned from outside the door. It sounded like an order so I hastened to obey.

"Look, I'm not real good at offerin' excuses. I apologize, goddammit. Ya didn't do anything to deserve that."

"Well, I . . ."

"Listen. Lemme figure this out a second." He appeared calmer. His voice was deep and smooth, not agitated like before. In between sucking the life out of his cigarette, he spoke with resolve.

"I hate losin'. Always have. Cried the first time I lost a football game. My dad slapped the back of my head 'n told me to 'buck up' or not come home. Left me sittin' there on the end of the bench, chokin' slobber. Drove right home without me." He looked up at the sky. "I hate to lose," he repeated.

"Everybody does," I said.

"But y'know, Bubba, I go all to pieces if even *one* of our guys gets a scratch. Even though we got 'em in the end today, we just come from gettin' our dicks stomped." He frowned hard. "I hate this shit. And I took it out on *you* 'cause yer convenient."

"It's all right."

"Naw it ain't. We're in this shit together."

"Okay."

"I'm prouda ya. Didn't fall to pieces."

"Yeah I did."

He looked at me hard. "Do *not* let that getcha, Bubba. Dead is dead. Can't bring it back."

My eyes began to well up and sting. I started to speak several times but couldn't. A long silence left us both uncomfortable. Smitty finally changed the subject.

"This is a strange place, Bubba. I don't understand their religion or their culture or a damn thing about these people. One time, I patted a baby-san on the head. It was natural, like 'nice kid,' y'know? And this mamma-san came flyin' at me, cussin' with that whiny voice." He lit another cigarette and handed me his lighter. "I couldn't figure out why she was screamin' at me." He paused and filled his lungs with smoke. "But y'know what, Bubba? Every baby-san has an angel sittin' right on his head." He traced a ring with the fingers holding his cigarette, the smoke trailing a thin halo around his head. "A little angel, y'know? Protectin' 'em from dangers 'n curses." He stared at the ground. "And goddammit Bubba, when I patted this little baby-san, I knocked off his angel."

"Bad move."

"Nobody tells us shit like that."

"We're supposed to shoot these people, Smitty. Not understand them."

"You can be a real asshole sometimes, y'know that, Bubba?" Smitty shook his head.

"The only way I can live with myself, now and after, is to know that I didn't take anybody's life on purpose," I finally blurted out.

Smitty let that sit for a while, then went into triage and came back with two cold Cokes. "What if yer life's threatened? Or mine?"

"I restore breathing and stop bleeding. I don't even know how to use a gun."

"A rifle."

"See?"

"Dipshit."

"Serve my time and get out, that's all. I'm not a hippie. I never protested. Don't do drugs. Didn't burn my draft card. I just won't train myself to kill anybody. Won't pretend to. Don't intend to."

"What if somebody's comin' at us?"

"Well, we were under fire several times yesterday."

"And?"

"Did anybody miss my firepower?"

"I haven't fired my weapon in months."

"The difference is, I don't have one to fire."

"What if . . ."

"I guess I'd get greased. Everybody asks me 'what if.' I don't *know* 'what if.' But let me ask you," I turned it around, "what if the guy coming at you was your brother? Would you shoot him?"   .

"You think Charlie Cong's yer brother?"

"Could be."

My answer was too snappy. Smitty's jaw dropped. He looked left and right to make sure no one was close enough to hear my treason. Then he broke into a smile. "Have to think on that, Bubba. I know what yer sayin'. I get yer point. Just ain't *my* point, that's all." I was relieved to drop an argument I'd surely lose. "Keep doin' what ya *been* doin', 'n you won't have to worry about shootin' anything."

"Whaddaya mean?"

"That's a compliment, Doc. You're one strac medic in the field, okay? Kept yer head in. Yer ass down. Didn't go rabbit on us. That's gonna save ya from ever havin' to shoot Charlie, know what I mean?"

I hoped I did.

"We'll see how ya do on medevacs."

Two more zipper bags were packed into aluminum boxes. I guess we won. Two dead, eight wounded. The buzz on the *Nuaces* was that we called in a strike that destroyed an enemy stronghold. I'd been to war. My head couldn't shake the memory of the pool of blood in my open palm. I hadn't actually encountered the enemy, except for the shadow of a body slipping into the river. But I'd been out and come back. My thighs were raw, and I walked like an old rodeo cowboy. If I went to the field again, I would take more socks, fewer pants and shirts, a pair of jockey shorts, and a huge tube of Vaseline.

Midnight passed, day fifteen began. I took out my short-timer Old Glory calendar and blackened another box, then folded it away without looking at the rest of the flag.

51	52	53	54	55	56	57	58	59	60	61	62	63	64	65	66	67	68	69
70	71	72	73	74	75	76	77	78	79	80	81	82	83	84	85	86	87	88

89	90	91	92	93	94	95	96	97	98	99	100	101	102	103	104
105	106	107	108	109	110	111	112	113	114	115	116	117			

118	119	120	121	122	123	124	125	126	127	128	129	130
131	132	133	134	135	136	137	138	139	140	141	142	143

144	145	146	147	148	149	150	151	152	153	154	155	156
157	158	159	160	161	162	163	164	165	166	167	168	169

170	171	172	173	174	175	176	177	178	179	180	181	182	183	184	185	186	187	188	189	190	191	192
193	194	195	196	197	198	199	200	201	202	203	204	205	206	207	208	209	210	211	212	213	214	215

216	217	218	219	220	221	222	223	224	225	226	227	228	229	230	231	232	233	234	235	236	237	238
239	240	241	242	243	244	245	246	247	248	249	250	251	252	253	254	255	256	257	258	259	260	261

262	263	264	265	266	267	268	269	270	271	272	273	274	275	276	277	278	279	280	281	282	283	284	285	286	287	288
289	290	291	292	293	294	295	296	297	298	299	300	301	302	303	304	305	306	307	308	309	310	311	312	313	314	315
316	317	318	319	320	321	322	323	324	325	326	327	328	329	330	331	332	333	334	335	336	337	338	339	340	341	342
343													358													

16

Steam

"We're goin' to Dong Tam, Bubba."

My next shift found me in the middle of losing yet another game of chess to Dr. Guenther. "Good. Anything's better than this."

"Oh yeah? Next we do medevacs."

"You going too?"

"Yep. Ain't finished teachin' ya the ropes. Choppers next, Bubba. Ya like choppers, don'cha?"

"Choppers can't be worse than the beating I'm getting here."

Smitty and Dr. Guenther both laughed and nodded. "That's what *you* think!"

"Okay, I get it. When do we go?"

"Tomorrow mornin'. Then we sit in a standby tent 'til our call comes. Borin' as shit."

I looked down at the chessboard. "That'll give me time to find some nongenius type to play."

"Doesn't take a genius to beat you at chess, Ben," Dr. Guenther said. He picked up his medical journal and quickly lost himself in an article. My previous four days in Dong Tam had been spent in the morgue tent. It might be nice this time to get a haircut and find a poker game.

I spent the rest of the night smoking cigarettes out on the deck, watching the sky slowly grow lighter. I remembered sitting in that exact spot an eternity ago. No three days of my life had packed in so much yet moved so slowly, minute by minute, sometimes breath by breath. I couldn't shake the image of that handful of blood. The loss of color. The fragile failing breath. Someone's beloved, slipping through amateur hands. I felt alternating hot rushes of guilt and panic, recalling vividly Sergeant Bailey's look of disgust, then the face-down statistic for the evening news, limp arms dangling off a stretcher.

Sharp pains bit into my side. Whenever my worry rose as I recalled the morgue attack with pangs of fear and remorse, my ribs stabbed. Had somebody opened a coffin and found Cornelius Jones yet? Did he have family? Did they know he was a sociopath? Would that make any difference? No matter how I tried to envision other things, I couldn't shake the image of his face before it disappeared behind that zipper.

Well after the first sign of the sun, I met Wally Thomas pacing on the pontoon dock. He said Smitty had already left for base camp. As soon as a shuttle jeep arrived, we jumped in and I drove it back along the bumpy dirt road I'd bounced in on ten days before.

When we arrived at Dong Tam, Thomas pointed to a large building next to command headquarters. STEAM BATH AND MASSAGE read the huge stenciled letters on the front facade. A steady stream of GIs was filing in the front door.

"There she is," Thomas said. "Steam 'n Cream. Park this sumbitch and let's go!" I followed him through the front opening to a desk manned by an ancient papa-san.

"Fie dollah," he said in broken English. "You pay now." His outstretched palm had the same texture as his face, which resembled an elephant's leg. The few teeth he had were black and brown, and I wished he hadn't smiled. It made my whole mouth ache. I ran my tongue over my front teeth and thanked whoever had invented fluoride. "Numbah one massáh, ten dollah," he added, leaving his hand out toward us. Thomas had given him fifteen before he even asked. I fished in my pocket for ten more dollars.

Heavily painted plywood rimmed a huge square steam room with a dripping low ceiling. Wood benches lined the sides and made rows in the center. A string of bright bare bulbs hung draped over a wall, the light diffused by the hot fog. There must have been fifty guys sitting in straight rows.

Nobody said anything or sat very close. The steam made it hard to see, which didn't help my frayed nerves. I'd felt uneasy leaving my money tucked into the lining of my boot and didn't like that people had watched me undress. I hadn't been able to ignore the Vietnamese locals walking freely in and out of the dressing area, old men and young girls seemingly oblivious to my situation, yet suspicious to me nonetheless. The rancid smell of feet and armpits hung in a thick, wet haze. Not my kind of room.

I tried to tell myself I wasn't there just for the massage. The steam would be therapeutic for my aching body. But the extreme heat mixed with the stench soon affected my breathing, and after three long minutes I headed for the door. Who wanted a steam bath with a bunch of smelly guys in the middle of the most hot and humid country in the world?

Outside, the tent opened and the walls shot up higher. Powerful fans kept the air moving, and it felt refreshingly comfortable. Dozens of partitions blurred together in a bleached assembly of cotton and canvas. White surrounded me. White towels, white floors, white walls.

The massage girls wore white sarongs and thongs that slapped their heels as they glided through the narrow halls between the cubicles.

I stepped up on a bench to see over the maze of partitions. I guessed that more than a hundred cubicles were packed into the tent building. After days in the muck and mud of the jungle, this eerie, pallid dreamland was a pleasing reprieve for the eyes.

A young Vietnamese girl appeared and beckoned to the guy on the end of my bench. He followed her. Everybody slid their butts to the left. When I finally reached the end of the bench, I followed another girl through the long aisles. I got only a second to see her face. She motioned, turned, and walked with purpose past rows of cubicles, then turned left and walked by more rows, moving farther and farther away from my clothes. *Slap slap slap,* her thongs popped against her heels. From each side as we passed, I could hear soft, husky murmurs coming from the cubes, mingled with girlish giggles. My guide parted the white linen hanging in a doorway and patted the table indicating where I should wait.

"One moment," she chirped in practiced English. I started to ask her a question, but she was gone.

Soft hands on my shoulders gently woke me.

"You sleep?" a tiny voice asked, removing the towel I had carefully draped over my bare butt.

"Naw."

"Wha'chew name?"

"Fred."

She giggled, slapping my butt and saying, "Okay, Fled," then hopped on the table and sat squarely on my bottom.

"You in fight?"

"Uh huh."

She began to push my back muscles toward my neck very slowly, carefully avoiding the splotches marking my ribs and kidneys. For a small person, probably barely eighty pounds, she had good strength in her fingers and hands.

"You lost!" she giggled.

It actually felt okay to laugh. I hadn't for a while.

"Jus' take it easy, Fled. Numbah one massáh."

Fantasies blurred behind my closed eyes, snapping one to another like a slide show of flashbacks. I saw wounds. Was I *actually* a medic? Did I carry a body over my shoulder through the jungle, my muscles screaming in pain? Could I possibly be in Vietnam, when only a few months ago I ran around Disneyland in a Goofy suit? How could I have earned four times as much for clowning around with children as they paid me for carrying dead bodies?

Pictures circled. Tiny fingers slid through my defenses. Images from my past rolled behind my closed eyes.

I laughed with screaming kids, riding rides together, spinning in giant teacups, their long hair flying in their eyes. Gleefully, they waved at their parents, who stretched their necks trying to find them in the viewfinder of their Instamatic cameras. Later in the hot afternoon, framed by the magnificent carousel behind me, "Goofy!" the children would shriek as they ran up to hug my legs, mugging while their parents jockeyed for photo opportunities. Tidy and clean and orderly and safe, Americana swirled round and round in the California sun. Would anyone ever be as delighted to see me again?

Tomorrow medevacs. I couldn't be Goofy without my legs.

The baby-san balanced herself by holding one of the flimsy walls, then lightly stepped onto my back and began kneading my larger muscles with the balls and heels of her feet.

"You okay, Fled?"

I could only moan approval. The tiny feet at my neck were soft, cool, and penetrating. She stepped all the way into me now. I could feel her in my chest even though I lay on my stomach.

Fourteen years old, maximum. Light as a feather.

"Numbah one," she twittered again, then hummed a light soprano tune, agilely, delicately prancing on my back and legs, pausing briefly to knead a tight buttock with her practiced toes. Somehow she avoided my soreness. Everything she touched felt better.

My mind continued to play in-and-out games with an avalanche of lost days. My brain and body were both suffering from sleep deprivation. I could feel every muscle. Her small feet dug deeply, a sweet feeling. When nothing could feel better, everything became even more delicious. She changed her technique again. She bent to her elbows and knees, then began to crawl gradually on all fours. Sliding her thighs between my legs, she coaxed them apart. Kneeling behind me, she began to roll her chest along my back as her arms and hands smoothed me from my rib cage along under my armpits to the full extent of my hands and fingers, now stretched far above me. I could feel first the brushing of her linen shirt against my bare bottom as it fell forward in front of her. Then the smoothness of her chest rolled on contact, trickling shivers from the bottoms of my feet to my head. Her breath against my neck completed her plunge. With most of her body lying against mine, she hesitated for a few magical seconds, then pushed up and repeated her full body-roll again, smoothly and deeply. Then again. Pampering me a little bit more each time. Again, and again, and again. Long, rolling, crawling, lying, waiting, embracing. Full body therapy.

Sliding to the floor while trailing one finger behind my knee, inside my thigh, and lightly across my exposed privates, she sang, "GI no horny? No hang jaw?"

"Tired," I half explained, involuntarily pulling my legs together.

Totally all right with her, she patted my naked bottom lovingly and said, "You rest. They come say 'go,' twenny minutes." In a whisk of linen brushing linen, she disappeared forever.

I met Wally Thomas getting dressed in the changing room, smiling peacefully. "Pretty nice, huh?" he grinned, rolling his eyes.

"Like heaven," I hummed.

"What it cost ya?"

"Same as you. Fifteen bucks."

"No, Doc, I mean the hand job. What it cost ya? I got mine for another seven. Best I done yet."

I shook my head, and the radio operator looked at me funny. We sat in silence for the short drive to the barracks, where he dropped me off, gunning the engine on the jeep as if he couldn't get out of there fast enough. When I caught up with Smitty a few hours later, I told him that Thomas probably thought I had "trouble." He started laughing. "Oh, Bubba, let Uncle Smitty tell ya the facts of life."

"I know what a hand job is, for chrissake," I said. "I just wasn't thinking . . ."

"How could you *not* think. Man, with a little babe running her hands all over ya?" He looked at me seriously. "Have we got a problem here?" Sergeant Smith made a limp-dick sign with his little finger.

I didn't respond, though I'd been wondering. I hadn't

even thought about sex since arriving. Nothing about being in Vietnam felt sexy to me. Not in the least. As a twenty-three-year-old with a more than generous dose of testosterone, who usually began each day with an involuntary erection, it didn't seem natural that I hadn't been slightly aroused even once since I had arrived.

On my second night in Dong Tam, working in the morgue, I was invited to go off base for a little local action. I had absolutely no inclination to join them. After plugging butts with cotton balls all day, I wondered how they could feel horny. I didn't want to see anything naked, regardless of gender.

On the *Nuaces* the boys in the recovery ward showed porn movies late at night. I tried watching once. I remember an Asian couple positioning their copulating so the camera could have a better view. Their sex act looked uncomfortable and affected to me, with the woman clearly drugged and her partner grimacing at the camera. I trailed the herd as the guys in the ward cheered them on. Again, I had to excuse myself. I figured there were only us guys on the ship, so why get worked up?

The Dong Tam steam and massage tent defined for me the difference between sensual and sexual. Something secret in me had been found. The baby-san touched me deeply. I trusted her. I think she pacified me, especially my fear of the Vietnamese, the kind that could paralyze me in the jungle. Merely a child herself, she embraced my childhood fear that hid under the covers, trying not to be scared of the dark. The one where the house creaked in the wee hours, shadows threatening that maybe both parents would be dead when I checked in the morning. I had closed my eyes and felt wholly protected, like swallowing an antidote to the bone-aching horror of the field. And this calming came at the end of a tiny teenager's fondling fingers and toes. Any act of sex with that child would have violated it.

"Here, Bubba," Smitty said, offering me a set of photographs from his wallet. "Take a look at these."

He handed me Polaroid shots of a slightly chubby woman with a pleasing smile. Her frosted hair rose high on her head in a style that's been popular in the Bible Belt for decades. She wore a red bow where her hair parted above her forehead. She stood in a room with pine paneling and a large oil painting of Elvis Presley, a martini glass in one hand, a lit cigarette in the other. She stood totally naked.

In the second shot, she had bent over to give a better view of her private parts. The third picture had been shot from behind, through her legs, her breasts falling in front of her.

"My wife, Bubba," Smitty smiled ear to ear. "Fine, huh?"

I forced a smile and returned about a dozen pictures after having seen only three. "Look, Smitty, I don't think you need to worry. I'm not interested in guys, but I'm *really* not interested in looking at your wife."

"Why not? She don't care. Hell, she told me to show 'em around to the boys."

"I'll be okay. Really. Please don't take offense."

"None taken," he said, sliding his treasures back into his wallet.

I tried to change the subject. "That steam place is a thriving business."

"Steam 'n Cream?" Smitty grabbed the bait. "You bet. That place brings in thousands every day. Did some figurin' first time I went in there."

Totally different from the sergeant in most ways, that's exactly what I'd been doing when I saw all those cubicles.

"A hundred forty-four rooms," Smitty continued, grabbing a scrap of paper and the stub of a pencil out of his pocket. "I counted." He thought for a minute, then spoke in practically a whisper. "Let's say they do one guy an hour in about half of 'em." He began scribbling numbers. "Seventy-five, bein' conservative. They're open from nine to nine. That's seventy-five times twelve hours times fifteen bucks. Five for the steam 'n ten for the massage."

"Everybody gets a massage?"

"Bubba, why the hell go? Shit, you can get a steam bath standin' outside." He laughed and asked, "What's that come to?"

"Thirteen five." I did the math in my head.

"Exactly! That's what I got." He hadn't quite completed his multiplying. "How'd ya do that?" He shook his head and continued. "Plus at least half the boys are gettin' yanked for another, say, ten bucks average. What would that be?"

"Another forty-five hundred, and I think you're underestimating."

"Prob'ly." He put away his pad and pencil. "So that makes about twenty grand, right?"

"Eighteen five."

"Bein' conservative."

"Right. Okay."

"Seven days a week," he added.

"One twenty-nine five."

"A hundred 'n thirty thousand dollars?" Smitty whispered, eyes wide. "That's some kinda grand-theft dust."

"Conservatively. Rounding all the way."

"Got any idea what those gals make?"

"Not counting tips?" I asked.

"They don't keep tips. One of 'em pockets a buck, she

gets her ass whupped. They get ten dollars a day, Bubba. That's it. Damn good money for 'em too."

"How do you know *that?*"

"Mamma-sans cleanin' the barracks 'n mess hall get mighty pissed at those little whores. Talk about 'em all the time. *They'd* like ten bucks for doin' our dirty work, but only get five a day. It's all bullshit, though. They all go home 'n divvy it up, no matter what they make."

"How many girls they got working there at ten bucks a day?"

"Three truckloads leave Steam 'n Cream every night with at least twenty-five in each. I think we gave about seventy, eighty of 'em cholera 'n tetanus shots a couple months ago."

"Where do they all come from?"

"All over, Bubba. This here's big business. The U.S. Army's in town! These people come from everywhere to make money on this base."

"Seventy-five baby-sans at ten dollars a day," I multiplied. "Seven-fifty a day. So somebody does a gross of a hundred and thirty a week, with expenses around five grand. That's a tidy profit."

"Yeah, Bubba, it is. Nice little business. Every week. Here's the real bitch. Every day, papa-san loads his trucks 'n watches 'em leave out the gates. Then he goes right to HQ."

"He's paying rent," I offered.

"You betcha. Through the back door, though."

Suddenly the war became a little more understandable. Reduced to the lowest element—greed—there wasn't much to ponder. How many bases? How many colonels? How many generals? How many millions of dollars? How many tiny Asian fingers stroking lightly over angry, throbbing penises?

"Steam 'n Cream," I finally said. "Nice little business

indeed. I had an English teacher in high school who told us that when Eisenhower left office in 1960, his last words to the American people were, 'Beware the military-industrial complex.'"

"No shit," Smitty chuckled, then tried the words himself. "Beware the military-industrial complex." He nodded then smirked. "And grunts get jerked off payin' for it."

"Yes, we do. Nice metaphor, Smitty."

"Nice what?"

"Never mind."

17

Medevac

Our medical support company worked in two-man teams. Smitty and I remained partners after our first trip into the field. He could have made it easier on himself and paired up with someone who didn't leave him with all the rank and responsibility. But then, Smitty didn't fit any of the stereotypes I had about ranking sergeants. When I asked how it worked, he shrugged and said that each team had equal odds of getting blown away.

In the barracks at base camp in Dong Tam, I had my own bunk and could actually turn around in the shower, but the food was lousy compared to the great navy food on the ship. Everyone in the medevac building waited on-call and had no assigned daily duties. We played cards and sat around telling lies about life in the World. Smitty and I were assigned to a helicopter team that included a pilot, a second officer, and two machine gunners. We smoked cigarettes and took catnaps in full field uniform, anticipating a call from medevac dispatch. Somebody explained that most missions happened in the morning hours, from seven or so on, as daylight came and Charlie discovered the night movements of our troops. Taking turns once an hour, one of us would walk fifty yards across the street to the NCO club to get cold Cokes.

Amid a long, boring game of gin rummy, just after a

196

huge breakfast on the second morning, our call came. The overhead speaker squawked, "Unit Three, lift off!"

"That's us, Bubba," Smitty grinned, grabbing his gear. As usual, more prepared than I was, he stood holding the door, sucking hard on a cigarette, looking frustrated with the time it always took me to gather myself. "Today?" he pleaded.

The chopper had no red crosses and there were gunners at each door. We were in the air before I had a chance to ask where we were going. Hotdog chopper pilots loved to jeopardize comfort by pressing their skills. Hueys were easy to maneuver, ear-piercingly loud, and filled with their own exhaust on takeoff. Surrounded by armored steel, there's no luxury in a combat chopper.

Smitty motioned for me to strap up, each of us unable to hear anything. I clumsily hooked my belts around both shoulders and straightened tall to strap the waist belt in place. I gave my jaw some relief by loosening the chin strap on my steel helmet. Smitty looked at me from across the cabin, medical gear between his legs, straps across his chest, helmet barely above his furled brow, tight and straight, a steel trap set to snap. Fastened to the walls in the small, noisy cabin, we really had nowhere else to look. I returned his gaze and made a quick face by crossing my eyes and curling my lips. Smitty's white teeth brightened for a second, then quickly hid behind terse lips. One thing about him differed from when we were in the jungle, and I noticed it immediately. Rather than his M-16, he was carrying only a handgun in a hip holster.

As we approached the landing zone, both pilots hollered into their mikes. The door gunners also had helmets with earphones and microphones. Smitty and I had nothing. I figured that when we got closer, they'd tell us what we were supposed to do. I was wrong.

Smitty unhooked and motioned for me to do the same. He moved to the opening, slid onto his butt, and dangled his legs out until they balanced on the landing skid.

The old pro perched there, holding himself motionless from a handle by the door. I flailed around behind him as close as I dared, trying to find purchase by grabbing grommets on the floor. The chopper cornered, tilting into the turn, lifting Smitty directly above me, his feet pointing up at the blue sky. I started to slide backward and my fists went white as I clenched the handholds. My feet flailed just as Smitty looked back at me and laughed, firmly wedged into his position at the door.

"LZ's secure!" the copilot yelled to us. "We're goin' in! Purple smoke! Purple smoke!"

Fine with me. Already struggling to hold my breakfast on this roller coaster, I didn't need more excitement. We flew past red smoke, then the skids hit the ground and Smitty leapt out of the chopper, sprinting through a light violet fog with his head ducked. My face stayed six inches behind his butt as we ran. I had no idea how he could tell where we were going. All I could see was smoke. We led four ambulatories back in a hurry, hoisted them onto the floor of the Huey, and were off the deck with our damaged human cargo in less than two minutes.

Once in the air, the pilot headed straight up over the tree line and gained altitude, flying more smoothly than he had on the way in. He knew his medics were moving freely about the cabin, checking wounds and bandages. The four casualties had caught a booby trap. Other than being extremely pissed off, they weren't critically injured. Some superficial burns and deep scratches. One guy had caught shrapnel in the side of his neck, and the field medic had done a good job of plugging the bleeding.

If this was a routine medevac, I liked it a lot more than the bush-humping of the past week. But as I strapped myself in for the ride home, I realized we weren't returning to Dong Tam.

"Where we going?" I yelled to the copilot.

"28th Evac. They called for medic support." He pointed ahead.

The 28th Evac, a mobile unit, treated seriously wounded soldiers who had little chance of surviving a fifteen-minute ride to the base camp hospital. When we landed, other choppers with big red crosses stood by, blades turning, unloading or ready for takeoff. Everywhere, people were running.

"I hate this," Smitty yelled as he leapt from the door.

Casualties lay on stretchers, sat on the ground, or limped along by themselves in three tents, open on all sides, each with tables draped with dark red sheets that had once been white. Several doctors dressed in fatigue pants and green smocks tended to the wounded in the open air. They were moving as fast as they could and immediately pressed Smitty and me into service. In serious battles there could be so many wounded that there might be no room for medics on the helicopters. Ground troops carried their wounded back to a secured LZ and loaded them in. The copilot and gunners did what they could to keep the wounded alive until they set down. This mobile surgical hospital might have been within a three-minute ride of the battle site.

"A couple Marine units and the 82d Airborne are getting run over north of here," a medical officer shouted as we delivered our minor casualties. "Been receiving wounded all night."

At least fifteen people needed immediate attention. Smitty and I went to work. Medical supplies lay strewn in open boxes between the tents. Anybody, medic or not, who wasn't badly wounded tried to help. Over my shoulder I saw our chopper lifting off.

"Seein' real war here, Bubba," he said as we both bent to lift a litter, then head for the tents at a half run. "North toward DMZ. Near Da Nang, Hue, Quang Tri, places like that. They fight regulars up yonder." Smitty explained that the NVA (North Vietnamese Army) fought by using a more traditional trench-type of warfare. "Got Russian-made tanks 'n shit. Major artillery. *Real* war stuff."

"Vinh Loc," the kid on the stretcher said from under a wad of head bandages. "Took us six days to secure the southern beach at Vinh Loc. Now they're takin' it back."

"Cocoa Beach," Smitty added. "Supposed to be light duty up north."

"That's what we thought. They came in from the south. Whole shitload. I seen more dinks than I could count."

"Charlie stays in the bush in the Delta," Smitty explained.

"Not in the north, Doc," the kid replied. "We seen whole battalions there. Half the time we're in retreat or gettin' airlifted to take 'em from a flank. Got six, seven battalions up there tryin' to keep what we took yesterday. Vinh Loc's supposed to be like REMF duty. It's a fuckin' island. How do they keep comin'?"

"How long ya been there?"

"Dunno, Doc. Lost track. Was countin' NVA attacks swarmin' over the beach. Just kept comin' like waves. Lost count. What day is it?"

"One day closer to goin' home, son," Smitty said as we laid him on a surgery prep table. He hollered when the doctor started removing his bandages.

"He's outta here," Smitty said.

"Naw, he's okay. He'll make it," I said.

"I mean he's outta here *home,* Bubba. What does he care what day it is? It's Day One of Real Life."

Smitty and I returned to the chopper area. Medevacs were landing and taking off, and the wounded kept pouring in. We worked near the landing pad to determine who needed immediate attention and who could get by with minor aid. We were up to our armpits with every kind of injury imaginable, coming in a steady stream off the choppers. We didn't have time to even wipe our hands, much less scrub. We would check for color and bleeding, change a bloody bandage, then send a casualty to either the surgery tent or the prep area outside. A few times we had to detour a patient directly to the morgue hut behind the tents.

As I pulled away from the mouth of a blue face, I hollered to Smitty for help. He leapt to my side and began pounding the guy's chest. I started to blow into his open airway again and caught a load of puke right in the face, swallowing half of it. The man gurgled, gasped, spit, hacked, and choked to life.

On one knee, I heaved the double helping of watery scrambled eggs I had gobbled that morning in Dong Tam. Shaking my head at Smitty, my expression said, "Will I ever learn?"

"Turn yer face away, dipshit," Smitty instructed a few seconds too late, trying not to laugh. He reached out with the back of his sleeve to wipe puke off my cheeks.

We rolled the guy onto his side and Smitty struck him firmly on the back. More repulsive fluid drooled out of his mouth. He coughed and choked, then started breathing on his own. He sucked in hard, then labored to exhale. He had one tiny hole near his chest pocket. His right side heaved while his other side lay limp.

"Collapsed lung," Smitty said. "Move it!" We rushed him to the tents.

"Dead on arrival, sir. Don't know how long," Smitty informed the surgeon as he met us coming in.

"Fine work, soldier," the officer said, placing his ear directly to the man's chest. "Somebody bagged my 'scope. Blast!" He looked around, then shouted, "Collapsed lung here!" Everybody yelled in the tents, trying to be heard over the din of soldiers howling and physicians snapping orders. There were too few medics to respond.

"Hang on a second, guys," the doctor said as he rushed off to prepare a place to treat the soldier. Smitty placed his hand lightly against the limp side of the man's chest. He leaned forward and whispered in his ear. The heaving relaxed a bit and his breathing became less labored. Smitty kept whispering. The heaving lessened even more.

"Could you do that again?" a voice behind me asked.

"Do what?" Smitty turned around.

"Your buddy there. Could he do that mouth-to-mouth thing again on that colored guy?"

The man behind the voice stood there in his clean, starched fatigues and polished single bronze bar on each lapel. Battlefield officers had their rank sewn into their fatigues with black or gold thread. I hadn't seen the shiny bronze of a second lieutenant since I left the Alameda transport station. He motioned with his camera.

"You know, put your mouth over his again. Just for a second." He indicated that he wanted a picture, as if we didn't comprehend.

"Get yer sorry ass outta here," Smitty warned. "Unless ya wanna wear that camera home stickin' outta yer ass."

The photographer fled backward in a wordless, hasty retreat.

"Jesus, Smitty. He's an officer."

"Je-ee-sus, Bubba. He's an asshole."

We worked until well after dark without a break, the only time I ever saw Smitty go that long without a smoke. We saw at least seventy or eighty wounded and probably a dozen or more KIA.

The 28th Evac looked like medical hell compared to our tidy little triage and operating room on the *Nuaces*. We had no place to scrub, no orderlies or surgery technicians, no X-ray room to determine internal damages, no disposable gloves or shoe covers, no fluorescent lights or stainless steel. We didn't even have hot water.

As a dying man entered the tent, a doctor would yell "Ten minutes!" If he died after that, he would be listed as DOW (Died of Wounds), a different classification from KIA. The evening news in the World reported only the KIA from that given day, not the number of DOW. The doctors had been ordered to list as many as they could as DOW.

When human organs are exposed to open air, they change texture and appearance immediately. Blood and intestines congealed and became slippery on the hard dirt floor. If a gut wound oozed innards, we might try to shove them back in, then cover the open wound. But if a piece of flesh or bone or part of an arm or leg or hand became separated from a body, it might not make it back onto the stretcher. If we couldn't instantly identify who it came from, it would remain on the dirt floor. A medic wearing a surgical mask would occasionally come by with a plastic bag and collect spare parts. One soldier with no medic training helped out by scooping up gobs and carrying them away in his hands. Another used the

wood side of a push broom to shove the mess from under the doctors' feet.

This was a butcher shop. Dried blood was hardened
on everything. On the ground and the wooden boxes.
On every litter and every soldier. All over the fronts of
our shirts and pants, forearms, necks, and faces.

A medic with a box full of morphine Syrettes moved
swiftly to anybody screaming, then pacified him with a
full dose of about half a gram. One pant leg had four
needles stuck through it, and I wondered if anybody
could even *survive* two full grams of morphine. In training, we were instructed to administer no more than two
doses.

The dead were stacked in a shelter behind one of the
tents. Soldiers from Graves Registration hurriedly tagged
their toes and zipped them into bags, but they couldn't
keep up. When more choppers landed, they left their
post to help the living. When they returned, another
body would be waiting for them. They were working in
heat over a hundred degrees with equal humidity. When
Smitty and I delivered a body on a litter, we escaped as
quickly as we could.

A small canvas lean-to with a wooden toilet seat suspended over half an oil drum served as the latrine. By
my count, this one hole served about sixteen medical
people, sixty or seventy ambulatory patients, some waiting chopper crews, and probably fifty infantrymen on
duty at the perimeter of the evac. There was always a
line with a few guys waiting. The half drum filled up
continually.

The other half of the drum had been dragged twenty
feet away and held burning human excrement ignited by
a generous dose of diesel fuel. Anything swept or
scooped up from the ground in the tent helped fuel the
fire, although blood-soaked gauze and body parts don't

burn quickly. I had known the odor of singed hair from my forearm once when it got too close to a gas burner. That's maybe one percent of the stench of human flesh and organs burning. The reek loaded down the air. Every few hours the fire would die out and someone would switch the two cans, then gas and ignite the full can. Haze from diesel-burnt excrement and guts hung like a London fog.

As the 82d Airborne retreated to lick its wounds, Smitty and I boarded another Slick and fell into a heap of exhaustion as it headed to Dong Tam. Somehow I managed to strap myself to a wall. The vision of bloated bodies and scraps of meat being pushed along the floor grabbed hard at my own intestines, causing convulsions. I dry-heaved several times into my throat, then swallowed hard against the hot stomach gases. The vibration of the chopper rattled everything inside the cabin as well as my stomach. Looking across at Smitty's chin comfortably bouncing against his chest, I lowered my head to try to relax. I asked God to make this nightmare go away. A flood of tears instantly and involuntarily spilled to my shirt. I tried to think of something I could bargain with, something I could offer the Almighty in trade, if He would just make this stop. Instead, I got dizzy, choked again on dry puke, and spit up between my legs on the floor of the chopper. I wiped my eyes and face and caught a glimpse of Smitty watching me. He quickly shut his eyes.

Somebody on the ground called for help, and our copilot replied with a lot of "Rogers." The second officer shouted into his mike, asking for directions. We were going in again.

The chopper abruptly pitched sideways. Feeling the

negative G-force of an elevator falling forty floors, I tightened all my belts, including my chin strap.

Able to hear only the copilot's side of the conversation, it sounded like a hot LZ. He repeated "Give us two minutes!" several times. Using sign language with the pilot, he wound his finger in wide circles, indicating that we needed to make a broad turn. As we leveled out, he shouted again into the headset and the two gunners yelled "Roger" in unison. They grabbed their ammunition belts, locked and loaded their weapons, then spun into position, watching out their side doors. The second officer left his seat to lean back into the cabin and shout, "You guys set?"

"Roger!" Smitty returned two thumbs up. I sat mute. I couldn't even nod. My stomach still vaulting into my throat, I didn't think I could do this again.

The gunner next to Smitty tapped him on the shoulder and offered him his headset. Smitty took off his helmet and listened to the second officer yelling above the roar. Smitty relayed the orders to me. "We're comin' in hot. Two ambulatory, maybe more." He pointed at me. "Yer side down, Bubba. Be ready. We got no time." He returned the earphones and relayed a thumbs-up to the gunner.

Smitty unhooked his belt and approached my side, motioning me to unhook too. He pushed me into the door beside the gunner and yelled in my ear. "Stand on the rail, Bubba! We're goin' fast!" He crouched behind me with his hand on my back. "Wait 'til I say go!"

I could see red smoke ahead, filling the landing zone. We were maybe two hundred yards out. The second officer hollered at us, but I couldn't understand him. Smitty's hand grabbed my backpack.

"Incoming fire! Roger that!" the machine gunner yelled into his headset. Both sides of our chopper let go with ear-shattering outgoing M-60 fire. Yellow tracers were flying away from the gun above me and hitting the tree line faster than my eyes could follow. The gunner shook to the cadence of his weapon and screamed. He didn't seem to be aiming at anything as he spurted out a line of fire, warning anyone out there to keep his head tucked.

We flew right through red smoke and into bright yellow. Two colors to confuse Charlie. As our nose straightened and forward momentum stopped, I could barely make out the ground below me as the smoke swirled in the downdraft of the chopper blades. I sat in the doorway, feet firmly on the skids, suspended in the eye of a whirlpool.

Smitty yelled, and his hand left my shirt. I fell forward, letting go of my hold on the frame of the side door. As I flew off my perch, I heard a dreadful clattering of metal on metal behind me. The chopper had been hit.

My free flight didn't last long. Gravity makes the ground jump up quickly. I barely had enough time to realize my situation. Way too high. Twenty, thirty feet. Try to turn . . . get feet under . . . no time . . . not sure anyone could drop that far without . . .

Then I lost the light.

18

Nightmare

Can't see. Can't hear. Smells like burnt hell.

Pain inventory: Massive chest pain. No deep breath. Cramping, ankles to hips. Straining crotch ache. Innards tight. Arms asleep. Kidneys, lower back, bladder . . . tense. Excruciating.

Senses inventory: Abnormally dark. Mute. Sightless. Soundless. Stillborn. Dead?

Inventory complete. You're a mess, Ben. Hello? Ben? Buddy? Anybody in there?

I couldn't hear my voice, but something bit my esophagus as an involuntary moan gurgled up, begging for Mommy. Any movement, even to breathe, caused jerking sensations of crushing chest pain followed by a frozen stillness, waiting for the next sharp jab of pain.

Flat on my stomach, chills prickled across the back of my neck. It was a poor excuse for fear and took too much energy, so I gave up and fell off the side of the world, drowning in my own sleep again.

Waking found me not so much afraid as alone. In some hollow refuge, I became the only person who would never leave me. Time passed. Not like a dream, where I'd flown from stair landings, done flips in the air, walked through walls. Never had I dreamed physical pain.

So, this is what hell is. The smell. The taste. Dry, lurid, fiery. Like smoldering tar. Rank and heavy. Even the dirt smelled burnt. I blinked and could feel my eyes flicker, but saw only black. So, hell is also blindness. And deafness? I couldn't hear a sound, not even my own breathing. How could damnation be so peaceful? Who's in charge here? I want some answers. . . .

Waking again, this time to a flash of fear, I knew I had to get away from where I lay. Something bad could be close. But my legs wouldn't move. When I tried, sharp spasms pinched my groin and butt. One side of my face was plastered to the ground, the other side was stinging and itching. I tried to raise my head and felt a terrific tug at my chest. Another breath caught me short, left me claustrophobic. My lively imagination had always served as my friend. But in this dark silence, it turned on me. My thoughts crawled all over themselves like a sack of snakes.

Maybe I'm not dead. Too many factors supported this notion. I remembered falling through the air and knowing I would hit face first. This explained the powerful tightness in my chest. Maybe I'm a tough sumbitch and this death is just a fright. "What dreams may come once we have shuffled off this mortal coil." Yes, of course. Thank you, Hamlet. Except I hadn't shuffled off anything. I had wiggling toes and my chest hurt. Odor and taste couldn't be imagined. The mind is capable of playing great tricks, especially in times of trauma. But this smelled acrid. Awful. It tasted pungent, like lighter fluid. How could my mind manufacture what I'd never experienced before?

No, I wasn't dead. Just beat up again. And way out where I shouldn't be.

Some people have a run-as-fast-as-you-can reflex to fear. Others freeze. Some fight. Some scream. I kept dropping into a large dark hole called sleep. Each time I woke up, I didn't know how long I'd been out or if I had actually been dreaming.

Finally, I awoke to the light of a bright, gray day. In the night I had been blind only because clouds covered the stars and moon. Despite the pain, I lifted my head enough to look around me. I lay in a clearing where the chopper had tried to land in the middle of a shallow, mostly dry rice swamp about the size of a football field. The hot LZ. Something had burned the jungle across from me and on two sides. Smoke still rose from the blackened trees. The smell of fuel and fire still filled the air. Clearly, I was very much alive.

And very much alone.

I still had no hearing. My head was a dull blob. Shifting my body a little at a time, blood began to flow into my limbs. I wiggled thirty or forty feet to the only green patch I could see, opposite where the jungle smoldered. Crawling headfirst into a tangled mess of bushes, it felt a lot safer than being out in the open.

My medic bag was still hanging around my neck, but my backpack was gone. I managed with some difficulty to turn myself around in the bush so that I could see where I had been. The all-important pack that had been firmly strapped to my back as I perched in the door of the chopper was nowhere in sight.

Looking out over the field, I sensed someone's eyes on me. I felt cold all over, and my overactive fantasies flew again. Was I being used as a decoy? Was I in somebody's sights right now? I clutched the medic bag and pushed backward into the bush line, and tried to cover my legs and chest with light foliage. I stopped before I could faint from the exertion. I pulled an elephant-ear leaf to my chest and fell backward, turning my head as far as I could, searching the stillness for any movement.

My thoughts turned to Hollywood images of prisoners of war. Beatings. Interrogations. A single naked bulb hanging over a small table with a snarling commander slapping his black knee-boots with a riding crop. Somebody in basic training had described bamboo cages filled with American POWs dangling above the ground as rock-throwing targets for laughing children. Why did that asshole suggest such an image?

I closed my eyes tighter to force my thoughts elsewhere. I tried to remember the names of girls I'd dated. No one came to mind. I could remember only the light song and strong feet of the lithe baby-san at Steam 'n Cream. Sleep caught me again.

I awoke to darkness. I tried hard to remember what day it was, what time, what place, but couldn't put it together. I knew every blood vessel and muscle group in the body. I knew how to treat shock, flush out eyes, minimize heat exhaustion, plaster a sucking chest wound, protect burns. And just yesterday, or the day before, I had breathed the gift of life back into a dead man. Yet I hadn't had one single hour of training on survival. Medics weren't supposed to get lost.

The sky had cleared and there were so many stars that they seemed to all touch each other. I lay motionless, like a statue perched forever on a mausoleum. Fear had no shape or substance. It took over and left me helplessly lost. At any moment, one of those sets of eyes looking at me would come and pump a full clip of bullets into my chest.

And if they didn't, I'd sit here and slowly starve to death, because I sure as hell wasn't going to move. This was where it would all end.

Maybe even more than being afraid, I was bone weary and sad. I couldn't ever remember feeling so alone. For the first time in my twenty-three years, I felt totally and utterly abandoned.

My friends back home had gone on to their protests and love-ins, rejecting me and my short hair before I left the country. My family couldn't reach me, even if they had known that I was lying here waiting to die. The drill sergeant had said that the army would be my mother, father, priest, and only friend. Yet now, even the army had left me unprotected out in the middle of nowhere.

I curled into the fetal position, reached my hands into my fatigues to hold my testicles, and wept myself to sleep.

"Hey, Ben!"

Few people had called me by my first name since I'd been drafted. My whole body shuddered as I tried to focus on a figure squatting on his haunches ten yards from me. I could see only his silhouette in the moonlit pale. He scared the crap out of me, yet he knew my name. Who the hell . . .

He waved a hand. I froze. He came to his feet and walked up slowly. Again he squatted, looking directly in my face.

"What's happenin'?" A chill frizzled my forearms. "What's up, Sherm?" It was Ricky Bright, a buddy shot dead in Vietnam four years before.

"Rick, is that you?"

"Fuckin' A! Well, I mean . . . *sorta*."

"Whaddaya mean *sorta?*"

"Yeah, well, don't shit or anything but . . . umm . . . I'm very much dead, y'know."

"Jesus."

"Yeah. *I'm* dead, and *you* aren't really awake."

I reached below to feel my legs. My hand slipped through them. I felt another tingle behind my ears.

"I can see you and hear you and . . ."

"Illusion," Ricky explained. "You been through a major trauma, little buddy. All those bodies, dead 'n half-dead. Arms 'n legs 'n blood 'n brains 'n crap. Spent all day thinkin' about me 'n Terry 'n Mr. C."

Terry Nelson, my best friend. Mr. Clemenson, my high school English teacher. Both had died young.

"I'm here to tell you that you're not dead."

"I know that." I almost believed it.

"Just figured that since you couldn't hear anything, maybe you thought you were."

"I can hear *you*."

"I'm dead, asshole," Ricky teased and stood up to light a cigarette. I reached for a puff on his smoke. He ignored my outstretched hand.

"This is pretty far out for me," I said. "I'm not ready for talking to dead guys."

"I've missed you, man." He leaned forward, close enough to touch. I didn't dare.

"Yeah, me too. Damn, Rick. Why couldn't I dream up Marilyn Monroe?"

He laughed. "Same ol' Sherm." I could see his face a little better now. There might have been a light from somewhere, or my eyes were finally adjusting. "You're too fucked up to do Marilyn Monroe right now. Shit, you're lucky you survived that crash landin' out there."

"We were supposed to be roommates."

He shifted his weight and sat on his butt, stretching his legs out to meet mine. "Yeah, I missed out on college." He wore the same boots I did, but his fatigues were camouflage. He had no gear, pack, canteen, or rifle. His shirt was open, exposing a bare chest. "I probably would've failed at that too. Who knows?"

"You *joined* the army."

"Tried to get into the Marines."

"I thought you were smarter than that."

"You know me, youngest of four boys. Had to prove myself. Be a hero."

"Got hit by a sniper?"

"No way. My own guy. I took a piss, he panicked and shot me right in the forehead." Ricky touched his fore-finger to the middle of his brow. "Didn't feel a thing. Didn't even hear the shot."

"Jesus."

"You out here by yourself?"

I didn't want to answer.

"You *are* out here by yourself. Trust me."

"Okay."

"What are you gonna do?"

I shrugged my shoulders.

"They probably saw you hit the ground 'n figure you're dead," he said. "You oughta wait another day, then head east."

"East? I can't move."

"If you're careful. Move slowly at first light, then just before night. Charlie don't move much then."

"I can't hear. I mean, I can't hear when I'm not dream-ing up dead guys."

"You will, Sherm. It's temporary." Before I had a chance to rub my eyes, Ricky backed away, smiling, into the night.

"Where's east?" I begged. "Ricky?" My voice rang out in the darkness. I could hear again. "Rick?"

When the sun woke me, I looked to where my friend had been sitting. There in Ricky's place sat Bill Clemen-son, smoking a pipe in the full light of day. In the middle of the sweltering jungle, he was wearing the moth-bitten cardigan sweater I'd seen him in a hundred times.

Mr. Clemenson had been my English teacher in both

junior high and high school. He was my hero. He drove too fast, smoked too much, laughed too loud. Class was always filled with stories and metaphors, often one innuendo tied to another and another. We would laugh until we cried. Mr. C was constantly getting hauled onto the carpet for having too damn much fun in school. We loved him. One night, at over one hundred miles per hour, he lost control of his Ford Lotus and was dead on impact. He was the first person close to me to die.

"Hard, isn't it?" he asked, responding to words I hadn't spoken.

"You're an illusion," I sighed.

"Like Ricky?"

"Yeah."

"Are you sure?"

"Don't mess with me. I'm freaked enough already."

He chuckled. "This is *so* like Dickens, isn't it? I'm the Ghost of Christmas Past!" He laughed at the image, then reached forward to lightly pat my knee. I couldn't feel it. He seemed live in full color and high fidelity. "Well, technically, I would be the Ghost of English Teachers Past." He threw back his head to cackle and was halted by a spasm of coughing. After clearing his lungs, he savored a puff off his pipe. "Don't sweat it, Ben. I'll be gone in a minute."

"Why is all this happening to me?"

"Maybe you have to remember."

"Remember what?"

"I don't know. What are you forgetting?"

"Jeez, everything. People are dying."

"That's exactly right, Ben. But not you. You're not dead. You're just curled up, holding your jewels, crying yourself to sleep, *waiting* to die."

This wasn't a conversation I wanted to have with anyone, much less a dead person. I wanted him to go away.

Instead, he was joined by someone else. Someone I missed more than anyone in my life.

Terry Nelson was wearing a broad smile and a pilot's jumpsuit with the word NELSON stenciled on the breast pocket. He looked bigger than life.

"Why are you doing this?" I asked the two ghosts.

"Because you're starting to lose it," Mr. C replied, then disappeared.

"Remember the Oak Park boys?" I asked Terry.

"Oh yeah. The games at the Y. That big asshole Mike somebody . . ."

"Saloy. Mike Saloy."

"The Franchise."

"We sure hated him then. Beat us up every game."

"I *still* hate him," Terry chuckled.

We tried to remember the names of the girls we took to the movies on our first double date, but all we could remember was that they wore red lipstick and stuffed their bras. We relived the night I stole my dad's '55 Ford convertible and tried to get Terry to go joyriding with me. But he knew better. My dad might have popped me, but his would have killed us both. We laughed about the junior prom, when our dates, the Lewin twins, switched clothes, glasses, and hairstyles, and fooled us for most of the night.

"You're wondering if this is all worth it," Terry said, pulling us out of yesterday and back to today.

"It's hard being the one who lives," I said. "All our old friends look at me, but they don't see *me*. They see *you* and me. And that reminds them that you're gone."

"It's gonna get worse, Ben. People you don't even know are gonna wonder why you made it and a bunch of us didn't. It'll be tough to return to a normal life. You gotta be yourself and put all this shit behind you."

"Am I gonna get that chance?"

Mr. C had returned. "Wait one more day," he advised. "If nobody comes, get up and walk out of here."

"East," Ricky Bright chimed in from behind me. "Just get up and start walking."

"East? Toward the sea?"

"That'll do," Terry said. The others nodded.

"I think the Mekong River is south of here," I suggested.

"Go east. Stay quiet. Move along tree lines." Rick was insistent.

"You can make it, Ben," Terry added. "Remember when we'd play 'ditch' every night in the summer?"

"Oh yeah. Ditch and hide-'n-seek."

"For hours. 'Til way after dark."

"You're unarmed, son," Mr. C reminded. "They won't shoot you if you're alone and unarmed. They'll take you prisoner maybe, but you won't get shot."

Little comfort there. I closed my eyes.

When I opened them, all three were preparing to leave.

"Don't go," I begged. "Don't leave me here."

"Sleep," Mr. C said, reaching his hand toward my eyes.

I wanted to stay present, wanted to hold their images, but his fingers had power. My eyes relaxed. I slid backward into a pool of fond memories.

19

Buttshot

Waking suddenly, I coughed hard and spurted warm water onto the lap of someone holding my neck and head. Everything looked blurry. I couldn't see who was holding me.

"Drink slower," he urged, holding my head higher. Cradling me in the crook of his elbow, he poured sips of precious liquid into my blistered throat. "You alone?" he asked. I recognized the voice from somewhere.

"Uh huh," I stammered, trying to focus on his face in the sun. He shaded me, but it didn't help. His voice had a very distinctive raspy growl. I searched my past. Which era of my life was he from? High school, college, church, sports, work?

"You AWOL out here, son?" It was Captain Buttshot, the ill-fated platoon leader with the pockmarked hindquarters.

"Captain!" I sprayed.

"Sam Riley," he answered. "Captain Samuel Franklin Riley, U.S. Army Infantry."

"More?" I asked, craning for the water.

"Save it," he replied. "You'll upchuck."

I could hear him plainly. I could feel his hand under my neck. Another dream? Why him? He dropped my head on the ground and deftly screwed the cap on his

218

canteen. I twisted my neck to face the notorious captain and stammered, "What're *you* doing here?"

"Three hundred sixty-five days," he laughed. "Just like you!" He positioned himself so we could talk. This couldn't be a ghost. Sweat soaked through his shirt and he smelled like a locker room.

"Exactly forty-two and a wake-up," he boasted of the time he had left on his hitch. "Then take me to Jersey, Mama. I am by-god outta here. I'm so short I could sit on a dime and swing my legs." He laughed at himself.

"Why've you come out here . . . out this far? Where's everybody else?"

"Well, Doc, it wasn't by choice. You seem to be the only show in town." He looked around. "You sure you're alone?"

"I don't know . . ."

"Of course you are!" he laughed louder this time. "Shit, man, Charlie vacated this area days ago."

Could I possibly have been alone for days?

"Forty-two days and a wake-up. God-*damn*. I'm so short, I could sit on a dime and . . ." He paused. "Already said that, didn't I?" He surely looked real. At least as real as Rick, Mr. C, and Terry had. "You got smokes?" I couldn't speak. Soon I'd wake. "Gooks ambushed us bad over there." He waved at the forest across from us. "Then you cowboys come ridin' in. Hi ho, Silver! Beautiful!"

Not only could I hear the captain, I could hear wind in the trees above me. I could hear my hands rubbing against the ground and my pants and chest and face. That must mean . . . it meant . . . what *did* that mean?

It meant I probably wasn't imagining Captain Buttshot.

"Some gook bastard shot up your chopper. Sittin' in a tree about three fuckin' inches from my nose. Shot you up then beat feet. Ran like a wild boar. I chased his sorry ass through the woods. Almost lost him. Tripped a claymore. Runnin' so goddamn fast, nearly outran a fucking claymore mine! Probably had it aimed too low. Can you *believe* it? Caught a small load in my ass. Probably ricochet. Fourth fucking time!"

"You're hit?" I asked.

He shrugged. "Anyway, I caught that dink bastard and greased him. Where are your smokes?" He reached for the medic bag but I clutched it tight to my chest. The captain knelt right in front of me and pulled something out of his pocket.

"Lookit here," he said, tossing it into my lap. "Cut off the slope's ear."

I reeled away from the piece of meat that fell in my lap.

"Aw for chrissake, don't be so jumpy. Here, give it to me." He reached forward to scoop up the trophy from the ground and snatched my medic bag in the same move. The ear went back into his top pocket.

"I saw you drop outta that chopper. Damn! You hit the ground, *bam!* Bounced like a rag doll. Thought you were toast. When I turned you over, your whole front was matted with fresh blood." He was right. I had dried blood from head to toe from the 28th Evac. "Look at you. You're a mess. Sure you ain't wounded somewhere?" I felt around my chest and shook my head.

"I know you ain't AWOL. Just messin' with ya. Now goddammit, where are your *smokes?*" He started rifling through my bag.

"We can't smoke," I mumbled.

"Why not? Charlie ain't within fifty miles of here. Dinks got out in a large hurry when the napalm came in."

"Napalm?"

"Fuckin' A. You can't smell it?" He took a whiff.

"God-awful. Look at that tree line." He pointed to where the jungle still smoldered.

That's what was caught in my throat.

"You're lucky you were out there in the middle of the LZ. They hit that tree line over there," he pointed again, "and all over there," indicating with a long sweeping motion the area behind us. "That shit's still smolderin' over there. They surrounded your ass with firebombs, Doc. You're lucky to be breathin' anything except ashes."

The loss of hearing. The smell. The burnt feeling on one side of my face. Now it all made sense.

"Where were *you*?" I asked the captain.

"Charlie's hole. I chased that papa-san dink forever!" The captain pounded his chest like an ape and stomped around like he was running through the woods, whooping as he went. "Bastard ducked down a hole and I went right in after him. Cut his throat. Pulled him back up and used his body to block the opening. Worked too. I'm alive to prove it."

He continued to jabber. "Got his ear right here. Blocked the hole. Burnt his ass to a crisp!" He paused, looking around as if he'd heard something, then continued. "Hell, my own men tried to send me home early. Now they even called in a whole ton of napalm, knowin' I'm still out here. Can you believe that? I could grow to be pissed at the whole army."

"I had smokes in my other bag," I said, motioning to where I'd hit the ground.

He threw the medic bag back at me. "Shit, Doc, I smoked them two days ago." He had taken my backpack. I looked around for it. Buttshot squared to look at me, interrupting my search. "They're good men, y'know. I love 'em. Every one." His voice softened. His eyes watered. "Misguided. Free love. Protests. Sex all the time. That's all they talk about. They're just drafted hippies, y'know?"

He breathed heavily a few times to regroup.

"Smokin' that marijuana. Either busy gettin' stoned or gettin' their dicks whipped over at the Steam 'n Cream. Free love and weed messed 'em over, that's what I think. Cambodian red. Bad shit, Doc. You don't do that shit, do you?" Before I could answer, his mind caught up with his mouth and he changed expression again. "Napalmed our butts good! Even that couldn't kill me!" He looked at me with a wild eye. "I'm invincible! Bullet-fucking-proof. I'm so short, can't see my shadow. I'm outta this godforsaken hole in forty-two days. Ain't even got time to piss." He laughed, then demanded, "Gimme a smoke, soldier. That's a direct order."

"You smoked all I had, sir. Let me see where you're hit." I leaned up on one elbow, still hurting all over, and opened my medic bag to see what I had left.

His fatigues had several small holes in the back, but his wounds were superficial, not nearly as menacing as the ones he had when I saw him a few days earlier on the *Nuaces*. Those wounds were scabbed but not yet healed. A couple of tiny gray pellets stuck in his skin were easily dislodged. Red marks showed where other stuff had hit and dropped. They might have been from the claymore or just secondary rocks from the path. He repeated how lucky he'd been to be running so fast and that a clay-more is usually about ninety percent deadly. He truly be-lieved he had outrun the explosion. I almost pointed out that he would have had to be running about eighteen hundred miles per hour, but thought better of it. His fanny showed a pocked map of purple scabs and old scars. This captain had quite a history tattooed to his behind.

"Hurts like shit," he insisted.

"You're okay. They're mostly shallow." I motioned for him to pull his pants up, then shifted to my back, dizzy from the pain on the side where I'd been leaning.

"Easy for you to say," he grumbled.

"You know, Captain," I began after a long pause to breathe, "begging your pardon, but something seems to be very wrong with your command."

"No shit, Sherlock! Those boys don't get this war." He glared down at me for a response.

"Does anybody?"

"I *do*, dammit! This whole worthless piece-a-shit country is infested with communists. Hell, half of America is crawling with commie-lovin' hippies. This entire backward godforsaken rice-eating country is communist. The whole damn thing. That tree over there," he pointed above me. "That's a by-god communist tree!" He laughed at himself.

"We should wipe the whole lot clean. I wish whoever's in charge of this war would let us drive out the whole damn communist mess!"

"Like we're not trying?"

"What?" He halted his pacing, studied me for a moment, then exploded again. "What the hell do you mean?" He paused and pointed. "Where's your weapon, boy? Did you lose your piece?"

"I'm a medic."

"You'd never medic a day in my platoon, soldier, if you lost your weapon. I don't care how hard you hit the ground." He leaned forward threateningly, shaking his jowls at me. I had been squeamish at the severed ear and irritated with the captain in general. But now I actually began to fear what he might do.

"Every swingin' dick in my crew spits fire like a dragon. Like a *dragon*. Hear me? Medics. Radio operators. Lieutenants. Commanding officers. That's what we're here for."

"I'm a medic. I don't carry a weapon."

"Jesus Christ, 'medic' don't mean shit to me. You shoot whatever commie pig walks in front of you, then you can patch him up all you want. You grasp my meaning?" I looked away. "What're you lookin' at, son? I'm talkin' to you. I oughta cut *your* stupid ear off and show you my meaning."

He caught himself. "Naw. Never mind. I didn't mean that. I don't mean you. I just guess I got no use for . . . well . . . we all gotta grease as many of these gooks as we can." He paused to reload his thoughts. "Y'know, I ain't that bad. I'm mostly just a lotta smoke."

Buttshot began to stomp away, then clicked back as if a switch had gone off in his head. "I'm just a trained killin' machine, Doc! A straight-up, military-minded mad dog, y'hear?" He saluted quicker than I could respond, then shot me with his finger. "Bang! You're DOA."

What was I dealing with here? Why hadn't I paid more attention in Psychology 1A?

"It's all a matter of will. My will against theirs. I fight the communists. I fight the coward draft dodgers. I fight the chicken draftees they send over here to fight."

He paced around, searching the ground as if he'd lost something, speaking to himself almost too low for me to hear. I tried to straighten myself and sit up, but my chest and stomach were still cramped. My arms and legs were weak and useless.

"We oughta bulldoze this jungle right to Hanoi. Cover over every livin' thing. Line up the big tractors side by side and flatten this whole country." He watched me watching him. "Am I right?" he hollered at the trees, not waiting for a reply from me. "Shoot every livin' thing that jumps outta the bush." I didn't react. "Shoot even the blood-suckin' mosquitoes!" He cackled again and flailed his arms, making flapping sounds like the flutter of quail coming out of a bush. Then over and over he cocked and fired an imaginary shotgun from his hip. "I could teach you to shoot, Doc. You come be part of my team. We'll make you a crack shot." He spun on his heel and shot six more ghost birds out of the sky. "That's a captain's promise."

"I'm a medic," I whispered.

He shook his head. "That's the sorriest whiny-ass lament I ever heard in my life." He fell in a heap of sorrow on the ground in front of me.

"I've been too busy to shoot anybody," I said.

Now I was making *him* sick to *his* stomach. He changed the subject.

"We got blown away by an eight-year-old baby-san with a grenade in her basket. No more'n eight. Walked right up to four guys eatin' their C's and put her little basket with sticks in it down right next to 'em. They thought she'd brought 'em firewood, y'know? A gift or something."

"And . . ."

"Here, GI," he imitated a child. "Here's some firewood for your cold C rations."

"And . . . ?"

"And she killed two of 'em and sent the other two home with legs and arms gone. Little commie shit. She even smiled when she put that basket down. Smiled real sweet, like, 'Here fellas,' y'know? Then skipped away like it was a normal school day." He lost himself in a daze, then returned. "It was my first platoon. I'd been in country two, maybe three weeks. Second patrol."

"What happened to the little girl?"

"You mean the baby-san communist commando?"

"The baby-san."

"Don't mess with me, Doc. I'm in no mood."

"Neither am I." My body hurt everywhere. I had no food in my stomach. I couldn't defend myself against a tick, much less a psycho-hysterical gladiator. I felt like I had in the morgue. Enough already. Put up or shut up. Kill me or back off.

He pretended not to hear me. He had rank; he didn't have to listen. "Slit her from crotch to neck. Cut her head off and stuck it on a pole."

I know I turned pale. I certainly felt like all the blood in my head was gone.

"I did it myself, Doc. Wouldn't let anybody else have the pleasure. Three weeks in country. *Damn!*"

The captain ran about twenty feet and stopped to shout back at me. "I chased that little bitch half a mile. My boys were shootin' at her, missin' my head by inches. Ricochets all around me. Mamma-sans screechin' outta their huts. I chased her down the road. Caught her right in front of the whole lot of 'em. Slit her right in half."

He fell forward on his knees, grabbed his gut, rolled his eyes, made a gagging sound, and fell on his back, letting out all his air. He didn't move. The captain had finished with me for the moment. He lay there looking up at the clear sky.

How could I make sense out of dreams and nightmares, little girls with bombs, heads on poles? My heart had held clotted emotion longer than I could remember. My head cramped in on all sides. I didn't just want to fall asleep. I didn't just want to go home. I wanted to die. I didn't want to spend one more second with this captain from hell. No wonder his own guys took target practice on his butt. If there was a postcard to depict everything wrong with this war, with any war, it would be a smiling Captain Buttshot holding a piece of some-body's body like an Oscar.

"You look like shit, Doc. If this bothers you, I really apologize." His sarcasm cut the air like a bad stink. "Hey, man, really . . . some guys just aren't cut out for this crap." With that, he regained his feet, marched out, and stood right in the middle of the clearing, about where I'd originally fallen. Plucking the pistol from his belt holster, he popped the clip out into his palm, then checked the ammunition and slammed it into its slot un-der the handle. He aimed at something, then put the pis-tol back into the holster. He drew it out quickly and aimed again. I'd seen this scene a thousand times. Cowboys on television. Wyatt Earp. Marshal Dillon. Billy the Kid.

As I watched this fantasy version of *High Noon*, I wondered if I was still dreaming. I half hoped maybe I was. What were all these confusing visions in my loneli-ness? Connections to the real world? First, dead people alive in my dreams. Now this outrageous B-movie char-acter, an alive person who probably should be dead. Myth had become real, and reality seemed like a myth.

On my third day in country, I had tagged and bagged some bully. How could I judge this captain? Conscien-tious objector, my ass. Without a sniff of regret, holding my crushed ribs, I had done my assigned task and tagged the man who had just moments before tried to beat me to death. I could rationalize it all I wanted. I had cer-tainly hated him. I had completely panicked. Afraid and battered, I went along with Vincent and Satterfield. And then I never said a word about it to anyone.

How did I differ from Captain Buttshot? By my third day I had become just as screwed up as he was. As screwed up as this whole war. After all I'd been through to plead my case and gain the distinction of noncombat status, how quickly I had let that go. I hadn't stood for anything. Not the war or the protesters, not the ACLU or the president. Not the flag, the resistance, or even my own beliefs. It had come down to "What would you do if you were getting the shit kicked out of you and you feared for your life?" And I had done the wrong thing.

Maybe this guy wasn't psychotic. Maybe the communists really were the bad guys. Could John Wayne have been right all along? As an American, did I have a responsibility to search out anybody in the known world who didn't believe in my way of life and shoot them? Is that how to save the world for God? Did I miss the whole point a long time ago? What side was I on anyway?

Peter, Paul, and Mary. Pete Seeger. Joan Baez. Bobby Dylan. All my favorites were against this war. How did I let myself get sucked into the army? Was it out of fear that I climbed those steps onto the bus to the induction center? Had I refused to shoot a weapon because I was afraid? Or did I actually feel some real commitment to what I'd been brought up to believe? Did I really believe in something more powerful than anger and fear?

I didn't have much else to offer this officer standing just a few yards away picking off imaginary foes with a very real loaded pistol. I couldn't talk him out of his position because I didn't understand it any better than I understood mine. Nothing in my life had prepared me for how I would feel when a commissioned officer threw somebody's ear in my lap. This one action opposed everything I had been raised to believe. I hated him for it. Would I shoot him in the butt if I had a chance? Would I knock him out cold with a six-foot aluminum box and then bag him without checking his pulse? Down here in the Delta, we cut off ears. Up in Hanoi,

American POWs suffered sleep deprivation, starvation, torture, and fake executions.

If there really was a revolution going on, something highly political and intellectual, it was playing out right here in the middle of an unknown jungle, not on the streets and campuses back in the World, or even in Paris around a big oak table. It was between Captain Buttshot and me: Can we survive without violence? I didn't know. And I had nothing to say to him. No political solutions. No doctrine. No explanation.

I hated the whole thing. Both sides.

"Really, Doc. You look like you're gonna puke. Got anything you can take?"

"Naw."

"Well, maybe you should get some sleep. Come nightfall, we're gonna walk outta here."

"Yeah," I whispered, curling into the fetal position, forearms wrapped around my neck and knees. I didn't feel like I could walk three feet. Under my breath, after he had strolled far enough away, I whispered, "Go fuck yourself, sir."

20

KIA

The sound of a helicopter cut through the jungle quiet. A Huey cleared the trees and hovered in a slow turn above the clearing. In the open sliding door, sitting with his feet dangling over the side rail, was SFC (Sergeant First Class) Robert E. Lee Smith, Jr., his right arm in a sling, teeth gleaming white, the brightest lights in my galaxy.

Rolling over onto my knees, my chest gave up on me and I couldn't stop coughing. Still, my eyes were riveted on Smitty. It took a thousand years for the chopper to descend its final ten feet, drift sideways for some reason, then rumble back. Captain Buttshot held his rifle high above his head, watching as the skids finally touched down and my boss dismounted, military chest riding high as he marched toward us, saluting with his uninjured left hand. Buttshot stiffened, drew his boots together at the heels, and snapped a return as fine as you'd see on any parade field.

"As you were, Sergeant Messiah!" the captain boomed.

"Gotcha!" Smitty joked as he tried to pluck me off the ground in a one-armed bear hug. "I *knew* you was out here, Bubba!" When my entire torso wrenched in his arm, he stopped and gently placed me back on the ground.

"Holy shit. Ya hit?"

"No, sir."

"Dammit, Bubba. I'm an enlisted man. Don't call me 'sir.' When ya gonna learn?" Turning to the captain, he introduced himself. "Sergeant Smith, sir. I fixed yer butt once."

"Who hasn't?" the captain countered. They laughed. I tried to smile.

"This right *here* is an officer, Bubba. You may refer to him as 'sir' until it stops rainin' in Southeast Asia."

The captain acknowledged Smitty with another quick salute as he turned to look out at the chopper. "Sergeant, is that taxi for us?"

"Yes, sir, it is! Looks like we need to carry our young doc here." Smitty bent to the ground on one knee, threw my arm around his neck, and hoisted me gently over his good side. Buttshot picked up his bags and mine. I was practically crying.

"How many times I gotta save yer happy ass?" Smitty yelled over the noise of the blades.

"Just this once, I hope," I croaked back.

"Twice," Smitty corrected. Twice? Did he mean the whistle at the river?

"What day is it?" I asked.

"Tuesday, Bubba. Owe the army three days of work for sittin' on yer butt out here." He was having a great time being my personal hero. Three days? I counted only two. I'd lost a day somewhere.

"Whaddaya mean twice?" I asked.

"Later."

My whole body felt dull and heavy. The noise of the chopper's engines and blades thumped in my already sensitive ears like hammers crashing inside my skull. It hurt worse to close my eyes, so I tried to create a distraction.

"I couldn't hear," I hollered.

"Huh?"

"My ears were shocked. Couldn't hear!"

"Eh?" he repeated, cupping his ear. Nothing had changed. He was still messing with me.

"How'd you know I was out here?" I hollered across the cabin. Smitty unsnapped his belts and moved to my side of the chopper. With no gunners aboard, he could close both long sliding side doors, shutting out much of the sound. It was still loud, but at least we could hear each other.

"Knew ya were too green to go anywhere. Knew ya'd stay put at least 'til ya got real hungry."

As we flew back, Smitty recounted for me the past three days.

While I was on my face in the clearing, Smitty was enduring a tricky wrist operation under general anesthesia at 3d Surg. The machine gun round that had hit him shattered the bones in his wrist just as I was leaning forward to jump from the chopper. Blood from Smitty's wound had doused the machine gunner's face and half the interior of the helicopter.

"Incoming! One down! One down!" the gunner had screamed as the pilot jerked out of the LZ, barely avoiding a line of tracers.

"Who's down?" the second officer barked, looking over his shoulder. "Aw shit! We lost a medic!"

The two machine gunners had sprayed everywhere they could reach. Incoming rounds clamored inside the cabin, barely missing everything, except the bullet that caught Smitty. He wrapped his sleeve around his wrist while trying to keep balanced as the chopper stood on its tail. Smitty crawled to his perch and strapped himself in with the help of one of the gunners. Fighting it as long as he could, loss of blood finally caught up with him, and he was unconscious when they landed at the hospital pad in Dong Tam.

He woke up with his arm in a cast, leaned over the side of his bed, and dry-heaved. He was weak, dizzy, incoherent, his entire arm hurt like hell, and Sergeant Smith had no idea where he was.

Smitty asked a nurse how long he'd been out.

"Out of jail?" she asked. "Out of luck?"

Even though groggy, Smitty managed to smile at her.

"Out of ideas? Out of money? Out of what?" He kept smiling, waiting for her to end her routine. "About a day and a half," she smiled back, picking up his good wrist to check his heartbeat. "How're you feeling?"

"Like I been kicked in the head or seen a real woman for the first time, one or the other," he winked. "Ya don't have anything against married men, do ya?"

"Not at all, Sergeant," she said. "Especially the one I'm married to."

He smiled and relaxed, then tried to remember what had delivered him. He recalled getting hit. Right before that, as tracer bullets came slicing toward the chopper, he was leaning forward, grabbing for a backpack as his whole right wrist exploded in bone and blood.

"Shit!" He leapt from his bed. "Bubba!"

He barefooted to the duty desk at the entrance of the ward. It was midnight, and an officer and an orderly were the only staff around. He insisted to the officer that there was a soldier missing in the field. The orderly stepped forward, answering the second lieutenant's wave to escort the patient back to the recovery ward. In hospital clothes, the top sergeant appeared to be just another wounded grunt whose medication was wearing off.

Smitty protested. The officer said that headquarters would be closed at this hour, but promised he'd look into it in the morning. Smitty barked some typical drill sergeant threats but didn't call the second lieutenant a ninety-day-wonder shit-ass-wimp, at least not to his face. Then he retreated to the recovery ward. Smitty retrieved his fatigues from under his bunk and found them caked in dried blood. He tracked down a corpsman and growled at him to take the clothes to the hospital laundry and have them cleaned and pressed immediately.

Within a few minutes the young second lieutenant from the desk arrived at Sergeant Smith's bedside to report that he had called headquarters and spoken with a duty officer. The pilot had reported large amounts of blood inside the chopper and a positive visual of my lifeless body as they took off.

"That was *my* blood," Smitty corrected the second lieutenant.

"Be that as it may, Sergeant. To save the troops on the ground, some of whom were wounded, all of whom were pulling out, a full ordnance of napalm and air-to-ground missile fire was directed on the area where numerous guerrilla forces were reported active. There is no hope for survival. Both men left out there are listed as KIA."

"Both? Who's the other?"

"Captain Riley and . . ."

"Buttshot Riley?!"

"The same."

"I'm tellin' ya, Bubba, the army likes to cover its ass promptly when we fire on our own people," Smitty interrupted his story to explain. "That officer he called knew exactly what happened out here. Everybody did. It was all over the officers club. Both the chopper pilot 'n radio operator from the field unit had filed reports."

"Why?" I asked.

"Because of that guy sittin' up in the copilot's seat right now."

"Buttshot?"

"Roger that. Turns out he's not popular *anywhere*."

"They left us out there on purpose?" I moaned.

"The captain, Bubba. *You* were reported KIA."

Smitty went on with his story.

Realizing he needed to take a different approach, Smitty somehow managed to talk the second lieutenant into finding out if Smitty's buddy Fred Frink was still stationed there at Dong Tam. Twenty minutes later the young officer returned with what he wanted to hear.

"Mr. Frink is still in Dong Tam. Hangs out most nights in the officers club. That's all I know." He didn't even wait for his salute as he turned abruptly and left, escaping any additional errands from Smitty.

Shortly thereafter, in the wee hours of morning, the hospital orderly returned with a neatly folded stack of Smitty's cleaned fatigues. Smitty dressed quickly with his one good hand, waving off help from the orderly.

"Umm . . . are you going someplace?" the orderly asked.

"No, Private. However, I do feel a good deal better with my fatigues on." He smiled at the youngster. "I would certainly hate to be under attack 'n have Charlie shoot my ass hangin' outta that nightshirt." Smitty nudged my shoulder and laughed, repeating, "I would just *hate* to have Charlie shoot m'bare ass hangin' outta m'nightie!"

As soon as the orderly disappeared down the hall, Smitty swung his legs off the bed, wrestled into his boots, and headed out the back door.

His first stop was the barracks where the radio dispatch team slept. After waking five guys, he found the one who had called in the fatal dustoff. The radio operator remembered the coordinates exactly, even though he was half asleep.

"Who could forget?" he mumbled. "That's where they called in the air force to finish off Captain Buttshot." Smitty wrote down the map coordinates on a scrap of paper.

Then Smitty headed for the officers club. Sergeants weren't allowed in, and they wouldn't want to go there if they were. Commissioned and noncommissioned officers didn't associate socially, and both groups agreed that this was determined at birth. Sergeant First Class Smith was no exception. "Rather kiss an alligator's ass than cross the threshold of an officers club." But on this particular early A.M., he walked right in as if he owned the place.

Fortunately, the club was too deserted for anyone to notice. A few men were smoking and playing cards at a rear table, and the bartender was half asleep on a stool, leaning against shelves of hard liquor. Smitty found who he was looking for in a booth, head on one hand, eyes closed in a stupor. WO (Warrant Officer) Fred Frink, everyone's favorite chopper pilot and somewhat notorious alcoholic, was right where Smitty hoped he'd be.

"Mister Frink!" Smitty sprayed into his inebriated face. "We have a mission."

An hour later Smitty and Frink exchanged glances as their chopper, obtained without permission from the deserted helo pad, cleared the trees leaving Dong Tam.

"Court-martial for sure!" Fred hollered.

"Only if we don't find him!" Smitty hollered back.

Robert Smith, AWOL from the hospital ward, was in a stolen Huey helicopter piloted by a half-drunk warrant officer. During his fourteen years in the military, Smitty had never committed the slightest infraction of military rules. This would pretty much make up for all that good behavior.

"This is *cake!*" Fred Frink shouted over the noise. Neither wore headgear since they weren't in radio contact with anyone. Flying barely above the treetops, the pilot watched his compass on the instrument panel and occasionally shifted his direction a point or two. The scrap of paper with the coordinates written on it was flapping in the wind, taped to the chopper window in front of them.

Smitty grinned. "This is *great!*" he yelled. "I've never rode up here!" He had been in a hundred choppers, but never in a command seat up front. As the copilot, he could see the jungle splayed out in front of him like a massive, bumpy green lawn.

"This is a beautiful country, Bubba, when ya don't have to look at it up close. Reminds me a li'l bit of the Mis'ippi Delta down near Baton Rouge. Used to go fishin' down there with my old man 'n grandpa. Didn't have a care in the world in those days."

Frink had flown right to the spot, and Smitty saw the captain waving before they touched down to get us.

"Bubba, you sumbitch!" Smitty kept saying all the way back to Dong Tam.

I couldn't stand it anymore. The sergeant wasn't himself at all. We were in serious trouble here, and he was smiling at me like he knew something very big and wasn't telling me.

"Was it the river? When you whistled for me in the river?"

"Awww," Smitty smiled. "Ya still workin' on number one?"

"Yeah. You know me. Always curious."

He knew I would bug him, so he took a deep breath. "Naw, if yer gonna count the river, that makes three."

"Huh?"

"Man, yer some piece of military work," he laughed at me again. My chest ached so much I dared not join him. "Yer in this shit-hole for barely a couple weeks 'n already ya seen more than most of us in a couple years."

"I gotta agree," I whined, trying to shift my weight so I could breathe easier.

"You carry a dead man a mile without a complaint."

"That's my job."

"Hell it is. Don't ever do that again. They was just testin' ya. Next time, get two grunts to load their buddy back to the chopper. Next time, *you* deal with what's happenin' next. Understand?"

"Uh huh."

"Ya walked in more blood back at the 28th than most people see in a lifetime. Hell, most *surgeons* don't see that much red."

"Okay, so when was the first time?"

"Now ya get yerself listed KIA without even tryin'. Hell, yer somethin', Bubba! Okay, Private Curious. I gotta tell yer ass sometime anyway."

"*What* already?" This made him burst out laughing.

"Remember when I first saw ya in the morgue tent?"

"Yeah, sure. You brought my orders to the *Nuaces*."

"Ever look at 'em?"

"Yeah, I guess." I swam through hunger and a blurry head to pull out that memory. "Oh yeah. You kept my orders. I never saw them."

"That's right, Bubba. 'Cause yer transfer didn't come 'til we went to medevacs."

"What?"

"Just in time, Bubba. This makes twice!" He roared

with laughter again. "That sumbitch was comin' to put ya in the dirt."

"Who?"

Smitty tried to speak low. It was difficult over the noise of the chopper.

"The sumbitch ya threw in a body bag. Jones, was it? Cornelius Jones? Ring a bell?"

"Holy shit!" I screamed.

"Aw, he prob'ly deserved it. Ya looked like hamburger when I picked ya up. He come to in the baggage depot in Bien Hoa, bangin' 'n drummin' from inside that box. When they opened it up, he nearly tore six people apart gettin' outta there."

"Oh my god!"

"Took a whole mess of MPs to strap him down. That guy is bad news. Spent another night in the brig. JAG reassigned him to the same morgue duty."

"How did you know?"

"The guys who smacked him. They came into headquarters 'n told me everything. Vincent 'n Satterfield? I'm the first sergeant, y'know. That's what yer *supposed* to do, Bubba. I'm yer boss!" Smitty smiled and winked, almost like he was letting us off the hook for this one. "Before I came to getcha, I transferred Vincent 'n Satterfield to Saigon, waitin' for disciplinary action. They told me *you* had nothin' to do with smackin' him. That true?"

I confessed to Smitty that I tagged him.

"Why'd ya do a thing like that?"

"He looked totally dead to me."

"You check him?"

"No . . ."

"Didn't check his *pulse*?"

"He had blood running out his ears. His head was

smashed. He'd just beat me up. I could barely look at him. I didn't want to go anywhere *near* him."

"Doin' well enough to fill out a red *toe tag*, Bubba. Gotta hand it to ya."

"I've been seeing that guy in my sleep for weeks."

"Never mind. Like I said, the dipshit prob'ly deserved it. Anyhow, he ain't dead. I figured you were the only one left he'd recognize over at the morgue, so I snatched yer sorry ass outta there."

"With no orders?"

"I make the assignments. Got the orders eventually."

"And the other guys?"

"Charges dropped as soon as he turned up alive 'n punchin' out MPs. Nobody wants to punish Vincent 'n Satterfield. Hell, the MPs wanna put 'em up for *medals!*"

"Why didn't you say something?" I asked.

"I could ask *you* the same question."

"You think I'd bust two guys who saved my ass?"

"I just wondered how long it would take you to trust me."

There was a long look between us. He'd been holding this secret while personally helping me adjust to the war zone without going to pieces.

"We're here for each other, Bubba. That's all that counts for anything. Ya gotta believe that *some*time. Four days in country mighta been a little early. But ya gotta believe that now. We're only here for each other." I looked away, trying to peek out the tiny window in the door of the chopper. Smitty leaned closer. "That includes *me*, you roger that?" I turned my face to his and found him grinning at me like a long-lost brother. He had risked everything to come out here to find me. I turned away so he wouldn't see the tears swelling.

"What's gonna happen once we're back at Dong Tam?" I asked, voice cracking, shaking my head.

"Don't sweat it, Bubba. Everybody thinks yer KIA. We'll leave it that way for a while, 'til Jones moves out or gets his shit in another sling. Bound to happen."

Yeah, right. I could just stay dead. And how would we work *that*?

Smitty handed me a pair of dog tags. "We'll borrow these a while, Bubba. Put 'em on. Yer gonna be James Kline."

By seven o'clock that morning, Smitty was lying in his bed at 3d Surg and no one knew he'd been gone. I was checked into the bed right next to him, having been brought in by Frink.

"Dazed and walking around the perimeter," he told the officer in charge. "I thought he was drunk. Don't think he knows where he's at. Passed out when I got to him."

Ten minutes later Frink was asleep in the officers barracks, the chopper was securely tied down right where they had gotten it, and Captain Buttshot was busily stuffing clips of ammunition into his new pack as he prepared to join his troops in the field.

As soon as the orderlies had tucked me in and left, Smitty looked over and whispered, "Never left my bed. No idea what yer talkin' about."

"Smitty, we have got to talk."

"Can't."

"Come on, Smitty."

"Yer dead, Bubba. Somebody come in 'n hear me talkin' to thin air 'n they'll put me away forever."

Two trays of food arrived. Smitty swung around on the side of his bed and shoved my tray closer to me.

"Gonna eat all that?" he asked.

"Dead men don't eat," I mumbled through a cheek full of eggs and toast.

"Well, Bubba, what we gonna do with ya?"

"Man, I'm not going near the morgue, that's for sure."

"Smart move. Might not even be healthy anywhere outside for a while."

I told him I felt paranoid being in the exposed base camp. Stumbling along between Frink and Buttshot from the chopper to 3d Surg, the back of my neck prickled as if someone were watching or following me.

"You were out there *alone* for a while, right?" He grabbed a piece of greasy bacon and held it up to the light. "Where *does* the army get the shit they feed us? When did Buttshot show up?"

"Not right away. He saw me drop. Came out and got my backpack and did all the smokes in it before he came looking for my body."

"He prob'ly woulda ate ya too, if ya wasn't alive."

"No shit."

"That captain is somethin' else."

"He wants to bulldoze South Vietnam . . ."

"I know, right up to the DMZ. I heard all that shit before. He's an asshole."

"How'd he ever become an officer?"

"Why, Bubba, ya'll of a sudden got some *high opinion* of officers?"

I ignored that question and finished all the food on my tray, then exchanged the empty one for a full tray that was getting cold next to a sleeping patient a few beds down. Smitty frowned at me in jest. He was thinking, his cheeks pulsating as he worked the rear muscles of his jaw.

"Phil Weber," he finally said, a beam replacing the frown. "We gotta go see Phil Weber."

21

Recovery

Sergeant Smith didn't think much of lying around in the recovery ward, and the young officer seemed happy to see him leave the next day. After a day of eating and sleeping, Smitty decided I had fully recovered as well.

"C'mon, Bubba." He pulled at my forearm. "We gotta find Weber."

"Who's he?"

"Phil Weber. The clerk who checked ya in."

"I just 'showed up' here, remember?"

"Not the hospital, dummy. Base camp. Dong Tam. He assigned ya to the morgue."

Looking back on that first day in country, it was all a blur. Incoming fire at Bien Hoa. Head wound in the bunker. An old medic and a new one. A long line waiting for a sleepy sergeant to find my orders. About a dozen of us catching a ride in a loud chopper just after sunrise, and my head spinning by the time I got to Dong Tam, where I pissed off my captain for not carrying a weapon and was assigned to the morgue tent.

Phil Weber's boss, a lieutenant colonel, managed the operations of base camp, directly under the full-bird colonel in charge of the whole base. This made Weber an important person to know. When Smitty and I entered the orderly room, I recognized him at once from the day I had stumbled in after the confrontation with the captain.

Smitty, however, was counting on Weber not recognizing me.

"Nice to see you, Sergeant Smith," Weber said. "Who's this?"

"We met when I first came in, I'm . . ."

". . . Jim Kline," Smitty interrupted. "From the 24th. Got banged up 'n needs reassignment. They sent him to 3d Surg 'n now *you* get him. Says he can type."

Weber smiled. "Jim Kline? You type?"

"Sure, a little," I said. "Spent a couple of months as an orderly room clerk waiting for orders."

"You a medic?" he asked.

"Yes." I looked at Smitty.

"Sure!" Smitty smiled.

"Noncombat?"

"Uh . . ." I didn't want to look at Smitty for every answer.

Weber shuffled some papers on his desk, then sat down and took a deep breath. "Your name's Ben Sherman. I just listed you as KIA yesterday morning. You're the only objector who's come through this base since I been here. You don't think I'd remember you?" He turned to Smitty. "Kline bought it on a beach up near Half Moon Bay. DOA at 28th Evac. He was a rifleman, not a medic, and he probably never saw a typewriter."

Smitty turned redder than usual. "Okay, okay. I guess y'know."

"That's affirmative, Top. That's what I *do*." Weber seemed edgy. "And I read the full KIA report every morning. Look for people I might know. I remember things like fourteen dead Americans in a single day."

Smitty stepped forward and dropped his voice low. "We're gonna let this guy lie low for a while, Phil Boy.

He's been through some shit 'n needs some extended R&R."

"I know, Smitty, I know. Back off. I'm on your side, man. Just pulling your chain. You're his first sergeant. You can do whatever you want."

My sigh of relief was so loud they both looked at me.

"But, Smitty, you might wanna take a look at that letter in his wallet."

"What letter?"

"The letter from his congressman."

Smitty stretched out his hand to me. "Hand it over, Bubba." I hesitated, then slowly removed my wallet from my pocket. "The letter, Bubba!" I handed it to him.

Smitty carefully unfolded my only copy of the letter I'd carried every day since the day I received it, right before leaving medical training in Texas.

"Jesus, would ya look at this?" *Congress of the United States . . . House of Representatives.* "Saint Peter on a crutch, Bubba. Congressman Moss is chairman of the Foreign Operations Committee." He read the rest of the letter to himself. . . . *the Department of the Army assures me that Hospital Corpsmen are assigned to hospitals which are not in the combat area and are not subject to ground attack. However, if you find after you have reported to your assignment in Vietnam that the circumstances are not as depicted, please do not hesitate to contact me at once. Sincerely, John E. Moss, Member of Congress.*

Smitty carefully refolded the letter and handed it back to me. "Sorry, Bubba. Didn't mean to intrude on private correspondence." He looked tired all of a sudden. He turned to Weber. "He's been in the field with me, 'n we did medevacs . . ."

"I know."

"Are we in a worlda hurt here, Phil?"

"*I* put him in the morgue."

"You said every medic started in the morgue," I protested.

"I assigned you there to keep you out of the field," he shrugged. "You were supposed to stay put right there." He scratched his head, tousling red hair that was longer and more unruly than generally allowed among enlisted men.

"Yeah, well, Bubba had his own way of workin' himself outta the morgue."

"You're his sergeant, Smitty. You're responsible for his assignment."

"So, now what?"

"Nothing. Nothing at all." Weber turned to me. "That okay with you, Sherman?" I wasn't sure what he was asking. "That letter stays in your pocket, and we keep you here, okay?" I turned to Smitty. He suddenly looked a lot less tired.

Smitty nodded as he gave Weber a slight, grateful smile. "Small-town folks . . ."

". . . stick together," Weber chimed in. "Lidea, Kansas. Population six hundred."

"Pachuta, Mis'ippi. Population I dunno, but it ain't six hundred!" The tension eased and Smitty continued. "What we need is for our friend here to disappear 'til some other heat is off. No big thing. Some shit's gettin' itself straightened out."

"Don't tell me. The morgue deal with Jones?" This guy didn't miss a thing.

"Just let it go," Smitty said.

Weber turned to me, smiling wildly. "Jeez, Ben, you were there! I forgot it was you. A blessed CO. Oh my god! Why didn't I put this together before?" He was scratching his head and grinning. "*That's* why you came and got him, Smitty. And you didn't even have orders for him yet! He sure *did* work his way outta the morgue. This is too much!"

He went on to explain that when Vincent and Satterfield were released after Jones showed up *not* dead, they returned to Dong Tam and told everybody about some unknown white medic going brain-versus-brawn with the formidable Cornelius Jones. Whether they meant to or not, they effectively diverted Jones's anger off themselves and onto the unknown and long-gone medic.

I must have looked very uncomfortable. Weber tried to lift my spirits by punching me in the arm and saying, "Hey, man, you're a flippin' folk hero at this base! Like the Lone Ranger." Weber laughed out loud. "Who was that masked man?"

I could only think about Cornelius Jones and the fact that *he* knew.

"I probably don't wanna know, but how'd you get on the KIA list?" Weber asked.

"In the bush by himself a few days," Smitty answered for me. "'Til this mornin'."

Weber thought for a few seconds, then his eyes grew wide. "Captain Riley checked in this morning to say he'd been missing the last few days in the bush. 'Til this morning. Word has it he was hit by friendly fire."

"Yeah, well, it's all very confusin', Phil . . ."

"Everybody on the whole base has been talking about Captain Buttshot finally buying the farm. Then there he was on my phone. Man, I about freaked. He wanted to be sure HQ took him off the KIA list so he could get back to his platoon. Wouldn't tell me what happened or how he got back. And didn't say a word about Sherman here. Is this connected?"

Smitty hemmed around a bit. "Well, we ain't really discussin' that entirely. Know what I mean?"

"You and Frink, no doubt." Weber gave a half smile and shook his head.

"That could be a roger. Who's to know?"

"Who, indeed."

"How can we cover this guy in some outta-the-way hole for a few weeks?"

"Look, you guys . . ." I finally said.

"Look *what?*" Smitty turned to me, scowling. "Wanna take it up with yer bag buddy Cornelius, or just lie low for a while?"

"I just don't want to get us in trouble," I said.

"Trouble? Goddammit, Bubba, no matter where the cow shits, yer stepping in it."

"Okay," Weber interrupted, "we can do this." Smitty shot me a "stick with me" look. "Clerk duty right here in Operations," Weber went on. "I got tons of paperwork."

Operations? How could this work? How could I get away with being a nonperson right next door to headquarters?

"Don't look so worried," Weber chuckled. "Ops is the best place to hide. We do all the morning reports here. I type them and send them to DC." Then his eyes lit up. "No, wait! From now on, *you* type them and send them to DC." Even I laughed.

I liked him. Short, stocky, curly red hair hanging down across his thick glasses. Quick to smile. Nimbly darting around the Operations orderly room, noticeably at home. A classic army clerk.

"I'll change your status in DC and put you on light duty here," Weber continued. "No one will know the difference." Looking at Smitty's injured arm all bound up in plaster and hanging in a sling, he announced, "We need to get Sherman into a cast."

"A cast?" I asked.

"Perfect," Smitty agreed.

"Yeah. Arm or ankle. Wait. Has to be ankle. Can't do a hand or arm because you need to type."

"Perfect," Smitty repeated. "No problem. I can do it over at 3d Surg tonight."

"A cast?"

"Sure. Nobody will ask any questions if you're injured. You're on special assignment. Happens all the time around here. Just means I get a temporary extra clerk."

"Okay! Now we're kickin' ass 'n takin' names!" Smitty beamed with excitement.

"I'm getting a *cast?*"

"Okay then," Weber said. "Where are you eating and sleeping?"

"Can't go to his old barracks just yet," Smitty said.

"Well, I got an extra bunk behind the mess hall where I stay. You're welcome there, Ben."

So my next assignment was temporary Operations clerk and Phil Weber's roommate, still with no official orders, if anybody asked me. But the more I learned each day, the more I knew Phil could cook any orders we needed. And officers and NCOs alike knew better than to mess with the division Operations clerk.

The next morning he updated the records to show my miraculous escape from the clutches of the jungle. He covered it with a note to the Pentagon, or whomever read those things, explaining my change of status on the morning report after I walked into camp all beat up and disoriented.

"You can just *do* that?" I asked.

"Army wants to know where we are, not where we aren't. Besides, what are they gonna do? Draft us and send us to Vietnam?" I loved that expression. He used it often. What *could* they do? It didn't hurt the army to know they had one less gone.

Phil and I worked mostly in isolation, which sat fine with me after what I'd been through in the first three weeks. For the next few weeks I hobbled around with a walking-cast on my left foot. Phil had been right about it aiding my anonymity. I didn't have to make up a name or lie to anybody, because nobody except Phil cared who I was. I obviously couldn't hump the bush or do any physical labor around base camp, so helping out as a clerk in the Operations orderly room looked like making the best of a bad thing. I wore new fatigues with no name badge.

Phil and I ate together during off hours in the NCO mess, where the food was a little better than regular food. We strolled through the PX usually when it was closed, a privilege reserved for those who worked for HQ. At night I returned to the room while Phil went to the movies or the club. He usually came back with a few beers and some chips, and we'd play Scrabble, chess, and gin until midnight. He never tired of whipping me at all three every time.

As his wrist healed, Smitty worked days in 3d Surg triage and spent most nights drinking beer at the NCO club. I missed working with him, but didn't miss humping the bush or flying in choppers. He came by the office once a day, just long enough to say hello but not long enough to attract any attention my way. I was soon able to sleep through the night without dreams of bodies in bags, exit wounds, or the 28th Evac.

Our days found Phil and me typing and filing and bored. We blew through typing morning reports and orders during the first hour of the day, then attacked any piece of work before it had a chance to land in one of our in-boxes. But we always had precious little to do. When the mamma-san came in to clean our office every day, we'd make her giggle by singing or whistling to the beat of her handmade straw broom as it whisked back and forth. She'd shake her head and call us *boo coo dinky dau,* which meant she thought we were nuts.

During the long hours with no visitors, Phil and I would play more Scrabble, chess, and gin, and talk. And talk some more. Phil had been drafted right out of college. "Weren't many draft-aged guys handy around Lidea, Kansas. Those old enough were needed on their farms. Every board has its quota, y'know?" His 2-S status got him through his first four years of college, but Selective Service didn't have much respect for those seeking doctorates. He became eligible as soon as he enrolled in graduate school.

We were both English majors. "Born under the same star," I laughed. On any afternoon we might try to remember every college class we'd taken, the professor's name, the textbook, and the grades we got. We'd list the girls we'd dated or the states we'd visited, compare best bowling scores, or just sit and read one of the classics from the shelves in Lieutenant Colonel Bambrey's adjoining office. In a month I read more than my sum total in three years of college.

Lt. Col. Thomas L. Bambrey came on like straight army, with the shiny brass buckle and spit-shined boots. He'd graduated from West Point near the top of his class and had the bearing, the walk, the language, and a born leader's eye. He could bark out orders without hesitation and demanded respect from civilians and enlisted men alike. But he'd been regularly passed over for promotion to full-bird colonel.

"Bambrey's good people," Phil assured me. "He looks

regular army, but must've missed school the day they made hawks. Not aggressive enough for full bird. Way too intellectual. Doesn't walk the walk."

Over the next few weeks I saw for myself a deeper side of the lieutenant colonel. He studied rather than practiced leadership. On the credenza in his office stood hard-bound copies of Cervantes's *Don Quixote* and Dostoyevsky's *Crime and Punishment* flanked by a New English translation of the Bible and a copy of Kahlil Gibran's *The Prophet*. He once waxed Phil and me at Scrabble by more than a hundred points. But he wasn't a physical competitor. He didn't push, he pondered.

Bambrey often joined our conversations if they turned to books, poets, or plays.

"You're both wrong," he once interrupted a Shakespeare discussion. "*Romeo and Juliet* was written ten years before *Macbeth,* sometime around 1596, I think. *Macbeth, King Lear,* and *Antony and Cleopatra* were all written around 1606." He stood rigid, looking for an argument, and saw only two young faces gazing at him with admiration. He bowed at the waist, clicked his heels, performed a perfect about-face, and marched out.

Nope. No hawk, this officer. He was literary, classical, intellectual, and terrifically softhearted on the two of us draftees. We adored him.

One early morning, from our quarters behind the mess hall right next door, Phil and I heard Bambrey playing his clarinet along with a swing-band recording. He didn't play very well, but you could tell he loved every note. When he came into the office after breakfast, I asked him about the recording.

"Hasn't been any real music written since 1949," he huffed.

"What about the Beatles, sir?"

"Bugs!"

One rainy afternoon, Phil and I were talking about the war. "I grew up believing in freedom, liberty, and democracy, but America is becoming . . ." Phil hesitated, swallowing his disappointment, ". . . has *become* materialistic and violent. This war isn't about democracy and communism. It's about capitalism and imperialism." Phil sounded like it hurt his feelings to sound so blasphemous.

"You're wise beyond your years, son," Bambrey said softly from the doorway to his office, before slowly closing the door. That was as close as he ever got to a statement about the war.

On a warm July evening, Bambrey invited Phil and me to join him in his quarters. He didn't actually live in the officers barracks, which was strictly off-limits to enlisted men. Like Phil, he had a private room, but his was attached to the back of headquarters. We accepted his invitation eagerly, mostly because we'd often speculated on what his room might look like.

We weren't disappointed. Nothing about it looked like the army. His bed had a regular old-fashioned spread. He had a finished-wood chest of drawers and a hanging oriental light. Nothing olive drab about it. Candles, paintings, a throw rug, and incense, it looked like a bachelor pad in the World. Normal, even civilian. On his tiny coffee table were a bottle of unopened Southern Comfort and three small shot glasses. Between the glasses lay three long cigars. Strains of solo violin music wept from a reel-to-reel tape player in the corner.

"You're just in time," Bambrey greeted us. He clicked off the music and, with a sweep, lifted the blanket shroud from a real live television set. Our mouths fell open.

"This is a special night, gentlemen. One I would like

to share with my only civilized friends in this forbidden nook of the good earth." Thick brown wires ran from the TV out the window. "We're connected on a downlink from NASA. Have a seat and relax, boys. You're not going to believe this!"

And there, in the middle of the Mekong Delta in South Vietnam, on a warm evening in July, the three of us smoked cigars, drank very smooth liquor, and watched in reverent silence as Neil Armstrong walked on the moon.

There were no commercials and no commentators. Our NASA downlink allowed us to hear all the communications between NASA sites around the globe as they each conveyed congratulations and heartfelt joy. These were fellow soldiers on a mission very different from ours. As colleagues in the military, however, we each felt very much a part of the drama unfolding before us.

Afterward, we walked outside and sat in three metal chairs on the porch of HQ. The sky was dark blue except for the moon, which shone like never before. When the quiet had said all it needed to say, Bambrey stood and stretched.

"You'd think they could end this war," he sighed.

Turning to face us, he smiled. "An honor, gentlemen." He reached out to shake Phil's hand, then mine. I shook hands with an army officer for the first time. He turned away and looked up, then saluted the moon. We heard him whistling as he walked down the street to the officers club.

22

News

After about six weeks, Smitty finally shed his cast and came by to get me. "C'mon, Bubba. Let's get that leg-iron off." Phil looked up and nodded in agreement. I limped behind Smitty to the casting room at 3d Surg. He had settled in as sergeant in charge of triage and, for once, didn't seem to mind rear support duty.

"Sure beats sleepin' in the paddies, but I hate that damned siren at night," Smitty complained.

"We just roll out and slide under our beds when there's incoming. Our quarters behind the mess hall are like a little bunker."

"Yeah, looks like some ol' army cook fixed it up so he'd be safe without havin' to run to the bunkers across the street. Two rows of sandbags should keep ya safe from any side blow," Smitty noted. "If there's a direct rocket or mortar hit, yer gonna be history, even in a bunker."

I stuck my fingers in my ears as the small handheld circular saw screeched through my ankle cast. It didn't take Smitty more than a minute to release me from what had been my constant companion night and day for more than a month.

"Better get some PT on that ankle, Bubba."

"Smitty, I really want to thank you for . . ."

"They took that Jones sumbitch outta here in chains last week."

"My man Cornelius?"

"The same. Punched out a lieutenant."

"No shit? What a head case." So that was why it was time for my cast to come off.

"Yer worries are over. He's shippin' to the World for court-martial 'n maybe a little hard time. Yer a free man now!" He swatted my bare ankle where the cast had been. It was skinny and damp and the color of white paste.

Phil put me in for permanent reassignment as a clerk for Operations. My field medic days were over. I celebrated with a quick trip to Steam 'n Cream. This time I took a little extra money.

Being an army secretary had a boring, stagnant, consistent appeal. Smitty liked to spice things up by occasionally borrowing Phil and me for some medical assistance. Late one night we delivered a mamma-san's baby in the mess hall kitchen, the cleanest place on the base besides 3d Surg. Afterward, Phil and I stayed up all night talking about women and marriage, commitments, finding our true loves, and someday having children. We both determined we didn't know shit.

When a large group of troops shipped out, Smitty set up a shot team to administer inoculations. Three tables of vials—one table each for yellow fever, cholera, and something else—sat waiting for the hundreds who lined up at our door. Two medics from 3d Surg prepared the hypodermic needles as Smitty and I administered the injections. It gave us an excuse to work together. From dawn to dusk we swapped stories and jokes while throwing darts into various sizes, shapes, and thicknesses of lateral deltoid flesh.

Smitty turned the successful completion of our twelve-hour shot marathon into a party. After cleaning up the tables and dumping six trash cans of used and broken needles, I just wanted to collapse into bed. Smitty had other plans. He hauled a case of beer and a bottle of Kentucky bourbon over to the small bunker where Phil and I lived behind the mess hall. Lifting the first shot of many, Smitty first toasted Phil.

"To Phil Weber, Lidea, Kansas! Small-town boy with a heart big as the Plains states. Sharp wit, nose for gossip, fingers faster than the naked eye can follow. Fine gentleman, scholar, friend, and HMFWIC of Dong Tam." Smitty grinned, then downed his first shot. Before I could ask, he explained. "Head MotherFucker What's In Charge!"

I gulped the shot and realized immediately that this was *not* Southern Comfort. The beer chaser didn't douse the instant fire in my throat. I tried to wave off another while my chest absorbed the heat of the first. But Smitty would have none of it. He poured until my glass spilled over, and continued his toast.

"Here's to Bubba, a walkin' talkin' conflict of a man! Short-timer since the day he arrived. Carries a calendar with the whole year on it!"

"Doesn't everybody?" I interrupted.

"When ya get under a hundred days maybe. Lemme finish," he teased. "Here's to a conflict of a man. Soldier without a gun. Clerk. Medic. Courageous under fire. More trouble than he's worth 'n a goddamn great partner!" He lifted his glass to us, to the heavens, then poured the liquor into the back of his throat. "I will swear-to-god drink to that!" Phil and I followed again.

And again, and again. We toasted the war, the flag, Mississippi, the American Red Cross, every beautiful woman we could remember, even Uncle Ho Chi Minh.

"May he die a peaceful death in his sleep very soon," Smitty offered.

The next morning our usual office chatter was muted by hearty headaches. When our boss entered shouting orders, we bristled. "Phil. Ben. My office. Now!" Bambrey stomped past us and left his office door ajar. We looked at each other. Surely we couldn't be busted for getting ripped with a ranking sergeant . . . we hadn't been late to work . . .

"I got news, boys. Great news! Get in here and close the door!" Bambrey paced in front of his window. We scrambled into the two wooden chairs facing his desk.

"We have an assignment." He cleared his throat and started again. "We have a *top secret* assignment. Just us. The three of us."

He began to ramble about political theories, hawks and doves, peaceniks rioting in the streets, congressmen and presidents, songs and movies, America generally coming apart. He finally wound around to his point. Newly elected President Nixon had made a campaign promise to bring the boys home from Vietnam.

"Our commander in chief was inaugurated in January and hadn't done a thing toward that promise . . . until yesterday." Colonel Bambrey explained that Nixon was growing frustrated with the lack of progress at the Paris peace talks. Diplomats weren't getting anywhere. Prisoners of war weren't being released. Fighting escalated on all northern fronts and in the southern jungles. And the president's unfulfilled promise was attracting more attention in the press every day.

This was all news to Phil and me. Campus riots and Senate speeches weren't covered in the pages of *Stars and Stripes,* our only source of information.

"The KIA rate goes up every day, and that massacre

of the 82d Airborne and a whole mess of Marines got Congress, the TV news, and the morning papers all in a fuss counting our losses over here. The White House is in trouble, boys. Big trouble." He was sermonizing, uncharacteristically, as if this speech were rehearsed.

"Yesterday the president made an announcement during a meeting with our allies on Midway Island. Said he's going to reduce the number of Americans in Vietnam by ten thousand troops by the end of August." Phil and I looked at each other, stunned. Bambrey paused to hold eye contact with each of us. "That's ten days, boys."

He leaned over his desk and dropped his voice low. "Phil?" He looked squarely at my buddy, then darted his eyes directly into mine. "Ben?"

"Sir?" we leaned forward.

"Phil, Ben, you have *got* to, from this moment on, tell *no* one, *no one,* what I'm about to tell you." He trusted us or he wouldn't have said this much. But he wanted to hear it from us. "I'm not kidding about top secret status here. This leaks, people get killed. Many people."

"Whatever it is, sir, you can count on us," Phil said. "Yes, sir," I added. We trusted him even more than he trusted us.

He leaned back and nodded. "As of tomorrow, the colonel is joining General Abrams in Saigon, and I'm in charge of Dong Tam." He leaned forward again, and again lowered his voice. "A thousand of those troops going home are coming right out of the 9th Infantry."

We were the 9th.

"That's us," he said.

"That's us," Phil and I whispered in unison.

"We're pulling ten thousand soldiers out of this division in ten days. Nine thousand will be redeployed elsewhere in Vietnam. But we'll make it look like the whole

9th is being pulled out. Only a thousand men will actually go Stateside."

"We?" Phil asked.

"We've been put in charge of the deployment home. Someone else is in charge of the nine thousand. Top priority. Top secret. They said I should use a couple of clerks I could trust. And that's you."

"Why the hush?" I asked.

Bambrey went on to explain that no one, not our South Vietnamese allies, not even our own officers and troops, could know what was up until the day or two before. If Charlie caught wind we were pulling out, he'd mount a huge attack to make it look like a communist victory and a U.S. retreat. We had to slip out without a fight. Bambrey began to revel in the intrigue. He had our rapt attention.

"We're in the middle of negotiations in Paris. We're playing hardball with the communists, and they're playing right back. Nobody's moving an inch. They've got all those POWs up in Hanoi, all our fliers they shot down over North Vietnam. And the press is printing horror stories coming out of those prisons, making the commies look bad. But they won't give an inch because they know those reports stir up protests back in the States, putting pressure on us to get out."

He paused to light a cigar and send a smoke ring sailing across his desk. "This whole deployment thing is a political ball game. The president needs to look good at home. Get some support out of Congress. Get the press to ease up on him, just long enough to get some breathing room from the protesters. He's using us as chips at the table, boys. This pullout is going to get played to the hilt."

"But, sir, if only a thousand are going home, where are the other nine thousand going?" I asked.

"Tan An. 25th Infantry. Headquarters Saigon is in charge of *their* paperwork." Bambrey paused again. "We'll take the men with the most time in Vietnam and send them to Hawaii. They'll make a big fuss in Honolulu with press and photographers when we get there. The rest will go north to Tan An and resupply the 25th. That way, we don't really lose that many bodies in country. Our force will be just as strong. In fact, with all the new recruits coming through Bien Hoa every day, we'll probably have more troops here after the 'pullout' is over. And the president will have kept his promise, so to speak."

Tan An. Where is Tan An?

"This is called 'Vietnamization,' a made-up word for giving a bunch of equipment and weapons over to the ARVN. Congress really wants to help these people, but they want us out of here even more." His voice dropped even lower. "What it means is, Dong Tam is going to be turned over to the South Vietnamese in a couple of weeks."

"Oh my god," Phil gasped.

"I know. Doesn't look good for Dong Tam." He paused, then repeated, "A thousand are going home, but we have to make it *look* like ten thousand are landing in Hawaii."

It took several times through for this to sink in. My only experience with army warfare was as a power drive right up the middle. This was a sleight-of-hand trick. The front-page headlines would read TROOPS PULL OUT and NINTH INFANTRY RECALLED.

"People won't be able to figure it out?" I asked.

"At the rate everyone's reassigned, who'll be counting?"

"Relatives of men in the 9th won't be waiting at the airports?" I was thinking about my own mother and father, who would certainly make the trip if it meant I was out safe.

"Do your folks know where you're assigned?" the colonel asked. Of course not. None of our families knew exactly where we were stationed. Strict military protocol prohibited us from disclosing location, assignment, company, or the names of anybody. It was part of basic training.

"Sir, what will be the cutoff date for the one thousand?" Phil asked.

"Start with ten months in country. Anybody with over ten months goes. If that doesn't get you a thousand, drop to nine months and so on."

I had been here barely three months. I was headed for Tan An.

Phil and I were to manifest a thousand troops to air force C-133 cargo planes. We'd need to schedule the flights and book the passengers, then type the orders and deliver all of them within twenty-four hours of departure. The 9th Infantry was spread out all over the Mekong Delta. Some were assigned REMF duty in My Tho and there were about five hundred stationed in Saigon. Others were on R&R. So the first thing we'd have to do is shuffle people to get those who were returning to the World all in Bien Hoa at the same time, no matter where they were currently stationed.

"No one can know about this up until the last day," Bambrey insisted.

A thousand orders in twenty-four hours? Two clerks?

"Impossible!" we whined.

Bambrey was insistent. "We can *do* this! All we have to do is schedule the planes with the air force. They land and take off all the time from Bien Hoa. We'll make them ours for a few hours. We can get over two hundred troops in one C-133 Cargomaster. The air force has lots of them."

Phil was beginning to perk up a bit. He had about eleven months in country. He would be on the list.

"I'll personally take care of the transportation from Bien Hoa to the States," Bambrey said. "You two just fill those planes."

My MOS read "91B-Field Medic." Clerk typist was a secondary job for me. I'd been in Vietnam less than three months and would be deployed to the 25th Infantry Division. Though it had been a while, I recognized the taste of my stomach as soon as it entered my throat.

After Bambrey finished, the realization of my going back into the field had me immediately crossing the street to 3d Surg in search of Smitty. I had to get some real information without breaking Bambrey's top secret trust.

Smitty showed no effects from the night before. "How's tricks, Bubba?" he beamed. I told him that Phil and I had started kinda late, given the poisonous night before.

"I can barely focus this morning, thank you very much." I forced a smile. "Usually don't understand half the stuff I read anyway, but we saw some reports come in about the 25th Infantry this morning. What do you know about Tan An?" Smitty took the bait.

Not far southwest of Saigon, yet not near enough to enjoy the armed protection of the big city, Tan An had the reputation of being a hot spot. Halfway between the Mekong River and the South China Sea, it was the capital of the most populated province in Vietnam and right in the middle of an abundant rice-growing region.

"Tan An is protected by III Corps, 25th Infantry Division," Smitty explained. "They're called the '25th U.S. '

so as not to confuse 'em with the 25th ARVN Infantry that operates in the same area. Motto is 'Ready to strike, anytime, anywhere,' and they're true to that. They are guar-an-*teed* to get into some kinda mess. Known for it. What happened this time?"

"I dunno. Just some troop movement down there."

"Dong Tam is R&R compared to Tan An, Bubba. That place is crawlin' with hurt." Smitty was pretty good at reading me, and I'm sure it showed that he'd scared me, but he didn't know why.

"Keep yer mind right here where it belongs, y'hear?"

"Yep." I let it drop. Not only would I be joining another infantry brigade, but it had to be a gung-ho, blood-and-guts bunch. Ready to strike? I was ready to puke.

23

Lists

The army can follow directions. It's very good at that. All you have to do is hand a commanding officer a pile of paperwork with a bunch of his soldiers' names, and he'll make it happen. Type enough orders, you can move anybody anywhere. But doing it without anyone knowing until the last minute is a stretch.

Bambrey was so excited he couldn't sit still. He rocked sitting down and standing up, puffing smoke like a sawmill. "A thousand troops out safe," he mused. Nine days to organize and write all the manifests, one day to deploy. Charlie couldn't know anything. A thousand boys going back to the World.

We knew we couldn't do any of the scheduling on paper until the last minute, so we needed a hidden, secured area where we could use the walls to draw up our plans. I suggested we could cover them with plastic ground-cover sheets and use grease pencils, like I'd done when managing parades at Disneyland.

"Perfect," Bambrey said. "All the reassignment paperwork can be done later when we land in Hawaii. We can issue permanent orders from there. We only need flight manifests to give to the commanding officers the day before takeoff." He stood up, indicating our meeting was over. "Pick a room that can be locked."

Phil and I commandeered a long, skinny supply room

behind headquarters, covered the only window, and put two padlocks on the door. We each kept separate sets of keys. I staple-gunned tightly stretched clear plastic ground cover to the interior walls, and Phil scrounged up some grease pencils. He brought stacks of lists with every name of every soldier in every company in the Mekong Delta. From more than ten thousand names, we had to pick a thousand.

Each C-133 Cargomaster could carry two hundred guys. We worked around the clock to cover the walls with rectangles, two hundred horizontal lines in each. It was going to take five full flights.

"Have we got five C-133s?" Phil asked Bambrey.

"Does a fat baby toot? We *better* have!" Within five minutes he hung up the phone and announced, "Five flights. C-133s. I'll be sharing departure times with you in due course."

We named the five flights Mickey, Pluto, Goofy, Peter Pan, and Donald Duck. At the top of the wall I wrote in big black letters, BAMBREY'S SURPRISE BIRTHDAY PARTY!

We began printing in the names of the one thousand. Using grease pencil on plastic allowed us to add, change, move, and reassign names as we went through the list. We couldn't have too many coming from the same company at the same time or it would tip off a pullout. Everything needed to appear to be business as usual, the Americans moving troops around again. In the final hour, Phil and I would type one standing order and attach individual lists to it.

By the end of the week we had compiled the list and begun assigning the lucky thousand to the five planes. Bambrey explained that C-133s didn't have seats. They were cargo carriers, wide-bodied planes meant for transporting armored vehicles. A large back door opened onto a ramp. I'd never seen one in person, but Bambrey reminded us of movies showing jeeps and trucks being parachuted out the back door of a huge airplane.

"That's the C-133. They'll put folding chairs in them Stateside. I don't think anybody's going to mind not having seat belts, do you?"

"Not on this ride," Phil said.

"Won't they slide all around?" I asked.

"Not as much as you'd think," Bambrey explained. "Those things fly like a big old barge."

Four Chinook helicopters would transport fifty men each, from different gathering points, to the airport at Bien Hoa, where the Cargomaster would be warming up for takeoff. In theory, each plane's manifest group should take less than an hour from collection point to takeoff. The hours were set starting at "minus five hours," and would be adjusted as soon as we got the first flight time from Bambrey.

We would move the four Chinooks in convoy five times. Five C-133 flights. Twenty Chinook shuttles. An incredible risk of error in a timetable this tight, even for the military. Bambrey loved the clockwork of our plan. "The tighter the better," he said.

"And what about Charlie?" I asked. "Can we depend on him to honor our schedule? Isn't he going to see something's up by the second Chinook?" I'd had nightmares of planes stacking up on the runway at Bien Hoa while Charlie pumped rockets at the departing short-timers. The precious cargo.

Bambrey assured us that any time we made large troop movements, as opposed to mere patrols, the guerrilla forces near Dong Tam sank into a protection mode rather than risk being outnumbered. We'd have to trust that when we started moving out so fast, Charlie would think we were after *him*. It would be a good time for him to duck and cover, or run all over the Delta warning his buddies that we were mounting some major offensive.

"We're assuming, of course," Phil said, "that Charlie doesn't believe what Nixon promised."

"Who does?" Bambrey replied in a rare cynical moment.

On our walls of plastic, each Chinook transport had a different color. Red, white, blue, green. Fifty men in each. Two hundred men in each C-133. Five flights. A thousand soldiers. The names leapt at me, darted in and out of my vision, haunted my every thought. Fifty names each, grease-penciled into twenty columns. I ate and walked and talked a thousand names. It felt like they were crawling over my skin. Dreams woke me as I searched the wall for my own name. It wasn't there. It wasn't *ever* there.

Each morning when Phil and I came into the room, I immediately checked for every person I knew on the wall. Smith, Guenther, Thomas, Sims, Frink, Cassidy, Bailey, Weber, Bambrey, Vincent, and Satterfield. I had to be sure their names hadn't disappeared in the night. I reflected on the brief time I'd had with each of them. I felt bad that none knew they were going home, except Bambrey and Weber of course, and they wouldn't talk about it. All talk about the World ceased as soon as we started posting the names. Loose lips sink ships. And I think they were mindful of the fact that my name wasn't there.

A few days before departure, Phil simply asked, "When you gonna get your stuff packed?"

"I'll stay with Bambrey, then catch a ride with the MPs. It's best not to look like we're leaving until everybody else gets the news. I can pack quick."

Then I carefully printed THOMAS BAMBREY on the bottom line of the manifest. The last Chinook, the Red

Team, the Donald Duck flight. As he requested, he would leave last.

I visited 3d Surg for the final time to pick up extra supplies for my medic bag. Smitty was sipping a can of beer with his feet up on a desk. It was nine o'clock in the morning.

"Drinking on duty?"

"It's happy hour somewhere, Bubba." He was grinning as usual. "Truth is, I'm off duty. Didn't feel like the NCO club. Just sittin' here decidin' what to do with myself all day."

"I need to restock my bag," I said.

"Sure. Right in there." He pointed to a supply closet. "Ya plannin' on hittin' the bush?"

"Naw. Just don't feel right having half a bag."

"Know whatcha mean. Feels kinda naked."

"Yep." I packed my bag with the essentials, as I'd seen Smitty do that first time on the *Nuaces*.

"Is there somethin' I should know, Bubba?" Smitty asked as I was leaving.

"Why?" I stammered.

"Ya got it written all over yer face."

"Just bored, I guess."

"Right." Smitty jumped up and approached me. "What's goin' on, Bubba? I *know* you. Ya either got a shitty letter from home or caught the clap from a toilet seat. Somethin' ain't right."

I couldn't hold him off. I owed him too much.

"Sergeant Smith, care to take a walk?"

Smitty was out the door before I could ask twice. Calling him by rank got his immediate attention. We walked down to his barracks and sat face-to-face on two lower bunks while I told him the whole story.

"Jesus, Bubba. Do any of the guys on the manifest get a choice?"

"Doesn't look like it. They'll get to choose their next duty station when they get to Hawaii. If they want to re-up for Vietnam, they probably can. But it'll be with another unit. The 9th is pulling out."

"I'll be all go-to-hell. I was short 'n didn't even know it!"

After things had sunk in, I asked Smitty to describe Tan An.

"That's where we got overrun my first time. I don't have great memories of Tan An."

"Well, that's where the rest of us are going."

"Figures. The 25th. 'Ready to strike, anytime, anywhere.' Trouble is, *they* get struck every time, everywhere. Charlie's been threatenin' to overrun that base for weeks. What we need up there is a *ton* of firepower. What's planned for Dong Tam?"

"We're giving it over to the South Vietnamese army."

"The ARVN? You serious?"

"Serious as a heart attack." I got that one from Smitty. "That's what all this 'Vietnamization' is."

"I saw 'em givin' Alpha boats to the ARVN. Navy was trainin' out there all last week. Man, this is comin' together now. 3d Surg is low on manpower. Most surgeons have gone to Saigon or other places. *Nuaces* left for the South China Sea last week. We been airliftin' patients all over the Orient. Saigon. Okinawa. Tokyo. Got nobody in the wards 'cept a few ambulatories."

"I guess the colonel, Phil, and I aren't the only ones walking around with a big secret."

Smitty whistled his little bird chirp. "Man, who'd have ever thought *I'd* be the last to know?"

I wanted to ask him more about Tan An. I wanted to ask him a lot of things. Like how I was going to make it in a new unit with new officers and sergeants, and without him. And what he thought a gung-ho unit's reaction would be to my "no-weapon shit," as he put it. But I didn't ask.

"Man, Bubba. I just figured out what I was sittin' around waitin' for today. You! Let's go to the club. I'm gonna getcha piss-ass drunk."

"Don't let me talk to anybody," I said, running to catch up with him.

My hangover finally slipped away two days later, just in time for a twenty-four-hour artillery show. From early evening into the morning, our rocket jockeys peppered the forests rimming Dong Tam, keeping Charlie's butt down. Nobody could sleep through the continual noise. Phil and I were awake all night anyway, typing final manifests to be handed to battalion commanders who had been briefed by Lieutenant Colonel Bambrey at noon the preceding day.

Dong Tam was closing down. Nine thousand 9th Infantry troops were riding in trucks and choppers to join the 25th Infantry in Tan An. The artillery command was still present and very active, though, lobbing rockets into the forests surrounding the base camp. MPs and a small company of Marines were flown in to secure our departure. A thousand men had been told they were going home. R&Rs were canceled. Orders rescinded. Field troops returned.

A thousand men packed after dinner, after all the Vietnamese who worked on the base had left for the day. Most of them probably stayed awake all night too, lying on their bunks, listening to the outgoing rockets, waiting for word of their ride to Bien Hoa. To get out early. To get out alive. They had counted the days, then the hours. Now they were counting each breath.

A few ARVN troops walked between the buildings in the first light of morning. They were already acting as if Dong Tam were theirs. 3d Surg was closed, as were all the clubs and mess halls. Steam 'n Cream had been entirely dismantled and packed onto trucks during the night.

Not a single Vietnamese citizen showed up for work on the base that morning, which made me very nervous. It reminded me of the afternoon a month before, when all the locals had left Dong Tam at four o'clock instead of five. Steam 'n Cream, the barbershops, and the PX had closed early. An intense night of incoming rockets and mortars lasted until close to dawn, and we suffered more than the usual number of casualties in the field. I realized then just how well the local Vietnamese knew the movements of the opposition guerrilla forces. I used the army barber from then on.

Starting at dawn, it took barely four hours for five Chinook helicopters to make four trips each from Dong Tam to Bien Hoa. Four C-133 Cargomasters spread their silver wings and lifted their all-important cargo out of the jungle, headed to the World. I hadn't said good-bye to Smitty. It wouldn't have been a scene either of us would have liked. Phil remained unusually quiet all morning then shook my hand, gave me a wink, and left before either of us could react.

One flight to go.

I walked outside. No wind. No dust. Even the sounds of voices and laughter were gone. Forty-nine soldiers stood across the street, smoking cigarettes near where Steam 'n Cream used to be, waiting for a truck to take them to the last Chinook. The Donald Duck Red Team, Bambrey's flight. They knew they were last, and were as silent as snowfall.

I returned to the Operations orderly room to help Colonel Bambrey gather the forms for the final flight.

"You set, sir?" I asked.

"Yes. You?"

"I'm going with the MPs as soon as you guys lift off. We'll be one of the last jeeps outta here."

"Tan An?"

"Yes, sir."

He nodded his head. "How many months do you have in country?"

"Not enough, sir." He had asked me several times before, but my answer and his silence never changed.

Our artillery's outgoing rockets had been breaking the silence periodically all morning. By now Charlie had to know something was up, but it was too late. We were about gone.

As Bambrey and I finished making final preparations, I handed him the manifest for the soldiers on his Chinook shuttle. In that instant a missile whistled over our heads and slammed directly into the group across the street. The detonation blew the colonel and me against the wall in a heap of arms and legs. Papers flew everywhere. Pushing his desk chair off us, I grabbed my medic bag and we rushed outside to the wounded. At least half the group was on the ground screaming. The others were either crawling to help them or seeking cover.

It all came flooding back to me. Grown boys begging for their mommies. Buddies clutching at them, not knowing what to do. Desperate people scratching at the hardpan dirt with their fingernails. Their wailing sent splinters into my heart. Again I looked into the gaping holes left by high-velocity metal slamming through muscle and bones. Human fluids were leaking everywhere, all over uniforms and packs and in the street. My eyes itched and blurred, stinging hot. Stomach gas filled my throat. *Goddammit!* Not *now!* They were out of here! They were almost home.

In minutes, medevac choppers appeared and landed right beside us. MPs were everywhere, sidearms drawn, directing traffic, shouting orders. Medic crews leapt off the choppers and began loading the wounded. More jeeps arrived. People came out of nowhere, piling out, trying to help. I had thought the base was almost deserted, but help seemed to come from everywhere. MPs, artillery gunners, even a few ARVN soldiers were picking up bodies and carrying them to waiting helicopters and jeeps.

"Get these men mobile!" Bambrey shouted above the roar of the choppers and the wailing of the wounded. He wanted the MPs to stop protecting us and start loading the choppers. He knew by the whistle of the rocket that it had been one of ours.

Bambrey grabbed medical supplies out of my bag, bandaged wounds, lifted guys onto stretchers. He spit out orders to an MP with a radio, calling for more choppers. "Chest wound over here," he called to me. He'd been here before. He knew what he was doing.

And to my surprise, so did I. In a matter of minutes, I plastered and sealed a hole in a guy's chest and bound up a spurting vessel under another's armpit. I tied a tourniquet high on his arm and stuck a roll of gauze between the wrap and his pit. As I cranked on it, the spurting stopped, but I had to keep hold or it started again. He was losing color fast. Two medics from a waiting chopper slipped him onto a litter and I ran beside them, holding the tourniquet with one hand while trying to read a pulse in his neck with the other.

"Think it's a brachial artery," I shouted to the receiving medic leaning out the chopper door. He reached for the litter and I waved him off. "Stick your hand up under his arm. I got pressure there." Blood started spurting again. The medic grabbed the wrap and gave it a sharp twist, and the blood stopped. We boosted the stretcher onto the floor of the chopper.

"Nice job, Doc!" he shouted. It was the same seasoned face that had handed me bandages in the bunker at Bien Hoa the night I arrived. He smiled and fired his finger at me as the chopper lifted off. God, that felt better than anything I'd done yet. He had been handing off his job to me in that bunker, and I had taken it.

Three dead soldiers lay in the street. A few shaken survivors cradled their buddies in their arms, rocking and weeping. Some of the group had escaped to the nearest cover, thinking there were more rockets coming. Others had been in base camp long enough to know that the rocket was outgoing, not incoming. A few wandered around after the all-clear siren, struggling to comprehend what had happened. Some had superficial wounds—shrapnel punctures, cuts, abrasions. I cleaned up a nasty gash under a guy's ear and applied a pressure bandage. He waved off a ride anywhere. No way was he missing his flight. Most of the surviving forty soldiers were in shock. Some were shaking like rabbits. I popped several amyl nitrate caps to stick under their noses. They were soon up helping others.

As the last chopper with the DOAs lifted off, everybody dropped to the ground, exhausted. We sat right where the rocket had hit, between the scattered duffel bags and the pooled blood. Less than fifty feet away was the supply room with the colorful walls listing the one thousand attendees of Bambrey's Surprise Birthday Party.

High speeding metal
Slamming through muscle and bone
How war begins, ends

"How did they know?" I sighed to no one in particular.

"They didn't," Bambrey said. "That was ours, Ben." The colonel bowed his head and allowed his tears to fall to the dirt in front of him.

The group's ranking sergeant and I sifted through the rubble and papers in the office until we uncovered the last list of names the colonel had been holding when the rocket struck. Finding it difficult to speak, the sergeant just ran his finger down the list and hesitated by the name of each dead soldier and each of the seven wounded as I crossed them off.

"We'll make the changes and bring you the new manifest outside," Bambrey said. He had come in behind us. "Sergeant, you better go load your men on the truck. They're looking pretty ragged. The last Chinook's waiting at the airfield."

The first sergeant, still looking totally lost, turned and stumbled out the door.

"Ben," the colonel said, "I'll be on the truck. Bring the new manifest when it's ready."

"Yes, sir. Three minutes."

"You all right?"

"Yes, sir. Of course."

"Of course," he repeated, then turned to follow the sergeant.

I put Phil's typewriter back on the desk, slid the manifest into it, and struck out the names of the three dead soldiers and the seven wounded. To the bottom of the list, I added my own name. It was my one hundredth day in Vietnam. Lieutenant Colonel Bambrey didn't say a word when I threw my medic bag on the truck and took a seat beside him.

• • •

That day in late July 1969, four C-133s made a quick landing for fuel in Okinawa and arrived twenty hours later at the Honolulu airport. Mechanical problems delayed the Donald Duck flight in Okinawa for four hours. Bambrey passed the time reading American newspapers and playing chess on a traveling set he carried in his briefcase.

When our transport finally bounced hard on the tarmac in Honolulu, a spontaneous cheer erupted. Folding chairs flew everywhere as men swept up their packs and duffel bags and shifted impatiently, waiting for the doors to open. I carried only my medic bag. We had been windowless for twenty hours, but we knew what was outside. A long covered airport terminal with open-air lobbies, and hundreds of small palm trees with giant leaves swaying in the cool ocean air.

Most of the men on the Donald Duck flight fell to their knees and kissed the runway tarmac. It tasted like petroleum, but we didn't mind a bit.

(Stars numbered 1 through 50)

51	52	53	54	55	56	57	58	59	60	61	62	63	64	65	66	67	68	69
70	71	72	73	74	75	76	77	78	79	80	81	82	83	84	85	86	87	88

89	90	91	92	93	94	95	96	97	98	99	100	101	102	103	104
105	106	107	108	109	110	111	112	113	114	115	116	117			

118	119	120	121	122	123	124	125	126	127	128	129	130
131	132	133	134	135	136	137	138	139	140	141	142	143

144	145	146	147	148	149	150	151	152	153	154	155	156
157	158	159	160	161	162	163	164	165	166	167	168	169

170	171	172	173	174	175	176	177	178	179	180	181	182	183	184	185	186	187	188	189	190	191	192
193	194	195	196	197	198	199	200	201	202	203	204	205	206	207	208	209	210	211	212	213	214	215

216	217	218	219	220	221	222	223	224	225	226	227	228	229	230	231	232	233	234	235	236	237	238
239	240	241	242	243	244	245	246	247	248	249	250	251	252	253	254	255	256	257	258	259	260	261

262	263	264	265																			315

24

Paradise

Wandering through one of the open-air corridors of the Honolulu airport, I saw his teeth gleaming white out of his deeply tanned leather face. I knew those pearls. His lips came together and chirped a bird whistle.

"Where's yer shit, Bubba?"

I waved my medic bag in his face. "All I need right here!"

In the bar of the Outrigger Hotel, Smitty and I spent our first night of freedom laughing and telling lies until the only people left were a few other guys from the flights and some honeymooners. "Ya went for it, Bubba," Smitty slurred. "I didn't think ya'd really do it."

"Then what were you doing at the airport?"

"Meetin' planes. First four came in an hour apart. I was curious who might be on 'em," he winked. "Man, you guys were really late. I musta had seven mai tais waitin' for y'all."

"I suppose I could be in big trouble."

"How's that?"

"The cutoff was ten months."

"Who decided seniority would be the cut?"

"Colonel Bambrey."

"Wasn't he on the flight with ya?"

"Yeah. We sat together."

"He say anything?"

"Nope. I did crosswords the whole time."

"You strac, soldier!"

"Yeah, I guess."

"Sumbitch, Bubba! Ya finally got all yer shit in one sock!"

"What?"

"You *out!*" He laughed loud and slugged my arm.

Smitty was the ranking NCO in the bar, and he swayed a little when he announced that the bus was leaving for the barracks. He'd decided we'd all had enough. Smitty and I found a seat in the back of the military bus that shuttled every hour out to Schofield Barracks from downtown and Waikiki. Almost everyone was smoking and laughing. When the driver left the city streets, several vets hollered for him to slow down.

"I'm goin' forty, you jerkoffs. This is the World, for chrissake. You guys been in the jungle too long." He was right. The roads in Vietnam made anything more than about fifteen miles per hour impossibly bumpy, so this bus ride felt like a roller coaster to us.

"Christ, Bubba, you *out!*" Smitty laughed again. As the bus heaved and swayed through the pineapple fields, I finally began to feel it.

"Well, *you out* too," I said, mimicking his accent.

"Yep. Ya saved yer *own* ass this time. And saved my happy ass too."

"Whaddaya mean? You said you *belonged* in the jungle. This was your third tour. I thought you'd be pissed that I put you on the list."

"I ain't the same guy I was in '65. Been lookin' at things . . . been thinkin' some shit. Got me wonderin' why I'm a medic in the first place."

"Yeah?"

"Well, in the *last* place, I guess. Did I ever tell ya I was a grunt in the Marines?"

"I assumed you were a medic."

"Don't have Marine docs. Navy corpsmen serve Marine units. All Marines are grunts. *Now* I'm a medic, Bubba. Wasn't always."

We both were lost in our thoughts for a while before he went on quietly.

"Uncle Sam trained me to kill people, 'n I was good at it. I trained myself to fix people, 'n I'm damn good at that too. But I can fix people in an ambulance or ER anywhere I want." He paused for several seconds. "Don't have to be in a war zone to do it."

"Smitty?"

"You heard me. I seen the last of Southeast Asia."

"You gettin' religion?"

"Choices, Bubba. Aw hell, never mind."

He cocked his hat down over his eyes to avoid more conversation and faked going to sleep. The bus rumbled past a sea of pineapple fields as we neared the barracks. The smell was thick and sweet, like breathing syrup.

"You was trouble before I even met ya," the sergeant murmured from under his hat. He leaned back farther and stretched, his weathered arms at full wingspan. He brought one hand back to his pack of cigarettes and the other to pull his Zippo. He took three draws, long and pronounced, knowing that I was waiting attentively for his next syllable. Only his mouth and cigarette could be seen under the hat.

"Ya *did* save my ass, Bubba," Smitty said from his hiding place. "I had four months to go 'n ya goddamn *know* it."

"Yes, sir, that's affirmative," I admitted.

Smitty flashed his pearly teeth. "Bubba, goddammit. Don't call me 'sir.'"

Epilogue

Robert E. Lee Smith, Jr., Gerald Guenther, Seth Bailey, Wally Thomas, Vincent Brown, and Rupert Satterfield were returned to Hawaii with the 9th Infantry Division before their tours of duty had passed ten months, which was supposed to be the official cutoff. I had made the decision to add their names to the lists. Bambrey and Weber, both past the ten-month line, never said a word.

I spent the subsequent eight months as an emergency room medic and admissions clerk stationed at Tripler Hospital in Hawaii. Military acquaintances slipped away as they were discharged or assigned new duty stations.

A few months before my ETS (Estimated Time of Separation), I put in for leave so that I could return to Southern California to begin to piece my life together. After the flight from Honolulu, walking through LAX in Los Angeles, I was the object of jeers and threats from peace advocates who blocked my way, grabbed at my uniform, and shouted questions in my face about why I had killed and maimed mothers and their children. I stopped to talk to a man in a robe who offered to take me far away, shave my head, dress me in clothes like his, and begin a long process that would eventually make me strong enough to save me from myself. I told him that somebody had beaten him to it.

Later, as I removed my dress greens, I found several strings of dried spit on the back of my coat and pants. Sitting on a thin mattress in a cheap motel, I thought about all the faces in the bags and cried until I couldn't make tears.

In 1985, three years after it officially opened, I visited the Vietnam Veterans Memorial in Washington, D.C. A friend who had not been in the war came with me. At ten o'clock on a drizzly Wednesday night, we found ourselves the only ones there.

In the alphabetical listings, I looked up Wilson, my first casualty. I returned to the wall to find the panel and line, and I found his name about face-high. Directly behind it was my faint reflection in the black night, lit only by the footlight at my feet. My face looked ghostly pale. While my friend shaded my paper from the wind and rain, I made a pencil-lead rubbing of his name. I held it tightly in my hand, as if I could somehow take a part of him away with me. Away from the names. Away from the dead.

Abraham Lincoln is quoted as saying, "Having absolutely no place else to go, I was driven to my knees." On the pavement, leaning my forehead against the ebony wall, I sobbed as I remembered my palm soaked with blood from his exit wound, the same palm that now clutched a rubbing of his name. I knew I wasn't to blame. Smitty had repeatedly assured me that he could not have been saved. I just yearned so deeply that it hadn't happened. I wanted more than anything to get that day back. I didn't know him, we had never spoken, but he mattered to me.

As I knelt, the reflection of a couple appeared behind me. A man about my age and his mother. I stood and backed away so they could touch the name they had located, the one name in fifty-eight thousand directly above where I knelt. His brother. Her son. The same name I held in my hand.

The next day, my friend and I returned to the Wall and told one of the Veteran Volunteers helping there the story of what had happened the night before. He offered a knowing smile and said, "It happens every day here, sir. This is Holy Ground."

Fellows

In Hawaii, SFC Robert E. Lee Smith, Jr. and I were assigned to different bases. We met for drinks and laughs a few times, then one day he wasn't there when I called. That's the way the army works. You get orders to another place, pack all your belongings in a waist-high duffel bag, and just leave. Sometimes we make promises to look each other up, but there are so many soldiers in a war. Army buddies come and go like the weather. In the last few years while writing this book, I tried a couple of times to locate Smitty with searches through Vietnam veterans groups, then more recently through the Internet. I called every Robert Smith in Mississippi, with no luck.

On August 29, 1968, two weeks after I was drafted, my parents received the letter my friend Dave Anderson sent to me saying the ACLU had agreed to take my conscientious objection case. He had apparently gathered copies and originals of all my papers and made the case to them. The letter had been opened and clumsily resealed with cellophane tape. My parents put it in a fresh envelope and sent it to me in basic training at Fort Lewis, Washington. They said they mailed it around the first week of September. I received it at Fort Sam Houston, Texas, in April 1969. Dave answered subpoenas for questioning by the FBI twice, once in 1968 and again in 1970. Although he made only twenty-eight hundred dollars net income in 1968, the IRS audited him. He was fired from his job soon thereafter, for no reason. Dave continued to work for the underground and the ACLU until the end of the war. He died in a car accident on November 11, Veterans Day, in 1975. He was thirty.

Phil Weber, Ph.D., is a professor of English at a small Midwest college. He says that occasionally he teaches a course on Vietnam War literature. He was stationed with me at Tripler Hospital in Hawaii for about five months before his service concluded and he returned home. I got luckier finding Phil after twenty-five years by calling a listing for Phil Weber in Lidea, Kansas. Turns out it was a number for his deceased uncle, but it put me in touch with Phil's aunt, who turned me over to her sister. After I heard all the news of Lidea, Phil's mom gave me his address and phone number and told me to tell him to call home. Phil read the first draft of this manuscript and helped me remember names and places. We agreed that I should use fictitious names for all the characters, which I have done with the exception of Dave Anderson and the ghosts of my three buddies from home who visited me in the jungle.

A few weeks after we arrived in Hawaii, Smitty and I saw Sgt. Seth Bailey in a small village on the windward side of Oahu. He was staggering dead drunk down the middle of a busy road, trying to find where he had left his car. I heard later that the army had given him six thousand dollars as a reenlistment bonus and that he spent it on a down payment for a brand-new Trans Am. On the day he bought it, he totaled the car into a tree on his way back to Schofield Barracks. He walked away uninjured and swore he had planned to get insurance the next day.

Radio operator Wally Thomas and I are still in touch. He worked with me after we got out, and we were roommates off and on for several years. He stood up for me at my first wedding, and stayed friends with both my ex-wife and me through hard times and a divorce. He taught me how to golf, and we played poker with a group of guys every Wednesday night for about ten years. He once told a mutual friend that I got him out alive before his tour ended, but he and I have never spoken about Vietnam.

In the early eighties, I saw Hoppy Cassidy on TV, winning an amateur volleyball tournament at Newport Beach. He looked exactly the same.

Vincent and Satterfield worked in the emergency room at Tripler, where we shared the same graveyard shift. We rented an apartment in Waikiki that we used as a bachelor pad on our days off. Vincent and I became close pals over the eight months we worked together in Hawaii, despite the racial tension all around us. When I mentioned that we should have a party for my approaching twenty-fourth birthday, Vincent said his twenty-fourth was coming up as well. We were stunned to discover that we were both born on April 10, 1946, a mere hundred miles apart, he in Oakland and me in Sacramento. He mentioned this coincidence in a letter to his mother, who wrote back that they *lived* in Oakland but, if he looked at his birth certificate, he'd see "Sutter Maternity Hospital, Sacramento, California." *My* hospital. In her next letter, Vincent's mom wrote that she remembered there were only two boy babies in the nursery of at least ten or twelve newborns. "And you were both so noisy and fussy that the nurses had to keep the two of you at opposite ends of the ward." What a birthday party we had in '70!

I visited Vincent in Oakland soon after we were discharged. Several times in the ensuing years, he and Satterfield brought carloads of friends down to Disneyland and stayed with my roommates and me. We partied and shared tales about everything except Vietnam. As years passed and we settled down from our wilder single days, we lost touch. I haven't been able to locate Satterfield or my "twin brother" Vincent, the guys who saved me from Cornelius Jones my third day in Vietnam.

When I got out of the army, I asked my father, who worked in law enforcement, to run a records search on Cornelius Jones. Sure enough, he had a long police record and was serving a sentence at a federal prison after being dishonorably discharged. Apparently, getting kicked out of the army was a violation of parole from previous convictions. Six years later, I got news from my father that Cornelius Jones had died in prison.

Most of the war stories you've heard, especially the really exciting ones, have likely come from the vivid imaginations of rear-echelon guys who never saw a firefight, never spent a day in the jungle, never slept in a rice paddy, never had their stomach turn over as they gawked at the open wound of a guy who'd bummed a smoke the minute before. Those who witness the raw hysterics of war up close tend to remain very quiet about it, forever. They think about it, you can be sure, but the words can't get around the clog in their chest.

There's a code. If you've really been in it, you don't

talk about it. Maybe that hasn't always been such a good idea. We don't talk to each other. We don't talk to loved ones. It stays in the bottle, corked tight.

As years passed, some have broken the silence. They've written books, both truth and fiction. A few have made movies, both accurate and not. Vietnam War literature shelves in libraries and bookstores bulge with rage, righteous indignation, continued political discontent, and who-owes-who. Vietnam poetry steams off the page. There's still a bunch of folks out there doing their yelling about a war we lost almost thirty years ago.

My story says little about courage under fire, brilliant strategies, right versus wrong, glory, regrets, or political necessities. It's mostly a story about a kid who got drafted and refused to kill anybody.

A fellow vet I once worked with had a T-shirt that read: SOUTHEAST ASIA GAMES, 1963–1975, SECOND PLACE. His wit replaced the flesh he had left on Vietnam soil for a cause he still couldn't articulate. Poorly stitched scars ran from his belly to his neck, then around his shoulder. Field scars. Deep, ugly raised skin ridges that were hard to look at twice. There had been no time in a field hospital to make them pretty.

When I told him I wanted to write it down, he told me that everything had already been said. We agreed it had been hammered to death in one way or another. Scratching gently at his shoulder, he said, "Just let it go."

I couldn't.

"No one has ever treated the infantryman's role in Vietnam with more sympathy or thoroughness."

—*Booklist*

A LIFE IN A YEAR

The American Infantryman in Vietnam, 1965-1972

by James R. Ebert

Finally, here's a book that focuses exclusively on the life of the "grunt" in Vietnam. The voices of more than sixty Army and Marine Corps infantrymen speak of their experiences, from induction to the jungles and rice paddies of "Indian country" to their return to "the World."

From I Corps in the north to IV Corps in the south, and from the early days of 1965 to the American withdrawal in 1972, *A Life in a Year* offers a unique look at the grunt's war in Vietnam—war as experienced from the edge of a foxhole, as seen through the eyes of the combat riflemen themselves. The experiences are woven together, giving the reader a true understanding of what it was like to serve in an infantry unit fighting Viet Cong guerillas and North Vietnamese regulars.

Published by Presidio Press
Available wherever books are sold

*An infantry platoon leader in
Vietnam tells it like it was*

MEKONG FIRST
LIGHT

by Joseph W. Callaway Jr.

December, 1966: Platoon leader Lt. Joseph
Callaway had just turned twenty-three when he
arrived in Vietnam to lead forty-two untested men
into battle against some of the toughest, most
experienced, and best-trained guerrilla soldiers in
the world. Callaway soon learned that most
events in this savage jungle war were beyond his
control. But there was one thing he could do well:
take the best damn care of his troops he knew
how.

In the Viet Cong–infested provinces around the
Mekong Delta where the platoon was assigned,
the enemy was always ready to attack at the first
sign of weakness. And when the jungle suddenly
erupted in the chaos of battle, the platoon leader
was the Cong's first target. Mekong First Light is at
times horrific, heartrending, and heroic, but is
always brutally honest. Callaway's account chron-
icles a soldier's painful realization of the true
nature of America's war in Vietnam: It was a war
that could not be won.

Published by Presidio Press
Available wherever books are sold

At last, the full story of Khe Sanh—from acclaimed Vietnam War historian
EDWARD F. MURPHY

THE HILL FIGHTS
The First Battle of Khe Sanh

While the seventy-seven-day siege of Khe Sanh in early 1968 remains one of the most highly publicized clashes of the Vietnam War, scant attention has been paid to the earlier battles of Khe Sanh, also known as "the Hill Fights." Based on firsthand interviews and documentary research, Murphy's deeply informed narrative history is the *only* complete account of the battles, their origins, and their aftermath.

"[A] VALUABLE ADDITION TO THE MILITARY HISTORY CANON . . . Murphy, who served in the Vietnam War, tells his story forcefully and with empathy for the American fighting men on the ground."

—*Publishers Weekly*

Published by Presidio Press
Available wherever books are sold

*On the front lines with the
bravest men in the bloodiest
year of the war*

WARRIORS

An Infantryman's Memoir of Vietnam

by Robert Tonsetic

It was the tumultuous year 1968, and Robert Tonsetic was Rifle Company commander of the 4th Battalion, 12th Infantry in Vietnam. He took over a group of grunts demoralized by defeat but determined to get even. Through the legendary Tet and May Offensives, he led, trained, and risked his life with these brave men, and this is the thrilling, brutal, and honest story of his tour of duty. Tonsetic tells of leading a seriously undermanned ready-reaction force into a fierce, three-day battle with a ruthless enemy battalion; conducting surreal night airmobile assaults and treks through fetid, pitch-black jungles; and relieving combat stress by fishing with hand grenades and joyriding in Hueys.

Published by Presidio Press
Available wherever books are sold